WRONG WAYS AND RIGHT WAYS IN THE STUDY OF FORMATIVE JUDAISM

Program in Judaic Studies
Brown University
BROWN JUDAIC STUDIES
Edited by
Jacob Neusner
Wendell S. Dietrich, Ernest S. Frerichs,William Scott Green,
Calvin Goldscheider, David Hirsch, Alan Zuckerman

Project Editors (Project)

David Blumenthal, Emory University (Approaches to Medieval Judaism)
William Brinner (Studies in Judaism and Islam)
Ernest S. Frerichs, Brown University (Dissertations and Monographs)
Lenn Evan Goodman, University of Hawaii (Studies in Medieval Judaism)
William Scott Green, University of Rochester (Approaches to Ancient Judaism)
Norbert Samuelson, Temple University (Jewish Philosophy)
Jonathan Z. Smith, University of Chicago (Studia Philonica)

Number 145
WRONG WAYS AND RIGHT WAYS IN THE STUDY
OF FORMATIVE JUDAISM

by
Jacob Neusner

WRONG WAYS AND RIGHT WAYS IN THE STUDY OF FORMATIVE JUDAISM

Critical Method and Literature, History, and the History of Religion

by
Jacob Neusner

Scholars Press
Atlanta, Georgia

WRONG WAYS AND RIGHT WAYS IN THE STUDY OF FORMATIVE JUDAISM
Critical Method and Literature, History, and the History of Religion

© 1988
Brown University

Library of Congress Cataloging-in-Publication Data

Neusner, Jacob, 1932-
    Wrong ways and right ways in the study of
formative Judaism.

    (Brown Judaic studies ; no. 145)
    1. Judaism--History--Talmudic period, 10-425--
Historiography. 2. Rabbinical literature--History
and criticism--Theory, etc. I. Title. II. Series.
BM177.N484   1988   296'.07   88-4546
ISBN 1-55540-228-3

Printed in the United States of America
on acid-free paper

For my friends, father and mother of my friends,
and for the family they have made
as their life's work

UDAH JACOB AND EDITH ZUCKERMAN

their children

SHIRLEY DAVIDMAN, MAY HER SOUL REST IN PEACE
MORTON AND SHOSHANA ZUCKERMAN
ALAN AND ROBERTA ZUCKERMAN

their grandchildren

PAUL AND ANNE DAVIDMAN
LYNN DAVIDMAN
MARK AND DEBORAH DAVIDMAN
CHANA AND AVRAHAM ROSENTHAL
ARYEH AND AVI ZUCKERMAN
GREGORY, EZRA, AND SHARA ZUCKERMAN

and their great-grandchildren.

The humblest of the humble,
asking nothing of anybody, but giving something to everybody,
they have lived their lives in love with each other,
in loyal faith in the holy way of life of Israel, the holy people,
and in devotion to their family, which is their creation and their monument.

They stand for everything that is good and enduring in
American Judaism.

I am proud and privileged to offer them
this book as a small token of respect for a great and lasting human achievement,
and as a gift of affection for them as friends
of my wife and my family and myself.

Bialik spoke for me of them:

yehi helqi imakhem...roqmé hayyehem beseter

Contents

Part Four
HISTORY OF RELIGION:
SOME INITIAL RESULTS IN THE DESCRIPTION OF
THE JUDAISM OF THE DUAL TORAH
IN ITS FORMATIVE AGE

Preface

   This is a book of a dozen free-standing, but interrelated, essays about right ways and wrong ways in the study of a Judaism in its formative stage. Giving concrete examples of both, deriving from (for wrong ways) other peoples' writing, and (for right ways), my own, I deal, in particular, with a single Judaism, the Judaism of the dual Torah that began to emerge in the first century and reached its final statement, for late antiquity, in the seventh. The results then will speak for themselves, both the wrong ways contrasted with the right ways, and the right ways tested against the announced premises and correct methods that are supposed to be followed. For it is time now to say, there are fundamental errors of premise, conception, and method, that have precipitated a wide variety of unacceptable readings and reconstructions of Judaism in late antiquity. And there also are fundamental principles that are sound and well considered, that will yield reliable and properly crafted results. In scholarship there can be no methodological pluralism: a set of questions are appropriate or irrelevant and indeed misleading; a set of premises, either well-founded or awry; a mode of thought either sound or flawed. In these essays I set forth what I think is wrong in other peoples' work and provide examples of what I conceive to be the results of the right way of framing and answering questions.

   Let me start with a wrong way of studying any religion, any Judaism, because the premise of all that follows is contained within my rejection of this single wrong way of doing things. The first, and worst, wrong way is to treat as one religion all the Judaisms of late antiquity, so let us begin there. While people commonly speak of "Judaism," in fact across time we find not one Judaism but many. And the same is to be said for "Christianity," "Buddhism," "Islam," and all the other convenient ways in which we treat as a single harmonious thing what are in fact many things. But here we do things in the right way, for we deal with only one Judaism among many. In showing the right way, we therefore take the Jews and their Judaisms as our exemplary case. Why is it wrong to treat all the Jews and all their Judaisms as one "nation" and one Judaism? The gap between one set of data, allegedly Jewish or Judaic, produced by a given group, in a determinate time and place, and another set of data, must impress anyone who stops to peer into the abyss that separates one group of Jews from some other. It is not a merely diachronic gap, in that "Judaism" in the time of Ezra is obviously different from "Judaism" in the time of the Essenes and "Judaism" as formulated by Maimonides. The synchronic problem is still more acute. The varieties of ways of life and world views exhibited by people who stoutly claimed for themselves the title, "Israel," must impress us not only in our own day but through history. The diversity of Judaisms generally characterizes not only the diachronic continuum but also the synchronic frame, which sets bounds around the data deemed definitive of, and appropriate to, (any) "Judaism." All solutions to the problem of difference and disharmony among Judaic data constitute statements of a theological (or ideological) judgment and bear no relevance to the requirements of description, analysis, and interpretation that dictate humanistic study.[1] That is why we speak not of "Judaism" as a single, encompassing religion, but rather *a Judaism*, that is, a particular religious system, with its own traits and definitions. Let me now spell out what I conceive to be the correct premises for the study of a religion, a Judaism, exemplified here by Judaism in its formative age.

A Judaism is a religious system comprising a theory of the social entity, the "Israel," constituted by the group of Jews who sustain that Judaism; a way of life characteristic of, perhaps distinctive to, that group of Jews; and a world view that accounts for the group's forming a distinctive social entity and explains those indicative traits that define the entity. Within this definition, I see the formation of a Judaism in three aspects:

[1]   the context of the social entity or group that constituted Judaism,

[2]   the components of the canon of that group, that is, of the literary analysis of Judaism as displayed in its sacred writings, the writings as they emerge at a particular time and place, and

[3]   of the system of questions and answers that served that group of Jews.

That context finds definition in the encompassing society, by contrast to which the distinctive social entity sees itself as different. The encompassing world constitutes the framework within which a given Judaism takes shape, and I call this "the ecology" of a Judaism. The social entity in the case of a Judaism always appeals to "Israel" and calls itself (an) "Israel."

What is at stake in this mode of analysis? As I see it, there are two quite distinct issues, each of them weighty. One is of a descriptive character,

---

[1] I spell this out at some length in my "Alike and Not Alike," in J. Neusner, ed., *Take Judaism for Example. Studies toward the Comparison of Religions* (Chicago: University of Chicago Press, 1983), pp. 227-236.

important in the history of religion, as to the classification of (a) Judaism. The other is of a theological character, consequential in our thinking not about but within Judaism, specifically pointing toward the correct modes of analyzing the theological structure produced by the Judaism of the dual Torah. But here we concentrate on the problem of definition, that is to say, (merely) secular description. And my point throughout is to show – through concrete examples in particular – the contrast between wrong ways of description and right ways of description.

I imagine that a Judaic system could treat as not essential a variety of rules for the everyday life. In modern times that indifference to rule-making for this morning's breakfast proves characteristic of Judaisms. Or it may fail to articulate elements of a world view to answer a range of questions others deem fundamental. Contemporary Judaisms do not treat as urgent philosophical questions found absorbing by earlier system-builders. But no Judaic system can omit a clear picture of the meaning and sense of the category, Israel. Without an *Israel*, a social entity in fact and not only in doctrine, we have not a system but a book. And a book is not a Judaism, it is only a book. But when we define a Judaism, we speak about Judaisms that Jews have created and that have sustained the lives of Jews. So let me repeat with emphasis, *a book is not a Judaism and a Judaism is not a book* – except after the fact.[2]

We ask how we may know one Judaism from some other. When we identify Judaisms in one period after another, we begin by trying to locate, in the larger group of Jews, those social entities that see themselves and are seen by others as distinct and bounded, and that further present to themselves a clear account of who they are and what they do and why they do what they do: the rules and their explanations, their Judaism. My simple premise is that religion always is social, and therefore also political, a matter of what people do together, not just what they believe in the privacy of their hearts. And a Judaism for its part addresses a social group, an Israel, with the claim that that group is not merely an Israel but

---

[2]The importance of this principle of selection cannot be missed. Let me explain by way of example. I do not see the writings of Philo as a Judaism, though they may represent a Judaism. We have distinctive books that represent social groups, for instance the apocalyptic writings of the Second Temple period, but our knowledge of those social groups – their way of life, their world-view, their identification of themselves as Israel – is imperfect. Consequently we cannot relate the contents of a system to its context or account for the substance of a system by appeal to its circumstance. We therefore know the answers provided by a system – that is, the contents of the book – but have not got a clear picture of the questions that the answers take up, or, still more important, the political or social forces that made those questions urgent and inescapable, in just that place, in just that time. In my work I always select those Judaisms that do allow for reasonably complete description, therefore also analysis and interpretation.

Israel, Israel *in nuce*, Israel in its ideal form, Israel's saving remnant, the State of Israel, the natural next step in the linear, continuous history ("progress") of Israel, everything, anything – but always Israel.   So a Judaism, or a Judaic system, constitutes a clear and precise account of a social group, the way of life and world view of a group of Jews, however defined.

So, as I said at the outset, the first and most fundamental error in the study of any Judaism is to treat all Judaisms as one.   And the right way is contained within my essential theory that denies there is now, or ever was, a single Judaism.   There is no linear and incremental history of one continuous Judaism, beginning, middle, end, for there has never been Judaism, only Judaisms.   But there was and now is a single paradigmatic and definitive human experience, which each Judaism reworks in its own circumstance and context.   What I have said requires the immediate specification of that single paradigmatic experience to which all Judaisms, everywhere and under all conditions, refer.   As a matter of simple fact, we may identify that generative and definitive moment precisely as all Judaisms have done, that is, by looking into that same Scripture.

All Judaisms identify the Torah or the Five Books of Moses as the written down statement of God's will for Israel, the Jewish people (which, as a matter of fact, every Judaism also identifies as its own social group).   I suppose that on the surface, we should specify that formative and definitive moment, recapitulated by all Judaisms, with the story of Creation down to Abraham and the beginning of his family, the children of Abraham, Isaac, and Jacob.   Or perhaps we are advised to make our way to Sinai and hold that that original point of definition descends from heaven.   But allowing ourselves merely to retell the story deprives us of the required insight.

Recapitulating the story of the religion does not help us understand the religion.   Identifying the point of origin of the story, by contrast, does.   For the story tells not what happened on the occasion to which the story refers (the creation of the world, for instance) but how (long afterward and for their own reasons) people want to portray themselves. The tale therefore recapitulates that resentment, that obsessive and troubling point of origin, that the group wishes to explain, transcend, transform.[3]   This seems to me a perspective nurtured within the history of religion as that discipline flourishes in America and Canada.

---

[3]Since all Christianities share the same books, the Torah, that for Judaisms portray the paradigmatic experience of exile and return, we have to wonder how the paradigm of resentment recapitulated makes its mark on the other family of biblical religious systems.   When the comparative study of religions comes into being, that will be an interesting question for reflection.

What led me to reach the conclusion that there really are wrong ways for the study of the history of Judaisms in late antiquity, which have now to be set aside in favor of right ways? It was in the 1960s that I perceived the problem of reading Judaism within the discipline of history of religion. Then, in my earliest years in the Department of Religion at Dartmouth College, prodded by Hans H. Penner and Jonathan Z. Smith, I began to wonder what one can possibly mean by the *-isms* and the *-ities* with which, at that time, we formed our descriptive, analytical, and interpretive categories, our "Judaism" as we taught "it," and our "Christianity" in the same context. We all recognized, of course, that "Christianity" covered diverse Christianities. The history of Christianity left us with no doubts that "Christianity" covered vast data defying harmonization and forming, each its own distinct history and social and political entity (as well as theological statement), and the present condition of "the Church" defined the problem. But no one then worked on the history of Christianity, read as a problem within the history of religion. Few even today have overcome the powerful heritage of theological harmonization to address an analytical program to that enormously rich and complex corpus of religious systems. And the same – we now recognize – is to be said of Buddhism(s), Hinduism(s), Islam(s), and all of the other artificial constructions that have simplified, for us in the West, our encounter with the complexities of a strange world beyond.

All of these *-isms* and *-ities,* we now know, were invented by the West, from the nineteenth century forward. They were to provide a way of making sense of strange worlds just then coming over the horizons of the West. Through a process of harmonization and simplification, of imposition of our categories and modes of category formation upon a world with its own categories and modes of category formation, we in the West proposed to explain for ourselves a world we just then had begun to encounter. Just then, as Jews entered into relationships with the politics and culture of the West, in Germany, France, and Britain, Protestant theologians were working out the meaning of the category "religion," as it applied both to their own Christianity and to the rest of the world. That is why "Judaism" was the first of those strange new worlds that Protestant scholars (there were few Catholics) in the new tradition of *Wissenschaft* found they had to classify and interpret. The *ism*-ization, in terms of systematic theology, of what Jews called "the Torah" resulted. Theologians of that "Judaism," first Reform, then Orthodox, later on Conservative, of course followed suit, and so a new classification was born, "Judaism," to which preachers would appeal for authority, from which discourse would flow along now well-defined lines. "Judaism" then would dictate this and teach that. That same "Judaism" would have its history, its symbolism, its sources. And all things Jewish would either find their place within the Judaism under invention and construction or would be placed into relationship with that Judaism, e.g., as heresies.

It was a particularization, for the Torah, of a much broader mode of thought about the social and cultural and political and religious worlds of those many "others," outside of the norm of the Protestant and later secular West, of which the West proposed to make sense. "Judaism" came first, to be followed by "Buddhism," "Hinduism," "Islam," and various other new categories and classifications, all of them deriving from the principles of category formation self-evidently valid in the Western tradition of philosophy and history we know as *Wissenschaft*. Research by such disparate scholars as Philip Almond and Wilfred Cantwell Smith has shown that fact, tracing the roots of those constructs so convenient to our mode of confronting the world, those *-isms* and *-ities* that have served to reduce to intelligible patterns what would otherwise lie beyond all comprehension within categories of description, analysis, and interpretation framed within our nineteenth century philosophical and historical heritage. Protestant theology had defined the study of religion and of history in such a way as to make sense of the world – for Protestant theologians. Pretty much everyone in the history of religion understands that fact today; learning does progress.

But as to Judaism, into the 1960s matters were in a still more primitive state than characterized, even, the study of Christianity or even Christianities. I recall long Sabbath walks with Abraham J. Karp, visiting at Dartmouth at that time, when I would press him with the question of treating as one thing – a single "Judaism" – what had begun to appear to me as many things. And what could that one thing be, I mean, what *sort* of thing was that one thing? And how does that one thing encompass so many? And why do people know what is in, and what is outside of, that single "Judaism"? For "the Torah," I knew the answers, because the canonical writings dictated them. But what was this "Judaism"? And that problem of definition, from within, formed only one part of the problem. The second part was the definition, viewed from without, of that Judaism as a species of something. But what? A religion, to be sure. But the usual use of "Judaism," in synagogue and scholarly discourse alike, involved the statement, "Judaism" believes. But then could all of the Judaic things be merely a set of beliefs, and was this "Judaism" species of the genus, theology? And was this "religion" a religion in the way that Protestant Christianity was a religion, or was it a religion in some other way? At that time, Wilfred Cantwell Smith's *Meaning and End of Religion* had not yet formulated this matter for me, nor could I find in the theoretical writing in the history of religion a suitable reading of matters.[4]

But the sources on which I was working, universally held to be classic and normative, did not talk about theological subjects very systematically, or at all. I perceived the -ism at hand in a different way altogether. Its literature presented me with a social and political problem, as my work on the rabbinic literature of late antiquity had begun to show me that that literature spoke for a single, political group within Jewry, but not for "all Israel," as it pretended to. In the 1960s I saw matters as essentially historical problems. In the 1970s I moved onward to a literary-exegetical program. The problem broadened for me in the 1970s, as I reached the conclusion that rabbinic writings had to be read, each on its own. That simple realization of the documentary character of the constituent parts of the canon of what we then called "rabbinic Judaism" and now call "the Judaism of the dual Torah" carried forward the analytical approach to category formation that was forming in my mind. In the 1980s I built upon the historical and literary results of the prior two decades' work and moved into the study of religion. As the 1980s unfolded, I realized that I had reached an inchoate and not fully articulated method pretty much of my own.

The intellectual tool I have called in my work *systemic analysis* in the case of a religion – in another context, I should prefer to say, in the context of the ecology of religion[5] – aims at allowing us to see whole, complete, and as a cogent statement, a system comprising a way of life, a world view, and the social entity that give reality to both way of life and world view. These we see in all their coherence and cogency, each by itself. But that means to see systems one by one, as a single and singular statement, each as distinct and distinctive. The alternative is to see as a single group – one Judaism – what are in fact elements of diverse systems or Judaisms. Then we combine systems that originally stood on their own, each facing its society. If we reflect for a moment on how one symbolic system excludes all others and conflicts with all others, we realize what is at stake in insisting that a Judaism make its own distinctive

---

[4]Wilfred Smith's theology of religion contains much with which I can identify. My forthcoming essay, "The Theological Enemies of Religious Studies," *Religion*, January, 1988, should in no way be read as a criticism of Smith's theology, upon which my paper has no bearing whatsoever. It is a criticism directed at modes of the definition of what we study when we study religion, a very different thing. Smith is in fact the model of the study of religion in its broader cultural and social context, and that is why I have found so much to learn in his writings.

[5]I spell out that category in my *From Testament to Torah. An Introduction to Judaism in its Formative Age* (Englewood Cliffs: Prentice-Hall, 1987).

statement, in its context, for its purpose, addressing its social entity, answering the urgent question that it has identified as critical.

In studying Judaism(s) and any one Judaism, therefore, I have sought to overcome the confusion brought on by thinking that all Judaisms really constituted, and today form, one Judaism, just as historians of religion, when they come to study Christianity, will sidestep the question of how all Christianities really are one Christianity. That theological question demands a theological answer, and historians of religion have nothing to contribute. That is to say, we should not allow ourselves to confuse one thing with something – everything – else. If we do, we lose sight of the distinctive and individual character of a system, its standing as one Judaism among several. We miss the particular questions it asked, the distinctive answers it supplied as self-evidently true for its society. We rather treat as one and the same a whole variety of Judaic systems or Judaisms, imputing connections where there are none. For theological discourse that act of harmonization defines the beginning of intelligibility. For the social description of religion over time which forms one principal task of the history of religion, that same mode of thought presents an insuperable obstacle.

The alternative, the systemic analysis of religious systems, is what I have contributed, in detail, as the way to describe, analyze, and interpret the histories of Judaisms. That my work has its roots in the tradition of Durkheim and Weber hardly requires articulation. Nor have I neglected their recent avatars and continuators. I read them all; I learn from them all. That what I have done is original to me is equally obvious, as a mere glance at any other contemporary writing, over the past three decades, on the definition and history of "Judaism" will indicate. Systematic description of any other Judaism, that is, Judaic system, besides the Judaism of the dual Torah, is difficult to come by, and descriptions of Judaism, as a single, unitary, linear, and harmonious "tradition" are commonplace. When we turn to other congeries of religions, e.g., a Christianity among Christianities, a Buddhism among Buddhisms, an Islam among Islams, matters seem to me not much better developed than among Judaism(s). That is why I conceive that I have a method to teach colleagues who work on religion. This I have exemplified in work on Judaism. Others will adopt and adapt the method in their descriptive, analytical, and interpretive work. I believe I am the one to identify the diversities of Judaisms and to devise a means of describing, analyzing, and interpreting those Judaisms, each in its own autonomy and each with its own integrity. By taking seriously the fact that "one of these things is not like the other, one of these things doesn't belong," and, therefore, should be allowed to find its place where it does, I have, I believe, framed an approach to the study of religion, that is, to the history and comparison of religions, that can well serve beyond the limits of Judaisms.

Now to this book in particular. I present twelve free-standing essays, all of them devoted to the same theme, namely, how, in our own times, the study of ancient Judaism has unfolded. I begin with the examination of two principal figures of the past generation, Saul Lieberman and Salo W. Baron, both of them transitional figures. I show that while they and their claques of admirers claimed that they innovated in fundamental ways the study of the received texts and history of Judaism, in fact they did nothing of the kind. In both cases we see the failure of the received modes of thought in the encounter with new ones. In Lieberman's case the logic of cogent discourse produced an illogic of free association. In Baron's instance the topical program of modern times yielded a rather crude and heavy-handed sloganeering, a misunderstanding of the fundamental issues of modern social science.

We proceed first to the literary, then to the religious, study of the generative writings of the Judaism of the dual Torah in its formative age.

On the literary study of the Judaism of the dual Torah, I contrast the Jewish circle of hermeneutics and its representation, and homogeneous reading, of the received writings with my own. That circle insists that documentary lines do not mark significant boundaries within the discourse of that Judaism, and I maintain that they do. In Chapters Two and Three, I spell out the position of the people who, in my view, do things wrong, and in Chapter Four I give a single example of how, in my view, to do things right, which is to read each document as a distinct and particular statement, with its own logical, rhetorical, and topical program. In the present case I concentrate on the logics of two documents and their authorships. I then turn to the historical study of formative Judaism, with special attention to the social history of that Judaism. I set on display two wrong ways of doing things, one the merely gullible, the other a wrong mode of category-formation. First, I provide a reprise of my argument in *Reading and Believing*, that much historical writing that lays claim to a critical attitude toward the received writings in fact replicates the familiar gullibility of the believers. Second, I review a book that claims to present Judaism "from the Maccabees to the Mishnah," and in seeing a single Judaism, fails not only to differentiate one Judaism from another, but, more seriously, the religion, Judaism, from the politics, history, institutions, culture, and everyday life of the Jews as a social entity. This exercise in utter confusion leads me to my two final essays in which I frame issues of the study of a Judaism, the religion, Judaism of the dual Torah, in what I believe is the right way and answer them in accord with methods I believe to be critical and sound. In the final section, I present results of the study of the Judaisms of late antiquity within the discipline of history of religion. These three chapters form an initial statement of how I propose to put together elements of diverse researches into a single coherent account. In this way I propose to do more than spell out both what I think is wrong, and also what I think is the right way to do things, in the study of a Judaism, a religion. I wish also to give what I believe will be the results of doing things the way, in this day and age, the consensus of critical scholarship concurs they should be done.

Jacob Neusner

December 20, 1987
In celebration of Hanukkah 5748
Program in Judaic Studies
Brown University
Providence, Rhode Island

Part One

CRITICAL METHOD:

WHEN INTELLECTUAL PARADIGMS SHIFT

Chapter One

Does The End of the Old
Mark the Beginning of the New?
The Odd Cases of
Saul Lieberman and Salo W. Baron

In the shift in a field of learning from one institutional setting to another, the field's paradigms, the modes of thought, manner of framing and testing hypotheses, the very thing that scholars want to find out about the subject at hand – all undergo drastic changes. For the institutional definition of what is important about a subject derives its norms not from the inner logic of the evidences of the subject, its sources and their structure, but rather from the institutional program itself. What the scholars and students wish to know about a subject will define their selection of data, their formulation of problems, and their judgment of hypotheses worth entertaining or worthy of neglect. Younger people in the time of shifts of paradigm, both institutional and intellectual, face the difficult task of moving from the old to the new world of learning. In doing so, they have to define for themselves a new approach to familiar knowledge. One solution to the problem is to ask new questions to old documents, or to do in a new way a task ordinarily done in some other, old way. Reading a familiar text in an unprecedented manner, the new generation then builds a bridge from the known but rejected to the unfamiliar but inviting mode of learning. Writing history in a fresh way, for instance, critically and skeptically instead of gullibly and credulously, or defining the historical agenda in new categories altogether represents a parallel way across what is in fact an unbridgeable abyss.

In the twentieth century, a very ancient tradition of learning found itself in a new institutional setting, and furthermore attracted to itself scholars bearing a quite unprecedented burden of interests. That field of learning is called "Jewish scholarship," meaning systematic study of the holy books of Judaism produced, after the Hebrew Scriptures of ancient Israel, from the second through the seventh century. These holy books, the Mishnah, a law code of ca. A.D. 200, various compilations of exegeses of Scripture, and, finally, the Talmud of Babylonia, a systematic exegesis of both the Mishnah and the Hebrew Scriptures, of ca. A.D. 600, had been studied in yeshivas, that is, "sessions," where law was studied and the theory of law evolved. Jewry constituted a political entity, and the institutions of learning served the polis. There the commentaries, codes of law, and basic texts formed the center of legislation and government, in theory and in practice, of the Jewish People. The institutional analogue to the yeshiva ("session") can be imagined if we set the Supreme Court judges onto the faculty of George Washington University, covering all subjects not only law, and, furthermore, declare them, or those subject to their authority, to be also the U. S. Congress, the Executive Offices and Heads of Federal agencies and departments, and on and on. The entire government of Israel, the Jewish People, consisted of these scholar-administrator-clerk-judges. The premises of their education and, consequently, scholarly study derived from the political responsibilities of these central figures and centered upon the amplification and theory of the law.

Now when the Jews en masse entered into the politics of the West, they carried forward the study of their received holy books. But the institutional basis shifted radically, for the political tasks entrusted to the scholars no longer pertained in Europe and in the USA (but they do, of course, continue in the State of Israel). Now the holy books were deemed part of the religious-theological or cultural heritage of the Jews, not to constitute political facts as the constitution and bylaws of a nation. Scholars addressed themselves to the study of the history and culture contained in those books, to the discovery of the correct text, the meanings of their words in historical context, and similar questions familiar from nineteenth century critical learning. A second and distinct task, connected to, but not continuous with, the first, required the scholars to carry on their studies not only or mainly in institutions sustained by the Jewish community, teachers' seminaries and rabbinical schools, for example, but also in universities. A new address for scholarship invited inquiry into questions of common intelligibility, in place of those issues particular to Judaic discourse that had defined discourse in the Jewish institutions for Jewish learning. The paradigm shift involved, therefore, both institutional and intellectual changes of a fundamental order. Here we inquire about the transitional generation, important figures born in one circumstance but active in the other.

I argue, through two exemplary figures, that the transitional generation, saluted in its day as harbingers of the new, turns out in retrospect not altogether successful in its enterprise of adaptation or renovation. For a paradigm-shift is just that: a fundamental change in how learning proceeds, for what purposes, under what auspices. The advent of a subject into a new institutional setting presents what is in fact an insoluble problem before those who have studied the subject under different conditions. Assuming that they know the old and have now to bring to bear the disciplines of the new, they turn out to grasp little of the new and only to go through motions they do not fully understand, like an untrained clog-dancer attempting a pirouette. The end of the old does not mark the beginning of the new. Where, how, and when the new generation undertakes its labors within the discipline of a new paradigm and a new institutional sponsorship for its subject, it derives from the immediately prior, supposedly transitional figures no useful model at all. The paradigm-shift, the advent of different institutional sponsorship for learning – these signal an abyss beyond all bridging, separating traditions of learning that address a single subject in common. So I shall argue by way of example.[1]

My examples, drawn from the history and sociology of learning in the literary and historical traditions of the Jews, originate in two long and influential careers, now ended, in the field of what is called "Jewish scholarship," meaning the study of the history, literature, religion, and culture of the Jews, from ancient Israelite to modern Israeli times. What we shall see is how two transitional figures struggled to find their way in the new intellectual and institutional world, bearing the crushing burden of the old. That new world was new geographically as much as intellectually, since both figures moved at the critical turning in their careers from European to American institutions. They found themselves, when they did, in circumstances, both institutional and intellectual, with no parallel in their European (including, in the first of the two cases, Palestinian-Jewish) careers. Each figure solved the problem of bringing the known into the framework of an unfamiliar world in the same way, by doing something new to a familiar subject.

The one read an inherited ("traditional") document not ordinarily studied in the old institutions, but he did so in accord with essentially the same exegetical and paraphrastic protocol in which he had been educated, and when he tried a to-him-new discipline, namely, history, he proved incapable of mastering it. The reason is that he was unable to think in those propositional and philosophical patterns that historical study required; he was all footnotes, no text. The other read a familiar subject in an unfamiliar way, showing as he did so that he had in no way become adept at that new way at all. Interestingly, both published their

---

[1]The implications of my argument for the study of the modernization of other fields of learning within the history of ideas in the twentieth century seem to me self-evident. We have to ask how new were the works of the first generation of new learning in a variety of traditional cultures in transition, both academic cultures defined by a textual community, such as is under discussion here, and also popular and political cultures.

most original and important work just as they turned forty. Each spent the
rest of this life repeating an early success, expanding, elaborating,
amplifying, but never doing anything new or even doing in a new way
something already attempted. I claim to explain that fact by appeal not to
the unfolding of the life-cycle of the scholar, but to the intellectual tools
accessible to each figure. Still, what we learn from these transitional
figures is that, when you leave home, you not only cannot go back. You
also cannot go anywhere else. For the true paradigm-shift takes place not
with the transitional figures. It makes its impact upon intellectual life only
with those who, from birth and through their education, proved to be
utterly at home in the new world of intellect and institutional setting alike.
There is no transition, no bridge extends across the abyss. The
transitional generation marks only the end of a tradition of intellect that is
always available for replication and recapitulation in terms of its own
paradigm. But, in terms of a new paradigm, the old tradition forever
remains beyond adaptation, let alone renewal. There not only is no
going back; there is no past, when paradigms shift.

I.
Saul Lieberman (1898-1982):
From Fixed Association to Free Association

The first of the two exemplary figures stands for the end of the old
paradigm of learning. He is Saul Lieberman, born Motol, near Pinsk, in
Byelorussia. Lieberman studied traditional Jewish sciences, the exegesis
of the Babylonian Talmud and related documents for instance, in the
yeshivas of Malch and Slobodka. Leaving that subject, Lieberman went on
to medicine at the University of Kiev in the 1920s, went to what was then
Palestine and promptly left for France, where he continued his studies.
He again settled in Jerusalem, in 1928, and reverted to his original
subject, particularly talmudic philology. But he added to his curriculum
Greek language and literature, and this represented what was new. For it
was not common for Talmud scholars to introduce classical philology
into talmudic exegesis, though from the time of S. Krauss's *Griechische
und lateinische Lehnwörter im Talmud, Midrasch, und Targum* (1898-9),
it was generally recognized that talmudic philology required knowledge of
Greek. Accordingly, what Lieberman did was new for someone of his
origins and interests, but was commonplace for learning.

In the yeshiva-world only one of the two Talmuds, the Babylonian,
was subjected to study. In defining the new approach to the received
literature, Lieberman chose to concentrate on the other, the Talmud of
the Land of Israel, a.k.a. the Yerushalmi (for "Jerusalem Talmud"). This
he did at the Hebrew University, where he was appointed lecturer in
Talmud in 1931. From 1934 he was dean at the Harry Fischel Institute for

Talmudic Research in Jerusalem.   His appointment at the Hebrew University terminated,[2] in 1940 he emigrated to the USA, where he became professor of Palestinian literature and institutions (meaning the Talmud of the Land of Israel or Yerushalmi) at the Jewish Theological Seminary of America, a rabbinical school for the education of rabbis for Conservative Jewish congregations.   In 1949 he was appointed dean, and in 1958 rector.

Lieberman's first book was called simply "On the Palestinian Talmud," and in it he emended texts and conducted a set of lower critical studies. While unconventional for the yeshiva-world, the intellectual enterprise – bits and pieces of novellae on isolated texts – hardly represented a new definition of work. As we shall see, when Lieberman did undertake work that was new in its very morphology, he proved unable to do it. A further set of studies, also mostly of a literary and philological character, followed. His greatest work was a systematic study of the Tosefta (1937-1939), a compilation of sayings in the name of authorities who occur, also, in the Mishnah. His analytical and exegetical work, covering the entire, sizable document, both proposed textual revisions based on a diversity of manuscript representations and also citations of the work in medieval commentaries, and also supplied explanations for numerous difficult passages. When Lieberman came to America, he took for himself the program of writing in English and also of writing on subjects of broad interest to his new scholarly environment, for example, historical and cultural topics. His work in English concerned historical and cultural problems.   *Greek in Jewish Palestine* (1942) and *Hellenism in Jewish Palestine* (1950) dealt with a number of concrete cultural matters, and his one important historical effort, on the history of the Jews in Palestine, will presently occupy our attention. He abandoned the effort to address the larger academic world of America, as I shall argue, because he could not accomplish that task of reframing not only his mode of address but also his mode of thought. In any event, in the 1950s and for the remainder of his life Lieberman reverted to Tosefta-exegesis, done in Hebrew of course, vastly expanding it in many volumes.

The work of the 1940s therefore captures Lieberman's effort at moving from one world to another, one country to another, and one paradigm of learning to a new one.   Lieberman represents the transition from one institution to two others, specifically, from the old-world yeshiva, which pursued the exegetical study of commentaries to, and codes of, the law of Judaism, beginning with the Talmud of Babylonia, to, first, an Israeli

---

[2]The decisive impact of that termination on Lieberman's life and career – he left the country and went to America, he had to learn a new language and to find a place for himself in a rabbinical seminary that was not Orthodox – cannot be overestimated.

university, and, second, an American non-Orthodox rabbinical
seminary. In making that move, he sought a fresh program of inquiry into
the received literature. He found it in making use of classical philology for
the exegesis of words and phrases of the Talmud and related writings, on
the one side, and presenting a compendious commentary to a critical text
of some of those same writings, on the other. So when he laid the
foundations for his abortive career at the Hebrew University, he
continued in a German-model university the philological work he was
trained to do in the yeshiva-world, but he did it on a broader basis and
drew upon a wider range of information. That is to say, in the move from
East European yeshiva to the Hebrew University, founded as it was on the
German model, he studied the old books in new ways. The American
move then challenged him to study new subjects in ways new to him, that
is to say, topics of history and culture. That he could not do. Lieberman's
move from yeshiva to university in the German tradition and onward to an
American rabbinical seminary carried him over considerable territory.

Here we can deal with only one dimension of his intellectual journey.
At issue is simply the received mode of thought concerning the making of
connections and the drawing of conclusions, and the mode of thought
characteristic of Lieberman's intellectual work, as represented by a single
exemplary article of his. What we shall see is the faulty, indeed
uncomprehending, replication, without any real understanding, of a rich
logical tradition. To explain the way in which Lieberman, in making his
move from a traditional to a modern intellectual climate, preserved the
form, but not the substance, of a received logic of cogent discourse, I
have to explain one paramount principle of cogency in the literature
studied in the yeshiva-world, and also in the university and seminary to
which Lieberman moved. The Babylonian Talmud, paramount
document for yeshiva-study, exhibits two traits of the mind in making
connections and drawing conclusions, one familiar, the other not. And it
is the unfamiliar one – specifically, the mode of connecting one thing to
something else in a well-composed and coherent statement of some
dimensions – that will occupy our attention.

The first trait of cogent discourse in the Babylonian and Palestinian
Talmuds is appeal to what is familiar indeed to us: rigorous propositional
argument at the middle range of forming sentences into paragraphs. That
is to say, when authors within the Talmud of Babylonia wish to make
connections and draw and present conclusions, they compose statements
and construct arguments in precisely the ways that we do in the Western
philosophical tradition. They present a proposition, amplify, illustrate,
test, prove, argue for it, just as we do. That is how they produce what we
should call "paragraphs" or "chapters" of thought. But there is a second
principle of cogency operative in the Talmud of Babylonia. It is one not

familiar to us.   It concerns the composition, out of well-formed proposition, of a sustained discourse, which we might call a chapter, that is to say, several paragraphs that flow in correct, logical order, one from the next, and make a single cogent point.

The (to us unfamiliar) logic of setting forth a sequence of propositions in the Talmud of Babylonia I call the logic of fixed association. Two or more propositions, unrelated to one another, may be set side by side because a text external to them both is thereby amplified. The association between paragraph A and paragraph X then is not because the one leads to the other and coheres in sense or meaning, but because both paragraphs join to a common text, which each one illuminates in its distinct way. The association between the two paragraphs then is extrinsic, supplied, conventional, and always fixed by a third, received statement, a text that is commented upon. When in the Talmud of Babylonia, therefore, an author wishes to join two or more propositions, that is to say, paragraphs of sizable discourse, the author may well affix both of those propositions or paragraphs to a fixed text, in succession to one another, even though the two propositions have not got the slightest connection to one another. I call this rather odd way of joining ideas a "logic of fixed association." What I mean is that an extrinsic protocol permits the association of two or more completed thoughts or propositions, even when those thoughts bear no intrinsic or logical connection.   In the Talmud of Babylonia, organized as it is as a commentary to a prior law code, the Mishnah, it is the order of topics (sentences, propositions) of that prior law code, and not of the unfolding and orderly argument in successive stages, that dictates the joining of this to that. This mode of thought then appeals to an *a priori* principle of connection, via fixed associations defined in a manner extrinsic to the proposition, at the broad horizon.

Now what can go wrong with this logic of fixed association is obvious. When the discipline of the protocol of fixed association is broken, what is left is merely *free* association. The faulty understanding of the logic of fixed association proves the key, since, when misunderstood, fixed yields free association. For if the logical sequence of propositions that connect and relate in an unfolding argument do not dictate connection between two facts or among three or more facts, so that the presentation of a statement encompasses facts, argument, and conclusion, then what does? In the received intellect, framed by study of the Talmud of Babylonia, it is the text that joins facts together within its own structure. For those who do not grasp the logic of fixed association that dictates what belongs and what does not, what is left is mere association without proposition.   That association beyond all rationality is what we call free association: there was this, and then, by the way, I just thought of that – but the other thing too comes to mind, and so forever and ever.

Training in the logic of fixed association did not teach Lieberman how to compose coherent arguments made up of sentences joined together in the service of a common syllogism, for example. In fact, he showed himself capable of exegesis of words and phrases, but unable to write history and treatises on culture. In this way, Lieberman shows us how, at the end of the received paradigm of learning, in the movement from one institutional setting to another, the *forms* of the old system persist, but are not understood and so enter a stage of decadence. Misunderstanding the received discipline of thought, he simply took for granted that sustained, continuous discourse, with one thought joined by proposition and logical sense to the next, defined no perquisite of cogent discourse. But then he found, in his progress out of the yeshiva world, no alternative principle of cogent discourse to take the place of the fixed association that, in the yeshiva-world made sense and provided self-evident connections between thought and thought. The result was that, when he had to address a Western reader and produce a set of coherent generalizations, e.g., of a historical order, he blundered, and, after a few efforts, gave up the effort entirely. What he was left to do, after the 1940s, was to revert to work he had already done, in the 1930s, and do it over again, only bigger and better.[3]

Lieberman shows in a concrete way how the logic of fixed association yielded to mere free association in the case of one who misunderstood the remarkably *disciplined* character of the paramount logic of fixed association. Lieberman of course recapitulated the form of fixed association, that is to say, the commentary. For if we review the literary form indigenous to the logic of fixed association, we note that the commentary or exegesis serves better than any other literary medium for expressing the discourse generated by that logic. The reason, self-evidently, is that once we have a fixed association defined by a text, then we do well to exploit what we have in hand, joining sentences one after the other not through shared propositions, nor even through a common teleological enterprise, but merely through appeal in common to an imputed cogency. But then, he also shows us what would happen when the entire conception of argument and proposition fell away, and when even the notion was lost that discourse of fixed association would register points, concerning the base-text, that were susceptible to generalization and systematic propositional statement. What would be left, then, would be simply the collecting and arranging of information pertinent to a given

---

[3]We shall see the same pattern with Salo W. Baron.

sequence of statements, for instance, a list of words or clauses or even whole sentences.

In attempting to write a historical article for the American university setting,[4] Lieberman found himself unable to conduct historical study and never again attempted to write a book or even an article on a historical problem. Nor, indeed do we find in Lieberman's corpus of writing much further effort to compose propositional discourses of a sustained character; his other work in English is essentially lexicographical and by nature episodic; the vast assembly of information in his Tosefta-commentary is conceptually utterly chaotic and bears no propositional character extending beyond two or three successive sentences. Over vast stretches of dreary fact-mongering, it is mere erudition, collecting and arranging lacking all logic. When we examine the sequence of topic-sentences of the sample at hand and secondary developments of paragraphs on an announced subject, we see how limited was the intellectual equipment provided to an exemplary figure of learning by training principally in the received canonical writings, secondarily in philology pertinent to them. Lieberman wishes to present an argument on "taxation and imaginary religious persecutions."[5]

A survey of his topic-sentences of sequential paragraphs yields the following:

We read in Aboth de R. Nathan, "Therefore shalt you serve..."

Similarly, we read in the Palestinian Talmud...

Here again the precariousness of riches at the beginning of the third century is well demonstrated.

We have already lost the topic "taxation," and persecution is not at stake. The point of joining the three topic-sentence, of course is that Lieberman appeals to an implicit text, or sequence of texts deemed to relate to one another, thus a fixed association, if one lacking an explicit text. So the procedure is not topical, even though the form is. But we proceed to recover the announced topic. Lieberman says, "The burden of *leitourgiai* of the third century is also well mirrored in rabbinic literature." Here the matter of taxation does emerge. We proceed to Lieberman's next topic-sentence:

R. Johanan himself summarized the situation....

Besides the liturgies, rabbinic literature of the time mentions a great number of taxes...

---

[4]Saul Lieberman, "Palestine in the Third and Fourth Centuries," *Jewish Quarterly Review* 1946, 36:329-370, 37:31-54.
[5]Pp. 344-370.

Similarly, Graetz gives a Midrash which demonstrates the crooked ways of the Roman legal procedure in trying the Jews.

Again, we read in the Palestinian Talmud: "Diocletian oppressed the inhabitants of Paneas."

The petition of the people of Paneas was probably worded according to the usual formula.

Similarly, we read in the Midrash:

Again, we read in the Palestinian Talmud:

I think it very probable that the purpose of Proclus' entering Sepphoris is revealed in another passage of TP [The Yerushalmi].

Moreover, the rabbis were not unaware of the fact that the Romans tried to put a face of legality on their robberies.

An interesting discrimination between the arbitrary and the 'legal' actions of the officials is noted in the following passage:

It is obvious from the names of the rabbis who visited the Hot Springs of Gadara that the question was raised in the first half of the third century.

Herein lies the main point of the discussion of the rabbis in the above passage of the Palestinian Talmud.

The Jews were in exactly the same situation as the other provincials.

The topic-headings of Lieberman's paragraphs leave the strong impression that we deal with a kind of stream of consciousness, not with a program and a well-crafted argument. The topic sentences do not produce the outline of a program, a propositional argument, a systematic inquiry – even a discussion of a sustained and orderly character. The topic-sentences attest to a stream of consciousness that in other circumstances we call free association. It is just this, that, and the other thing, starting somewhere, ending somewhere else. What has happened is that the dialectical argument as a mode of sustained discourse yields only the dialectic – the movement. The argument is lost, or left behind, or simply forgotten in the onrush of information and episodic, ad hoc observation concerning this and that.

That is not to suggest that Lieberman invariably proved incapable of composing a sustained argument, setting forth a well-composed statement with a beginning, middle, and end. Nor is it to claim that all he had to offer was an enormous mass of disorganized information, given some semblance of order by essentially meretricious appeal to a topic ("persecution," "taxation") or a text (the Tosefta). It is only to show that Lieberman exhibited an infirm grasp on the requirements of propositional discourse and relied rather heavily upon imputed connections which, a glance at his rather odd sequence of topic sentences suggests, look suspiciously like the outcome of little more than, "first there was this, and then, by the way, I just thought of it, also there was that." So much for the composition of a large-scale discussion, the counterpart to the resort to fixed association by the mind of Judaism. Let us then turn to the other principal mode of thought, the propositional, within the limits of a completed unit of thought, a paragraph. Here too we see the same evidence of a limited grasp, on Lieberman's part, of the mixed modes of thought of the received intellectual discipline in which Lieberman was educated and which he was widely held to embody better than anyone else in his time.

The reader may find patience to work through a sequence of two complete paragraphs, in which the full flavor of Lieberman's writing shows us how free association leads hither and yon but never to a cogently stated proposition, at best only to an implicit and somewhat confused one:[6]

> [1] We conclude our short survey with the position of the Patriarch and the Jewish scholars in the Roman system of taxation. [2] The role of the former in the distribution of the tax-burden and his responsibility towards the government are [sic!] not clear. [3] However, it is certain that the Patriarch had to pay vast sums to the government and offer gifts to the officials. [4] The Midrash relates that the Patriarch asked R. Simeon b. Laqish to pray for him, because "the government is very wicked," and this is demonstrated by the following episode: "A woman brought the Patriarch a small salver (diskarion) with a knife on it. He took the knife and returned the salver to her. Then a courier (beredarios, veredarius) of the government came and he saw it, coveted it, and took it."

I have numbered the sentences so that the simple point may be visibly clear. Numbers 1-3 form a cogent statement. The break at Number 4 is stunning. In fact we have no paragraph at all, only a set of generalizations followed by a case which in no way proves commensurate with, or even congruent to, the generalizations, and, in my judgment, has not been demonstrated to be even relevant to the issue.

Let us conduct the same analysis of the following paragraph in context, for we shall see precisely the same problem exhibited by Lieberman's writing in sustaining a thought and mounting an argument at the intermediate level of discourse, that of a propositional character, that we noted in mounting a cogent statement at the large level of discourse, that in accord with the logic of fixed association:

> [1] As for the scholars, there is enough evidence to show that they were at certain periods...exempt from some taxes and especially from *leitourgias*. [2] But it is unlikely that all scholars enjoyed the tax immunities. [3] It is much more probable that only the ordained scholars benefited from this privilege, scholars who could be placed in the category of priests, *sacerdotes*. [4] From the Palestinian Talmud we learn

---

[6]Pp. 359-362, pass.

that Simeon b. Abba was not ordained because he happened to be in Damascus when an opportunity to ordain him presented itself. [5] We also find that R. Jonah refused to be ordained prior to his teacher, R. Zeminah.

I simply point out that between sentence [3] and sentence [4] is an abyss, another between [4] and [5]. So the paragraph consists of three absolutely unrelated thoughts – and no proposition joins the thoughts. The pattern in both paragraphs is manifestly the same. Lieberman starts with something very like a generalization, then resorts immediately to a "case." But the case stands on its own. There is no clear connection between the case and the generalization. In the first paragraph, the "wickedness of the government" is not very clearly linked to the generalization, and Lieberman's reason for introducing the case is scarcely made explicit, nor are the conclusions we are to draw. But his persistent introduction of the Greek and Latin for the Hebrew counterparts suggests that a secondary motive was simply to show off knowledge of the Greek and Latin counterparts for the Hebrew, since that information plays no role whatsoever in making the point, if any, that he wished to make. In Lieberman's defense, I have to point out that the next paragraph refers back to "these incidents" and alludes to this and that, so that, if we stay the course, we can get some sense out of the whole.

But it seems to me amply demonstrated that Lieberman found exceedingly difficult the composition of a cogent paragraph, with a beginning, middle, and end, and that he was remarkably adept at collecting and posting interesting pieces of information. These pieces of information manifestly lacked all cogency between and among themselves, but were joined to some larger whole only by reason of an assumed composition, an implicit set of unstated associations of an-other-than propositional character. With no evidence of an available program of fixed associations (except as Lieberman's own mind defined for him the points of contact or intersection between one thing and the next), we have to conclude that the Judaic mind of the Bavli in our own day is imitated but not understood. For Saul Lieberman, exemplary of the world which received this kind of writing (whether in English or in Hebrew) and valued it, and Lieberman's audience too, obviously took for granted that free association, when executed by a scholar of sufficient public notoriety or political influence in the limited world at hand, constituted logical discourse. And that is not at all how the mind of Judaism was meant to think.

In his move from Yeshiva to an American setting, Lieberman faced the task of shifting from one intellectual paradigm to another. The former involved a somewhat modernized continuation of the exegetical-philological modality of the inherited system of thought. Just as in studying the Talmud, people read words and phrases and said things about them, so the so-called scientific (that is, *wissenschaftliche*) students of the Talmud did the same. They added attention to variant readings and they learned languages not ordinarily learned in yeshivas. But what they did with what they knew was not different in morphology, in fundamental mode of logical discourse, from what people in Yeshivas did. When he moved from Slobodka to Jerusalem, Lieberman moved to a world that was different from, but intellectually continuous with, the world in which he originated. When he left Jerusalem and came to New York, he encountered a different world altogether. He tried to meet its challenges, but did not have the intellectual equipment to do so, and so turned back to his earlier success with the Tosefta and recapitulated it. And as to the prior hope, namely, to present the Talmud of the Land of Israel with a critical text and an ample commentary, so opening it for contemporary study, beyond his earliest efforts, and excepting only some bits and pieces of apercus on this and that, Lieberman never even tried. Nor, of course, did he encourage anyone else to.

To state the matter simply, what we find in Lieberman is simply the incapacity either to generalize or to compose a competent paragraph, that is to say, present a propositional statement of a cogent character in which connections between two facts are made to yield a conclusion. Fixed association has in Lieberman's mind, as shown in his writing, given way to free association. He presents us with an exemplary figure who excelled at the hunting and gathering, the collecting and arranging of information, which is always best presented – predictably – in the form of a commentary. Even within the units of thought of the commentary, for example, on the Tosefta, Lieberman found it exceedingly difficult to state two or more cogent thoughts in not only succession but cogent relation. But Lieberman in English presents us with an accurate portrait of the workings of the mind.

What was at stake in Lieberman's (exemplary) failure to replicate the received logic? For him and those around him, what would happen, concretely, was that fixed association, with its remarkably subtle mode of effecting connection, was misunderstood as a license for *free* association in which nothing joined anything to anything else. Merely collecting and arranging vast quantities of information, without a semblance of a point or a proposition, is not the same thing as collecting what pertains immediately and directly to a sequence of words, phrases, or topics that stand in a fixed and precise relationship with one another. The logic of fixed association dictated not only what fit, but also what did not. Reduced to a scheme of collecting and arranging masses of information composing a whole of a merely thematic order, the logic of free association ended up no logic at all because no one could say what did not belong to discourse. Everything fit as well as everything else because, in a logic of free association, nothing was to be excluded on principle, on logic.

The long-term result was to yield public discourse, in the Judaic sciences, lacking all cogency, a mode of setting forth sentences in which beginnings and endings of paragraphs, that is to say, of whole discourses or expositions of ideas, played no role and served no purpose. For in free association, not only does any thing enter or leave merely as a matter of whim, but the very notion of connection is lost. And that forms the end of logic, of cogent discourse of a public character that, in one way or another, produces if not propositions then a kind of discourse deemed cogent and sensible with rules of intelligible exchange of thought, public laws governing what one may say and what is forbidden, in all, a syntax and structure of mind. In our own day the world made by the Bavli tended to lose sight of the discipline and order implicit in the logic of fixed association and to understand as the principle of intelligible discourse generated by the Bavli the legitimacy of utter free association. And that, by the way, was why he also could not write history.

II. Salo W. Baron (1895-):
Social Science and Conceptual Chaos

If Saul Lieberman proved insufficiently educated in the intellectual tradition he left and so unable to carry with him into the new world a clear sense for its logic, Salo W. Baron represents the counterpart phenomenon. When he entered a new world of mind, he merely imitated its language, without fully understanding it. Let me explain. Salo W. Baron was born in Tarnow, Galicia, in 1895, and brought to Vienna after 1914. He earned doctorates in philosophy in 1917, political science in 1922, and law in 1923, and was ordained a rabbi by the Jewish Theological Seminary in Vienna in 1920. He taught there at the Jewish Teachers College from 1919 through 1926, when he came to the USA to teach at the Jewish Institute of Religion in New York City, a rabbinical seminary. After a brief career there, from 1927 to 1930, he came to Columbia University, where he taught Jewish History in the Department of History at Columbia University. He also taught, from 1957, at the Jewish Theological Seminary of America. He was the first professor of Jewish history in a U.S. university history department. The institutional shift in Baron's career was not from yeshiva to university, but from a Jewish-sponsored school, whether the Vienna teachers' seminary or the American Reform Jewish rabbinical seminary, to a non-sectarian university.

Baron's importance for our inquiry lies in his representation of Jewish learning in the department of his choice, history. The problem before him was how to translate the subject he studied into the issues of his discipline. The answer lies on his interest in social history, so Arthur Hertzberg, "His emphasis has been on the social history of the people, rather than on the achievements of individual figures; on elements and areas of cross fertilization between Jews and their environment, rather than on pogroms and suffering; and on the Jewish Diaspora and Erez Israel [the Land of Israel], as the two centers of Jewish creativity, contrary to the views both of a Diaspora-oriented historian, such as Simon Dubnow, and the new school of Israel-centered scholars, such as Ben Zion Dinur."[7]

Hertzberg's accurate characterization points to the choice Baron made for himself. He looked backward, on a scholarly heritage that defined history as personal. So he proposed to introduce into the study of the Jews' history the interests of social science. That accounts for the title of his comprehensive and synthetic work, *A Social and Religious History of the Jews.*[8] He read the received corpus of history as the works of great men (never: women). He would concentrate on groups. The Jews were treated by their historians as isolated, living out their collective life in utter separation from their neighbors in the diaspora and in the Land of Israel as well. Baron would then seek commonalities, and, as any good social scientist, would ask about comparisons and contrasts. When we examine in microscopic detail what he actually did, as distinct from the topical program he defined for himself, we may assess the concrete record. What we shall see is precisely how competently Baron accomplished his goals. As I shall show, the intellectually alert and witty program proved beyond his capacities, so he went through the motions, without achieving the analytical goals.

One of the principal foci of Baron's work was economic history, and, it follows, the example in the case of Baron derives from the subdivision of social history that treats economics. Baron proposed, in particular, to write what he thought was "Jewish economic history." The facts that Jews' economies flourish within larger economies, on the one hand, and do not form a single continuum through time, on the other, did not prevent him from describing "Jewish economic history" portrayed through the

---

[7]Arthur Hertzberg, "Baron, Salo (Shalom) Wittmayer)," *Encyclopaedia Judaica* 4:254.

[8]This work, complete, originally appeared in three volumes in 1937. A second edition, considerably expanded and revised, began in 1952, and, far from complete, by 1983 had reached eighteen volumes. The "religious" part of the social and religious history defines its program without a serious engagement with the methods of history of religion. In 1986, Baron published a work on history and religion lacking sustained reference to anything written after 1971, and we may dismiss as trivial any pretense on Baron's part to study religion. Hence we concentrate only on his claim to write social history, and, as I shall explain, within social history, the economics of the Jews.

composition of pictures of Jews' economics and Judaism's economics. That was because an absolute given of his historical study was that the Jews form a continuing, uniform group, with a single, linear history, hence, "Jewish history," not merely Jews' histories, defined his work. Quite reasonably, the same conception defined for Baron the field of "Jewish economic history," a social scientific subdivision of the social and religious history of the Jews.

Since our interest in Baron is whether or not he actually gave evidence of grasping the social science he claimed to introduce into the study of Jews' history, we have to ask whether or not Baron produced a conceptually rigorous definition of the work. And the answer, as I shall show through analysis of exemplary statements of his, is that he went through motions that proved clumsy and imitative. Baron's works on this subject are characterized by fundamental faults of method, conception, and execution. As to method, they impute to all Jews everywhere traits demonstrated in a single case. As to conception, they take for granted that sayings attributed to authorities by texts composed long after said authorities lived actually were said by those authorities, and, further, that people did precisely what sages said they should do. As to execution, they display considerable difficulty in composing cogent paragraphs and well-crafted arguments. In all, a work on the economics of Judaism, not on Jews' economic behavior or on an alleged correlation between the economics of Judaism and Jews' economic behavior or economics or formation of economies does well to review how these subjects have been handled even by substantial figures of our own time.

One representative example of Baron's "Jewish economic history" as a chapter of his introduction, into Jewish learning, of historical generalization in place of (mere) exegesis of texts, with particular reference to Jewish social history suffices to show the essential incomprehension, on his part, of what was at stake. He presents [9] us with a claim to know about economic trends among Jews in the second, third, and fourth centuries. As evidence he cites episodic statements of rabbis, as in the following:

> In those days R. Simon ben Laqish coined that portentous homily which, for generations after, was to be quoted in endless variations: "'You shall not cut yourselves,' this means you shall not divide yourselves into separate groups...." Before the battle for ethnic-religious survival, the inner class struggle receded. [10]

---

[9] *A Social and Religious History of the Jews* (New York: Columbia University Press, 1952) II. *Ancient Times,* Part II, pp. 241-260.
[10] Baron, p. 241.

Baron's introduction of such categories as "class struggle" will strike the reader as odd. For he does not tell us what he means, for late antiquity, by "class" at all, and how the Marxian category of "class struggle" pertains is equally unexplained. But that error of a misplaced metaphor need not detain us, because it represents a sophistication to begin with not displayed in Baron's "Jewish economic history." Not defining for us the origins and character of classes and the generative source of the (consequent) "class struggle," Baron plunges forward:

> Age-old antagonisms, to be sure, did not disappear overnight. The conflict between the scholarly class and "the people of the land" continued for several generations...

> Class differences as such likewise receded into the background as the extremes of wealth and poverty were leveled down by the unrelenting pressure of Roman exploitation. Rarely do we now hear descriptions of such reckless display of wealth as characterized the generation of Martha, daughter of Boethos, before the fall of Jerusalem. Even the consciously exaggerated reports of the wealth of the patriarchal house in the days of Judah I fell far short of what we know about the conspicuous consumption of the Herodian court and aristocracy....

It would be difficult to find a better example of overinterpretation of evidence to begin with irrelevant to the point than Baron's concluding sentence of the opening paragraph of this abstract.

Not having shown that there was an inner class struggle or even spelled out what he means by class struggle, how he knows the category applies, let alone the evidence for social stratification on which such judgments rest, Baron leaps into his explanation for why the class struggle receded. That is not the only evidence of what can only be regarded as indifference to critical issues characteristic of writing on Jews' economies, but it is probative. The rest of the passage shows how on the basis of no sustained argument whatsoever, Baron invokes a variety of categories of economic history and analysis of his time, e.g., conspicuous consumption, class struggle ("inner" presumably different from "outer"), and on and on. When discussing economic policies, Baron presents a discussion some may deem fatuous.[11] Precisely how he frames the issues of economic theory will show why:

> Economic Policies: Here too we may observe the tremendous influence of talmudic legislation upon Jewish economy.

The premise that there was (a) Jewish economy, and that (b) talmudic legislation affected economic action, is simply unsubstantiated. How Baron knows that people did what rabbis said they should, or that Jews

---

[11]Baron, pp. 251-255.

formed an economy in which people could make decisions in accord with sages' instructions, he does not say. The premise of all that follows, then, is vacant.   More to the point of our interest in matters of economic theory, we turn to Baron's program of discourse on what he has called "policies:"

> The rabbis constantly tried to maintain interclass equilibrium. They did not denounce riches, as some early Christians did, but they emphasized the merely relative value of great fortunes....The persistent accentuation of collective economic responsibility made the Jewish system of public welfare highly effective. While there was much poverty among the Jews, the community, through its numerous charitable institutions, took more or less adequate care of the needy.

> Man's right, as well as duty, to earn a living and his freedom of disposing of property were safeguarded by rabbinic law and ethics only in so far as they did not conflict with the common weal....

> Private ownership, too, was hedged with many legal restrictions and moral injunctions in favor of over-all communal control....

> Rabbinic law also extended unusual protection to neighbors....

> Nor did the individual enjoy complete mastery over testamentary dispositions....

> Apart from favoring discriminatory treatment of apostates, who were supposed to be dead to their families, the rabbis evinced great concern for the claims of minor children to support from their fathers' estate....

> In a period of economic scarcity social interest demanded also communal control over wasteful practices even with one's own possessions....

How this mélange of this and that – something akin to economic policy, some odd observations on public priority over private interest that sounds suspiciously contemporary (to 1952), counsel about not throwing away bread crumbs – adds up to "economic policies" I cannot say. But the data deserves a still closer scrutiny, since Baron represents the state of economic analysis of Judaism and so exemplifies precisely the problem I propose to solve in a different way. Here is his "man's right" paragraph, complete:

> Man's right, as well as duty, to earn a living and his freedom of disposing of property were safeguarded by rabbinic law and ethics only in so far as they did not conflict with the common weal. Extremists like R. Simon ben Yohai insisted that the biblical injunction, "This book of the law shall not depart out of thy mouth, but thou shalt meditate therein day and night," postulated wholehearted devotion to the study of Torah at the expense of all economic endeavors.   But R. Ishmael effectively countered by quoting the equally scriptural blessing, "That thou mayest gather in thy corn and thy wine and thine oil." Two centuries later, the Babylonian Abbaye, who had started as a poor man and through hard

labor and night work in the fields had amassed some wealth, observed tersely, "Many have followed the way of R. Ishmael and succeeded; others did as R. Simeon ben Yohai and failed." Sheer romanticism induced their compeer, R. Judah bar Ila'i, to contend that in olden times people had made the study of the law a full-time occupation, and devoted only little effort to earning a living, and hence had proved successful in both.... R. Simeon ben Yohai himself conceded, however, that day and night meditation had been possible only to a generation living on Mannah or to priestly recipients of heave-offerings.... In practice the rabbis could at best secure, as we shall see, certain economic privileges for a minority of students, relying upon the overwhelming majority of the population to supply society's needs to economically productive work.

From the right to earn a living being limited by the common weal, we jump to study of the Torah as the alternative to productive labor. That move of Baron's I cannot myself claim to interpret. I see no connection between the balance between "freedom of disposing of property" and "conflict with the common weal," on the one side, and the issue of work as against study, on the other. The rest of the discussion concerns only that latter matter, and the paragraph falls to pieces by the end in a sequence of unconnected sayings joined by a pseudo-narrative ("two centuries later...") and an equally-meretricious pretense of sustained argument "...himself conceded"), all resting on the belief that the sayings assigned to various sages really were said by them.

This reading by Baron of how "the Jews" policies and behavior in economics are to be studied turned out to be not at all idiosyncratic. For Baron, unlike Lieberman, produced students and influenced colleagues. The result was that a whole field, "Jewish economic history," flowed from his definition of what one studies when one studies that subject. Since Baron did not really grasp the problems of conceptualization and the critical grasp of the character of evidence, the way in which economic history formed propositions and tested them, the work that flowed from imitating a language of thought that people really could not speak exhibited the same traits of uncomprehension. The obvious flaws of historical method, the clear limitations in even so simple a matter as the competent construction of a paragraph – these traits of Baron's construction of the Jewish economy and Jewish economic policy became representative. And any study of the history of ideas, the results of paradigm-shifts, and the consequences of the movement of a tradition of learning from one sort of institution to another will find important what happened in a case such as the present one.

What happened is that an entire field of learning took shape in which the fundamental flaws were replicated again and again. Only much later did new voices, trained elsewhere, enter the discussion. But, in circles well-pleased with the new tradition of learning, those voices would not be heard. Let us review some of the givens of the second generation, after Baron, in "Jewish economic history." The received conception first of all imputes to the Jews a single economic history, which can be traced diachronically. Proof lies in works in both English and Hebrew. Take for example the book entitled, *Economic History of the Jews,* assigned to Salo W. Baron, Arcadius Kahan, and others, edited by Nachum Gross.[12] Not surprisingly, Baron, inventor of Jewish social history, therefore also Jewish economic history, takes pride of place in this odd volume. Baron wrote Chapters One through Seven, Kahan, Eight through Ten, of Part One, "general survey," and the titles of these sequential chapters follow: "the first temple period, exile and restoration, the second temple period, the talmudic era, the Muslim Middle Ages, medieval Christendom, economic doctrines, the early modern period, the transition period, the modern period." That, I contend, is a program of diachronic economic history. These chapters can have been composed and presented in the sequence before us only if the author assumed that a single group, with a continuous, linear history, formed also a cogent and distinct economic entity, with its own, continuous, linear, economic history.

"Economic doctrines" as Baron expounds them are amply familiar to us: bits and pieces of this and that. The book's agenda replicates with precision the appeal to topics, that is, mere subject-categories, for the organization of data; there is, after all, no further analytical task to be undertaken through a nuanced classification of data. The remainder of the book covers these topics: agriculture, industry, services, and each part is subdivided, e.g., under services: "banking and bankers, brokers, contractors, court Jews, department stores, Jewish autonomous finances, market days and fairs, mintmasters and moneyers, moneylending, peddling, secondhand goods, slave trade, spice trade, stock exchanges." Here again, we may be sure, data on department stores derive from one time and place, those on slave trade, from another. But laid forth sequentially, the chapter-titles indicate a conception of a single unitary and continuous economic history, in which any fact concerning any Jew at any time or place connects with any fact concerning any other Jew at any other time or place, the whole forming a cogent economy.

Since Baron participated in editing the volume at hand, let us turn to one that he did not edit, since this one, in Hebrew, substantiates my claim that, because Baron successfully defined what one would do in writing a "social and religious history of the Jews," other people would, with equal uncomprehension, do the same thing. Nachum Gross, represented in the volume just now noted, edited *Jews in Economic Life. Collected Essays*

---

[12]New York: Schocken, 1975.

In Memory of Arkadius Kahan (1920-1982).[13] Here is the portrait of a field, as sequential essays outline that field:

The Economic Activities of the Jews

The Cardinal Elements of the Economy of Palestine during the Herodian Period

The Economy of Jewish Communities in the Golan in the Mishna and Talmud Period

The Itinerant Peddler in Roman Palestine

The German Economy in the 13th-14th Centuries: The Framework and Conditions for the Economic Activity of the Jews

On the Participation of Jewish Businessmen in the Production and Marketing of Salt in Sixteenth Century Poland and Lithuania

Economic Activities of Jews in the Caribbean in Colonial Times

Jewish Guilds in Turkey in the Sixteenth to Nienteenth Centuries

and on and on. Nor do I exaggerate the utter confusion generated by the conception of "the Jews" as an economic entity, continuous from beginning to the present. The juxtaposition of these two papers seems to me to make the point rather sharply:

Jewish Population and Occupations in Sherifian Morocco

On the Economic Activities of the Moldavian Jews in the second half of the 18th and the first half of the 19th centuries

There is no need to ask what one thing has to do with the other. We just take for granted that Jews are Jews wherever they lived, whenever they thrived, and whatever Jews' occupations were in Sherifian Morocco bears a self-evident relationship to whatever Moldavian Jews did for a living half a world and a whole civilization distant.

The upshot is simple. Baron began his career in Jewish-sponsored institutions of Jewish learning, teaching in the Jewish teachers seminary in Vienna, then in the new Reform rabbinical school in New York City. Then he moved to Columbia. His earlier education, in both Jewish subjects and also secular ones, exposed him not only to Judaic sciences but also to law, philosophy, and the like. Accordingly, Baron's mixed education equipped him to carry forward an old subject in a new way, and, as the institutional shift made it both possible and necessary for him to do so, he chose to work on "Jewish history," viewed as Jews had always (quite reasonably, from an ideological or theological perspective) viewed it, but do work on it in a way different from prior definitions. That is why

[13]Jerusalem: The Zalman Shazar Center for the Furtherance of the Study of Jewish History., 1985

Baron carried forward a received subject, namely, the study of the Jews' history, which, by the time he completed his formal education, in the case of the Jews had gone forward for more than a century. But that history was done by Jews and for Jewish readers, and constituted a sustained argument about rather parochial issues of group survival. Hence it stressed Jews' heroes and suffering, the books people wrote, the massacres other people carried out on them. The subterranean polemic is that Jews are cultured but suffer.

Taking up the study of history, Baron wished to reshape the subject and – appropriate to the ideal of entering a new institutional world – pursue the subject in such a way that others, not Jews alone, would derive valuable knowledge from it. To do this, Baron proposed to read texts for the purposes of social history, that is, for generalization, rather than for (mere) exegesis. But what he represented as social history scarcely corresponded to the sophisticated work of framing and testing hypotheses that others of his time carried on. When we recall that, in the very time Baron was writing the paragraphs we reviewed from his *Social and Religious History* Volume II (1952), and in the very same university, the Columbia of the late 1940s and 1950s, social science as we now know it was being redefined. In the very field at hand, in the same time and place, Michael Polanyi and Joseph Schumpeter were at work in the reconceptualization of economic history. That fact makes us recognize the stunning gap between Baron's work and that of others, on the same discipline, in the same university. Whether Baron did not understand, or was simply not interested, no one now knows.

Baron did not grasp the new economic history that Polanyi and Schumpeter were then creating. Rather, he found in economic history merely a new topic for the collection and arrangement of old facts, and then went about collecting and paraphrasing texts pertinent to that topic. What we find is not social history at all, but mere collections of references to texts deemed relevant to the theme at hand. Specifically, he came into a world of learning different from the yeshiva, but could not fully assimilate its methods, so he merely aped them. The result is an exercise in announcing a program that the sponsoring scholar himself did not really understand. In Baron's instance, the process of assimilation into the Western secular academy involved historical study of history, as against apologetic study of history. Once Baron had done his first go-around on his *Social and Religious History*, he had little more to do but to expand and amplify and augment, that is, merely more of the same. For he grasped little of the revolution in social science that took place in the late 1940s and beyond, so for him, social science was merely a set of topics, not a method and a way of thought, surely not a mode of framing hypotheses and testing them, identifying problems and solving them.

That is what I mean by imitating the sounds of a language without really speaking that language. No wonder that, like Lieberman, all that was left was to repeat an earlier success.

III. The First Generation Out and In

Flourishing in the first three quarters of this century, both Lieberman and Baron did their most original work in the 1930s, when they were, in fact, in the first third of their scholarly lives. But I think the reason was not biographical, but rather, intellectual. Lieberman's Tosefta-studies, 1937-1939, and Baron's first version of the *Social and Religious History,* of precisely the same years, would define the focus of their work in the second and third parts of those same protracted careers. Baron's second edition began its (as yet incomplete) journey in 1952, and Lieberman's expansion of his Tosefta-work started in 1955. Evidently, because neither man could find a second wind for his intellectual career, both could do little more than vastly improve upon their original efforts by covering much more detail than they had originally thought required. Lieberman's problem lay in an insufficient mastery of the logic of cogent discourse of the literature on which he worked; he imitated the form but found himself restricted to it. When he wished to undertake a different mode of discourse, he proved unprepared and retreated to a more comfortable and, for his purposes, appropriate framework: discrete comments on this and that, fundamentally lacking all method or system, deriving from the combination of formidable erudition, a fine memory, and guesswork. Baron, as I have shown, did not really grasp the new disciplines of social sciences but saw them as merely a source of neglected subjects, awaiting investigation, not problems demanding solution. That explains why he paid no attention, so far as the initial volumes of his *Social and Religious History* indicate, to the intellectual revolution under way in his own university, and among the social scientists who were his own colleagues. The names of Polanyi and Schumpeter do not occur in the index to the volumes, and, more to the point, the sophisticated conceptual issues of economic history and of the history of economic theory debated by them and their colleagues and students lay far beneath the horizon of Baron's vision of the economic part of social history.

More than this Lieberman and Baron have in common. They also, in their day, enjoyed exemplary standing as powerful political figures in the world of Jewish learning, Lieberman more in Jerusalem than in Conservative Judaism in the USA to be sure, Baron everywhere in U.S. university life. But despite their influence in their time, and despite even the claques ever ready to applaud their every word, neither defined an intellectual career that anyone afterward would follow. Lieberman produced no students at all, never directing a doctoral dissertation that in any way carried forward work he himself initiated, e.g., in Tosefta exegesis, in Yerushalmi-studies, and the like, and the work that he undertook ended with his death.   Baron's many students unanimously abandoned his conception of writing single, unitary, and linear histories of the Jews, whether social and religious or political and biographical. All of them chose to specialize in particular times and places and periods. The putatively compendious character of the work defined by Lieberman and Baron, in their moves, respectively, from the yeshiva to the German university (represented by Jerusalem) or from the Jewish to the secular academy, impressed no one as a worthwhile model.   The ideal of collecting and arranging whatever is worth knowing, represented for the study of the rabbinic literature by Lieberman's Tosefta studies and by Baron's history-volumes found no takers.

In the age of change in the institutional and conceptual setting in which the ancient tradition of Jewish learning would go forward, what we see in the two most important figures of the transitional generation is only the end of the old, not the beginning of the new.   The new generation in the subject in fact would have no past, and, the successors, none of them continuators, unanimously – a few explicitly, but most merely tacitly, – acknowledged no continuity with an intellectual past. And they were right. There was none.   The new learning began like archaeology, which leaps over centuries of silence to renew dialogue with the detritus of vanished ages.   The archaeologist is no more a continuator of discourse in the languages of Sumer or Akkad or the Rosetta Stone than the contemporary scholar of Judaic Studies carries forward the conversation of the Talmud in the language of thought of the Talmud.   Once the sands cover the

monuments, only the steel spade of another age can reveal them again –
but only for the inquiry of that new age, lacking all precedent in its
separation from the old, whether by one year, or by one generation, or
by a millenium. And so too when intellectual paradigms shift, the old
order passes into oblivion. And when the new begins, it is born *ex nihilo,*
in the minds and intellects of scholars without a past.

Part Two

LITERATURE:

WRONG WAYS AND RIGHT WAYS
IN THE STUDY OF THE LITERATURE
OF FORMATIVE JUDAISM

Chapter Two

Wrong Ways in Literary Study [1]:
Intertextuality and the Literature of Judaism

I. The Literary-Critical Issue of Intertextuality
and the Appeal to Rabbinic Judaism

The inquiry into the nature of intertextuality draws to itself the sustained attention of a circle of literary-critical scholars of Jewish origin who moreover appeal for their hermeneutics to traits they deem distinctive not only to Judaism in its classic literature but also to Jews, hence a Jewish circle of hermeneutics. These scholars appeal to the character of the rabbinic literature, particularly the biblical-exegetical writings produced by the Judaic sages of late antiquity, for roots and antecedents for the contemporary hermeneutic. The phenomenon is described by William Scott Green, who says, "It has become fashionable in some literary circles to depict rabbinic hermeneutics as allusive and indeterminate and to portray it as a harbinger of current dissenting theories of literature such as psychoanalysis and deconstruction. Consideration of rabbinic interpretive practices within the context of the religion that produced them calls that analogy into question. Rabbinic use of scripture was kaleidoscopic and the determination of textual meaning required and assumed a sealed sphere of reference."[1] As to the

---

[1]William Scott Green, "Romancing the Tome: Rabbinic Hermeneutics and the Theory of Literature," *Semeia* 1987, 40:147. Note also Howard Eilberg-Schwartz: "For some, rabbinic interpretation of Scripture is a forerunner of certain contemporary theories of reading. One school of recent criticism argues that all texts sustain a multiplicity of equally valid readings, each informed by its own set of assumptions. The text itself is said to exercise little control over its interpretation...This understanding of reading is said to be anticipated in rabbinic literature." See his "Who's Kidding Whom?: A Serious Reading of Rabbinic Word Plays," *Journal of the American Academy of Religion* 1987, 55:740. This matter of the text's "exercising little control over its interpretation" will prove crucial to the matter of intertextuality, as we shall see, and is central to the description of the rabbinic literature provided by Hartman and Handelman, whom we shall meet presently.

relevance, to the contemporary debate, of intertextuality in particular, Susan Handelman uses the following explicit language: "The rabbinic world is, to use a contemporary term, one of *intertextuality.* Texts echo, interact, and interpenetrate...."[2] The Jewish school of intertextuality therefore alleges that the peculiar traits of the writings of rabbinic Judaism, in the Talmuds and Midrash-compilations, prove particularly congruent to the conception of intertextuality. In particular, it is claimed, if we wish to find antecedent and precedent for the very notion of an intertextual reading of texts, we have to turn to that literature and learn, from its exponents today, the way in which intertextuality plays itself out in a vast corpus of writing.

Comprising both eminent figures, such as Geoffrey Hartman, as well as minor figures, such as Susan Handelman and James Kugel,[3] reaching out, indeed, to exegetes of rabbinic texts who stand entirely outside of the circle of literary criticism, such as Shaye J. D. Cohen and Lawrence H. Schiffman, the Jewish circle of literary criticism represents itself as authoritative in the exposition of intertextuality. For that circle lays claim to a literature that for nearly two thousand years – so this circle says – was read within an intertextualist hermeneutic. The ancient rabbis are supposed by them to have "anticipated recent developments in critical theory."[4] But are they right in their representation of the character of the rabbinic literature? Do the diverse documents of that literature relate in such a way that the boundaries between and among them prove invisible? And, further, how can we accurately describe the relationships between and among documents, if they do not relate in that intertextual manner that is currently imputed to them? The claim of this Jewish circle of literary criticism[5] concerning the intertextual character of the Judaic

---

[2] *The Slayers of Moses* (Albany: State University of New York Press, 1982), p. 47.

[3] I ignore Kugel in this article only because I have devoted to his representation of matters the chapter that follows, which summarizes the argument of my book, *Midrash as Literature: The Primacy of Documentary Discourse.* Lanham: University Press of America *Studies in Judaism* Series, 1987. In many ways his representation of the rabbinic literature is still less accurate than Handelman's.

[4] Eilberg-Schwartz, cited above, n. 1, p. 761.

[5] Eilberg-Schwartz imputes the following motivation to the circle at hand: "Recent interpreters of rabbinic literature have strong motivations for wanting to collapse the distance between the ancient rabbis and contemporary criticism. The emergence of post-structuralist criticism with its critique of the Western philosophical tradition provides a unique opportunity to rehabilitate the reputation of the rabbis. The claim that recent critical views are anticipated in rabbinic practice in effect asserts the superiority of this tradition to others, such as Christianity and Greco-Roman philosophy, which have had a more powerful impact on the Western intellectual tradition." I do not claim to know whether or not Eilberg-Schwartz fairly describes the motivations of the circle at hand. In any event, whether or not Jewish triumphalist ethnicism is more or less acceptable

writings, and not the definition of intertextuality, defines the issue before us. Specifically, are Hartman and his junior colleagues correct in their description of the literature at hand and of its distinctively intertextual character? At stake is whether or not in a vast corpus of ancient writings we find that precedent and example for the hermeneutic of intertextuality that these colleagues claim to have discovered. To assess the representation by these Jewish scholars of literary criticism, we turn first to the literature they claim to represent and then test their descriptions against the facts of the matter.

The relationships among the documents produced by the sages of Judaism, as we shall see, may take three forms: complete dependence, complete autonomy, intersection in diverse manner and measure. That second dimension provokes considerable disagreement and presents a remarkably unclear perspective, and it is the fulcrum of the debate on intertextuality in Judaism that I propose to precipitate here. For while the dimensions of autonomy and continuity take the measure of acknowledged traits – books on their own, books standing in imputed, therefore socially verified, relationships – the matter of connection hardly enjoys the same clear definition. On the one side, intrinsic traits permit us to assess theories of connection. On the other, confusing theological and social judgments of continuities and literary and heuristic ones of connection, people present quite remarkable claims as to the relationships between and among documents, alleging, in fact, that the documents all have to be read as a single continuous document: the Torah. Some maintain that the connections between and among documents are such that each has to be read in the light of all others. So the documents assuredly do form a canon, and that is a position adopted not in some distant past or alien society but among contemporary participants to the cultural debate. While I take up a community of texts and explores those intrinsic traits that link book to book, my inquiry rests on the premise that the books at issue derive from a textual community, one which, without reference to the intrinsic traits of the writings, deems the set of books as a group to constitute a canon. My criterion is simple but critical:

If I in advance did not know that the community of Judaism treats the writings before us (among others) as a canon, would the traits of the documents have told me that the writings at hand are related?

---

than any other is not at stake in this account of the matter, but, at the end, I shall point to the way in which the Jewish circle at hand has restated convictions of Orthodox Judaic theology as facts of literature and mediating principles of literary critical interpretation.

In the context of intertextuality as a description of the relationships between and among writings,[6] I have in mind indications of a quite objective and material character, such as decisions of an authorship to refer to or not to refer to Scripture, to compose an intersecting set of agenda or to talk about essentially diverse things, to cite a prior text or not to cite one, to make ample use of materials common among a number of prior texts or to use only materials not earlier used, and on and on. These matters of fact tell us whether, and how, autonomous documents connect with one another and so form a communion of authorships and give expression in textual form to a community. The connections include materials used in common, formal preferences dominant in two or more documents, substantive inquiries into topics interesting to two or more authorships, modes of intelligibility that characterize two or more sets of writers. In a word, we deal with rhetoric, topic, and logic, such considerations as symmetrical or asymmetrical plans of logic and rhetoric, programs of topic and proposition about a given topic, sharing materials, not sharing materials, and other perfectly objective and factual criteria.

II. Intertextuality

We do well to begin with a brief account of the matter of intertextuality, so that there will be a shared and clear notion of what, in the present context, the concept is meant to represent. In her article, "Is there an Intertext in this Text? Literary and Interdisciplinary Approaches to Intertextuality," (*American Journal of Semiotics* 1985: 3) Thais E. Morgan provides a clear account of basic issues of intertextuality.[7] Among the diverse theories at hand, the one of greatest relevance[8] is that of Genette, who defines the matter as "a relation of co-presence between two or more texts, that is to say,...the demonstrable presence of one text in another...." In that sense, the rabbinic writings are wholly intertextual, for, quite obviously, Scripture penetrates everything. But that does not establish a dimension of intertextuality that yields important hermeneutic, let alone heuristic, consequences. In fact, it is a merely formal fact, bearing no meaning at all. For it does not tell us how to

---

[6]This is a distinction to which we shall presently return.

[7]She was kind enough to send me a pre-publication copy of her excellent paper. I thank, her most cordially, as well as my colleague, Professor Robert Scholes, who drew my attention to her work.

[8]The others in her survey did not seem to me pertinent to the issues at hand. That is to state as a simple fact, theories of intertextuality do not illuminate that sizable corpus of documents that form a single canon, rich in reciprocal allusion and citation, of Judaism. The Jewish circle of hermeneutics under discussion here maintains the opposite view, as we shall see.

interpret a text that, not knowing that banality, we did not know how to read.

There are then these subcategories: quotation, which is explicit, allusion, implicit, and plagiarism, falling between the two. By that definition, of course, we correctly invoke the category of intertextuality. Let me stipulate at the outset: all components of the rabbinic canon quote from Scripture, and some of them quote from the Mishnah, or the Tosefta (the documents are identified and described in a moment). Allusion is another matter; I am inclined to think allusion always bears a material mark, e.g., a brief indication of a few words to direct attention to another passage. As to plagiarism, that seems to me to address the appearance of a single story or saying in two or more documents. Then either one has borrowed from the other, or both from a third authorship.

A further relevant point is Genette's notion of "metatextuality," by which he means, "the relation of 'commentary,' which unites one text to another text about which the former speaks, without necessarily citing it." This relationship presents difficulties in the reading of the writings before us. For it is one thing to identify a text on which another depends. We may even demonstrate that fact, e.g., Tosefta contains numerous passages that without actually citing them in fact comment on Mishnah-passages. Quoting, paraphrasing, commenting – these are not mysterious matters but subject to demonstration and exposition. The task of the exegete is to sort out precisely these matters. But it is quite another thing to show how texts relate when the authors do not clearly draw upon other, prior writings. Where we have difficulty is demonstrating that sort of inchoate metatextual-intertextuality in texts in which there is no clear paraphrase, citation, or commentary. Search as we may, we find it exceedingly difficult to specify concrete criteria to tell us where we do, and do not, deal with that sort of interpenetration of texts. How shall we know the difference between the presence of an allusion and our imputation of the presence of an allusion? Criteria, to be sure, can be defined – that is the work of sustained and rigorous scholarship.

Morgan cites the following: "Each literary or aesthetic text produces a palimpsest, superimposing several other texts which are never completely hidden, but always hinted it." The literary palimpsest hovers between originality and imitation, she explains. But, she judges, "The idea that the other texts can be seen transparently through the centering text is highly dubious." The conception of imitation as against originality yields a firm conclusion against the hermeneutic of intertextuality as applied to the ancient rabbis' writings, for no authorship of a single rabbinic document imitates any other. To state the negative: the authorship of the Tosefta does not imitate the Mishnah but cites it; that of Leviticus Rabbah does not imitate that of the book of Leviticus but cites it; and on and on.

There are paramount and definitive points of originality in *every* document. It is now time to turn back and introduce some of the writings to which reference has been made.

III. The Rabbinic Literature of Late Antiquity

The basic case framed by the Jewish school of hermeneutics these days rests on the notion that the canon of Judaism as it took shape in late antiquity, comprises documents that relate in a way we may call intertextual both to a single common book, the Hebrew Scripture or Old Testament, and also to one another. Consequently the holy books of Judaism in its formative period provide an ideal example of the meanings and uses of the critical initiative represented by thought on intertextuality. By the criteria supplied by Morgan and Gennette, that case proves flawed. For, as we shall now see with reference to several major documents, the criteria of intertextuality are not met. We briefly consider the Mishnah, ca. A.D. 200, which was the foundation-document of the entire literature[9] in addition to Scripture ("the Old Testament"), and two works of exegesis of Scripture ("midrash"), Genesis Rabbah, ca. A.D. 400, and Leviticus Rabbah, ca. A.D. 450.[10] What we shall see is that the final authorship of each compilation has imparted to its document distinctive traits of rhetoric and logic in working out on a particular topic a quite distinctive statement addressed to a defined circumstance.   On the surface, therefore, representing documents as of no consequence and claiming that individual sentences of paragraphs may freely float hither and yon constitutes a misrepresentation of the character of the literature that is adduced as evidence of intertextuality before intertextuality.

Let us begin with the Mishnah, the first and greatest work of the sages of Judaism.[11] Produced in the last half of the second century A.D. and

---

[9]Brief allusion to the Talmud of the Land of Israel, the first of the two Talmuds, will have to suffice for the present purpose.

[10]The description of the rabbinic writings that follows rests on a variety of writings of mine, including translations of the documents as well as studies of their rhetorical, literary, and topical-theological programs. I have now translated and written introductions for nearly the entire corpus of writings of rabbinic Judaism, including both Talmuds, all of the so-called Tannaitic midrashim, and most of the other midrash-compilations. Among these works, numbering more than 100 volumes of translation and exegesis, literary and historical study, five seem to me to cover the main points: *Judaism: The Evidence of the Mishnah; Judaism and Society: The Evidence of the Yerushalmi; Judaism and Scripture: The Evidence of Leviticus Rabbah; Judaism: The Classic Statement. The Evidence of the Bavli;* and *Judaism and Story: The Evidence of the Fathers According to Rabbi Nathan* (all: University of Chicago Press, 1982-1988, pass.).

[11]These sages bore the honorific, "rabbi," meaning, "my lord," and are homogenized by the Jewish circle of hermeneutics as "the rabbis." Since their

concluded at ca. A.D. 200, the Mishnah attracted to itself commentaries that ultimately became the two Talmuds, the Talmud of the Land of Israel, ca. A.D. 400, and the Talmud of Babylonia, ca. A.D. 600. The Mishnah is a kind of law code, covering six principal topics: sanctification of the economy and support of the priesthood, the holy caste, sanctification of time, with reference to special occasions, appointed times and the Sabbath, sanctification of the family and the individual, the proper conduct of points of social conflict, the political life of the people, the sanctification of the Temple and its offerings, with special emphasis on the everyday and the routine occasions, and, finally, the protection of the Temple from uncleanness and the preservation of cultic cleanness. These six principal subjects form the center of the Mishnah's six divisions and, all together, cover the everyday life of the holy people in the here and now.

A distinctive rhetoric characterizes the document and no other,[12] with the result that a Mishnah-pericope occuring in any other document is readily identified as to its origin. The Mishnah's discourse is made up of rules, and these ordinarily are phrased in the present tense, people do this, people do not do that, and, overall, the rules, framed descriptively, provide an account of an ideal world. The Mishnah's authorship rarely cites proof-texts of Scripture. Much of the Mishnah attends to topics of a utopian character. That is to say, the laws on the Temple and its conduct on an everyday basis, in the fifth division, and on special occasions, in the second division, on the support of the priesthood, in the first division,on the matter of cultic cleanness, in the sixth division, – all of these rules pertained to an institution that lay in ruins. Clearly, a century after the destruction of the Jerusalem temple in A.D. 70, the framers hoped and expected that, at some time in the future, the Temple would be rebuilt and its cult resorted. They prayed for that eventuality.

Not only is the Mishnah in the main, though not exclusively, a utopian document. It also deals, through discourse on practical details, with remarkably familiar issues of philosophy. For the Mishnah is a work of philosophy expressed through laws. On the surface the Mishnah

---

work extends over a period of six hundred years or more, we have in the present-day descriptions of "the rabbis," "their" thought, "their" hermeneutics, and the like, the equivalent of representing the whole of Roman Catholic Christianity, its theology and scriptural tradition, in all writings, from ca. 1000 to 1600, as "the Church," pure and simple. But everyone knows that, while perhaps pure, matters were never so simple as either usage, "the Church" or "the rabbis," suggests. But the Jewish circle of hermeneutics does not present whole texts, in translation and with systematic commentary; they simply cite "examples," without telling us how representative these examples are supposed to be.

[12]The Mishnah's closest friend, the Tosefta, cites Mishnah-passages verbatim and then adds amplificatory materials.

presents a set of rules, phrased in the present tense: "one does this, one does not do that." But when we look closely at the issues worked out by those laws, time and again we find such profound essays on philosophical questions as being and becoming, the acorn and the oak, the potential and the actual. Or, again, we will find reflection on the essential as against the actual, for instance, is the water in the stream the same water now that was there a moment ago, or is it different water? These and similar issues will have found a ready audience among the peripatetic philosophers who preached throughout the Mediterranean. But as we have seen, the sages were not merely philosophers, though many of their most profound exercises of thought concerned characteristically philosophical issues. They were holy men, and their philosophy sanctified.

While exhibiting distinctive traits of its own, the document precipitated a considerable process of amplification and apology, and in successor-writings, a continuous literary-theological tradition unfolded. On that account, the imputation of "intertextuality" is not entirely without its pertinence. But it was a political-theological, and not a literary tradition that unfolded out of the Mishnah. For the Mishnah took a position of centrality in the intellectual life of the Jews' sages. Applying some of the Mishnah's laws to the life of the Jews, these sages, many of them employed by the Jewish governments of the Land of Israel and of Babylonia, believed, and persuaded many, that the Mishnah, the constitution to which they appealed, formed part of the Torah, God's will for Israel revealed to Moses at Sinai. So the Mishnah, originally not a work of religion but of philosophy, attained the status of revelation. How did this happen? A look at the first great apologetic for the Mishnah, the Sayings of the Founders (Pirqé Avot), issued in ca. 250, approximately a generation after the Mishnah itself, tells us the answer. It begins, "Moses received Torah on Sinai and handed it on to Joshua...," and, the chain of tradition goes on, the latest in the list turn out to be authorities of the generations who form the named authorities of the Mishnah itself. So what these authorities teach they have received in the chain of tradition from Sinai. And what they teach is Torah. Now the Mishnah, which is their teaching, enjoys its standing and authority because it comes from sages, and, it follows, sages' standing and authority comes from God.

What happened beyond 200 and before 400 were two processes, one of which generated the other. Within these two processes we find a place for most of the writings of the sages in the formative period of the literature of Judaism, first, Mishnah-exegesis, yielding the two Talmuds, the one of the Land of Israel, noted above, the other of Babylonia, ca. A.D. 600., and second, Scripture exegesis, producing compilations of exegeses of biblical passages and books, those *midrashfim]* that are so commonly adduced in evidence as a corpus of writings lacking all differentiating traits.[13]   The Talmuds emerged from Mishnah-exegesis, the Midrash-compilations from Scripture-exegesis.   Later, in the final stages of the formation of the theological and literary tradition, both processes were identified as one and the whole was constituted as the single "Torah," or revelation, given by God to Moses at Mount Sinai, hence in the Judaic myth, "the one whole Torah, written [="the Old Testament"] and oral [=the Mishnah Talmuds, and Midrash-compilations]."

The Mishnah was extensively studied, line by line, word by word.   The modes of study were mainly three.   First, the sages asked about the meanings of words and phrases.   Then they worked on the comparison of one set of laws with another, finding the underlying principles of each and comparing, and harmonizing, those principles.   So they formed of the rather episodic rules a tight and large fabric.   Third, they moved beyond the narrow limits of the Mishnah into still broader and more speculative areas of thought.   So, in all, the sages responsible to administer the law also expounded, and, willy nilly, expanded the law.   As we noted just now, ultimately, in both countries, the work, of Mishnah-commentary developed into two large-scale documents, each called a Talmud.   We have them as the Talmud of the Land of Israel, which I have translated into English,[14] completed by about 400, and the Talmud of Babylonia, completed by about 600.

The second process – besides the work of Mishnah-commentary – drew attention back to Scripture.   This yielded not merely Scripture-exegesis but, more to the point, *compilations* of Scripture-exegesis, the so-called Midrash[im].   The precipitating cause of the making of such compilations lies in the character of the Mishnah itself.   Specifically, once the work of reading the new code got under way, an important problem demanded attention.   What is the relationship between the Mishnah and the established Scripture of Israel, the written Torah?   The Mishnah only occasionally adduces texts of the Scriptures in support of its rules.   Its framers worked out their own topical program, only part of which intersects with that of the laws of the Pentateuch.   They followed their own principles of organization and development.   They wrote in their own kind of Hebrew, which is quite different from biblical Hebrew.

---

[13]The word "midrash" stands for three distinct things, first, an allegedly particular midrash-hermeneutic, distinctive to the sages of ancient Judaism who produced, second, midrash-exegeses of various passages of Scripture, which they collected, third, in midrash-compilations.   I explain the distinct usages and how they are confused in my *Comparative Midrash: The Plan and Program of Genesis Rabbah and Leviticus Rabbah*. Atlanta: Scholars Press for Brown Judaic Studies, 1986.

[14]*The Talmud of the Land of Israel. A Preliminary Translation and Explanation* (Chicago: The University of Chicago Press, 1982-1991), thirty-five volumes.

So the question naturally arose, Can we through sheer logic discover the law? Or must we tease laws out of Scripture through commentary, through legal exegesis? The Mishnah represented an extreme in this debate, since, as I said, so many of its topics to begin with do not derive from Scripture, and, further, a large part of its laws ignores Scripture's pertinent texts in that these texts are simply not cited. When, moreover, the framers of the Sayings of the Founders placed sages named in the Mishnah on the list of those who stand within the chain of tradition beginning at Sinai, they did not assign to those sages verses of Scripture, the written Torah (except in one or two instances). Rather, the Torah-saying assigned to each of the named sages is not scriptural at all. So the sages enjoy an independent standing and authority on their own, they are not subordinate to Scripture and their sayings enjoy equal standing with sentences of Scripture.

The work of exegesis of the Mishnah therefore drew attention, also, to the relationship of the Mishnah to Scripture. Consequently, important works of biblical commentary emerged in the third and fourth centuries. In these works, focused on such books as Leviticus (Sifra), Numbers (Sifré to Numbers) and Deuteronomy (Sifré to Deuteronomy),[15] a paramount issue is whether law emerges solely on the basis of processes of reasoning, or whether only through looking in verses of Scripture are we able to uncover solid basis for the rules of the Mishnah. In that discourse we find the citation of a verse of Scripture followed by a verbatim citation of a passage of the Mishnah. Since this mode of reading Scripture is not apt to be familiar to many readers, and since allegations as to the relationship between Midrash and Scripture contradict the facts of the literature in general, let me give a concrete example of how the process of Mishnah-exegesis in relationship to Scripture-exegesis was carried forward in the third and fourth centuries. What follows is from Sifré to Numbers:

Sifré to Numbers Pisqa VI:II

1. A. "...every man's holy thing shall be his; whatever any man gives to the priest shall be his" (Num. 5:10).
   B. On the basis of this statement you draw the following rule:
   C. **If a priest on his own account makes a sacrificial offering, even though it falls into the week [during which] another priestly watch than his own [is in charge of the actual cult, making the offerings and receiving the dues], lo, that priest owns the priestly**

---

[15]I have translated all three documents; the translations have been published by Scholars Press for Brown Judaic Studies. Mine were the first and only ones into English for Sifra and Sifré to Numbers (in which William Scott Green participates for the final third of the document). In addition, Robert (Reuven) Hammer, *Sifré to Deuteronomy* (New Haven: Yale University Press, 1987) is available, with many excellent formulations.

portions of the offering, and the right of offering it up belongs to him [and not to the priest ordinarily on duty at that time, who otherwise would retain the rights to certain portions of the animal] [Tosefta to Mishnah-tractate Menahot 13:17].

What we have is simply a citation of the verse plus a law in a prior writing (in this case not the Mishnah, but the Tosefta, a compilation of supplements to the Mishnah's laws) which the verse is supposed to sustain. The formal traits require [1] citation of a verse, with or without comment, followed by [2] verbatim citation of a passage of the Mishnah or the Tosefta. What we have is a formal construction in which we simply juxtapose a verse, without or with intervening words of explanation, with a passage of the Mishnah or the Tosefta. So we see that, when sages proposed to provide for Scripture a counterpart, a commentary, to what they were even then creating for the Mishnah, they sought to build bridges from the Mishnah to Scripture. How what people claim is intertextuality squares with this is difficult for me to see, because the boundaries that distinguish three documents, Scripture, the Mishnah, and the exegesis of Scripture at hand, are clearly marked – and they would be even if I omitted the quotation-marks and references for Scripture and the bold-face type for Mishnah-Tosefta.[16]

The work of linking the Mishnah to Scripture was not the only kind of scriptural commentary. Sages turned to Scripture to seek the laws of Israel's history, to ask the questions of salvation, of Israel's relationship to God, that, in the Mishnah and in the works of amplification of the Mishnah, they tended to neglect. In the fourth century the sages produced the great works on Genesis, in Genesis Rabbah, and on Leviticus, in Leviticus Rabbah, to answer the questions of salvation, of the meaning and end of Israel's history, that the Mishnah and its continuator-writings did not take up. Why in the fourth century in particular? Because the historical crisis precipitated by Christianity's takeover of the Roman Empire and its government[17] demanded answers from Israel's sages: what does it mean? what does history mean? Where are we to find guidance to the meaning of our past – and our future? Sages looked, then, to Genesis, maintaining that the story of the creation of the world and the beginning of Israel would show the way toward the meaning of history and the salvation of Israel. They further looked to Leviticus, and, in Leviticus Rabbah, they accomplished the link between the sanctification of Israel through its cult and priesthood, which is the theme of the book of Leviticus, and the salvation of Israel, which is the concern of the

---

[16]Treated as a single protracted compilation for the present purpose.

[17]I have worked this matter out in my *Judaism in the Matrix of Christianity* (Philadelphia: Fortress, 1986) and *Judaism and Christianity in the Age of Constantine* (Chicago: University of Chicago Press, 1987).

commentators to that book. What they did was to place Israel, the people, at the center of the story of Leviticus, applying to the life of the people of Israel those rules of sanctification that, when observed, would prepare Israel, holy Israel, for salvation. Seeing these compilations of materials as purposeful and addressed to a particular context seems to me to call into question the premises of the intertextual representation of their authorships as speaking no where in particular to whom it may concern. The interchangeability of sentences and paragraphs may work quite nicely, to be sure, in the mind of the exegete, but the authorships of the several writings will then have found puzzling this reading of their writing. For they demonstrably delivered a finite message to a particular age in response to a distinctive and urgent question. The persistent relevance of that message is because of the persistence of the question, not because of the indeterminacy of the language at hand.

Take, for example, Leviticus Rabbah. In the aggregate and in detail, the framers of Leviticus Rabbah in ca. A.D. 450, a century or so after Constantine, imparted to the book of Leviticus the message, in response to the destruction of the Temple, that the authors of the Mishnah had addressed two hundred years earlier: Israel's holiness endures. Sanctifying the life of Israel now will lead to the salvation of Israel in time to come: sanctification and salvation, the natural world and the supernatural, the rules of society and the rules of history all become one in the life of Israel. And consider Genesis Rabbah, ca. A.D. 400, in the midst of the Theodosian revision of Israel's long-standing position in the Roman empire. In Genesis Rabbah sages read the book of Genesis as if it portrayed the history of Israel and Rome – and (now-Christian) Rome in particular. Now Rome plays a role in the biblical narrative, with special reference to the counterpart and opposite of the patriarchs, first Ishmael, then Esau, and, always, Edom. For that is the single obsession binding sages of the document at hand to common discourse with the text before them. Why Rome in the form it takes in Genesis Rabbah? And how come the obsessive character of sages disposition of the theme of Rome? Were their picture merely of Rome as tyrant and destroyer of the Temple, we should have no reason to link the text to the problems of the age of redaction and closure. But now it is Rome as Israel's brother, counterpart, and nemesis, Rome as the one thing standing in the way of Israel's, and the world's, ultimate salvation. So the stakes are different, and much higher.

What about the claim that, in the Midrash-compilations, there is no interest in order, so that everything is interchangeable with everything else? In Leviticus Rabbah, true, Scripture as a whole does not dictate the order of discourse, let alone its character. In this document they chose in Leviticus itself a verse here, a phrase there. But these then presented the pretext for propositional discourse commonly quite out of phase with the cited passage.   The verses that are quoted ordinarily shift from the meanings they convey to the implications they contain, speaking about something, anything, other than what they seem to be saying.   Leviticus Rabbah presents thirty-seven well-argued propositions, each proposition worked out in a highly-orderly exposition.   In fact, sages presented a new order for the world, a reconstruction of existence along the lines of the ancient design of Scripture as they read it.   What that meant was that, from a sequence of one-time and linear events, everything that happened was turned into a repetition of known and already experienced paradigms, hence, once more, a mythic being.   The source and core of the myth, of course, derive from Scripture – Scripture reread, renewed, reconstructed along with the society that revered Scripture.   Enough has been said to render plausible the claim that the rabbinic writings form, each on its own, a cogent and coherent statement, with a particular logic, rhetoric, and topic, suitable to the purposes of the authorship at hand.

IV. What Is at Stake in the Intertextualist Reading of the Rabbinic Literature

As we shall presently see, proponents of the intertextualist approach to the canon of Judaism claim to discern such deep connections between one document and the next, so that all documents impose meanings upon each, and each demands a reading solely in the setting of the whole literature.   But what *intrinsic* traits of the entirety of the corpus of Judaism in late antiquity validate an intertextualist reading of that corpus?   Of interest is not merely the well-known (but hermeneutically-trivial) fact that one text relates to another.   As we now recognize, that truism will not have surprised anyone who has ever opened a single text, since all texts cite Scripture, or any passage of the Talmud, since the Talmud cites the Mishnah.   The position at hand addresses the *entirety* of the writings of "the rabbis," all together, all at once, everywhere and all the time.   But viewed from the angle of their intrinsic traits, the documents scarcely connect at all.   We can read these texts one by one, we do well to consult points of intersection with other texts of the same canon where relevant, but we have no reason as a matter of a literary interpretation to invoke that invitation to chaos represented by the counsel: read everything in light of everything, everywhere, all at once.

This brings us back to the observation offered at the outset.   The writings of the sages of Judaism in late antiquity form a vast literature, each document exhibiting its own integrity, but in addition connected to others, and also continuous with the entire canon of which it forms a part. It follows that if you pick up any book written by ancient Judaic sages, you rightly expect to read what that book says on its own, beginning, middle, and end. You also will want to know how that book relates to others of its setting. That is because each book bears points in common with others. These include citing a common Scripture and addressing a shared program of interests. And, finally, one will wish to see a book in its broader role as part of the canon of Judaism, that is, of the Torah. For no document of the Judaism under discussion, that which came to its original expression in the Mishnah, ca. A.D. 200, and reached its full statement, in late antiquity, in the Talmud of Babylonia, stands on its own. In all, therefore, we discern three dimensions by which any document of that Judaism may be measured: autonomy, connection, continuity. Accordingly a book in the canon at hand stands by itself, within its own covers; it also relates to other books of the same canon through specific connections, indicated by intrinsic traits of rhetoric, topic, and logic or by shared materials, common to a number of documents. And it also forms part of an undifferentiated canon, that is, the Torah, or Judaism, through the dimension of complete continuity. Hence among those three dimensions, autonomy, connection, continuity, when we speak of intertextuality we address the second dimension in particular: the second, not the fourth!

V. Autonomy, Connection, Continuity, versus the Theory of the Intertextuality of the Rabbinic Literature

To clarify this perspective, let me invoke the analogy of a library. Books brought together form a library. Each title addresses its own program and makes its own points. But books produced by a cogent community constitute not merely a library but a canon: a set of compositions each of which contributes to a statement that transcends its own pages. The books exhibit intrinsic traits that make of them all *a community of texts.* We should know on the basis of those characteristics that the texts form a community even if we knew nothing more than the texts themselves. In the Judaic writings, moreover, the documents at hand are held by Judaism to form a canon. As I explained, later theology maintains that all of them find a place in "the Torah." But that is a fact we know only on the basis of information deriving from sources other than the texts at hand, which, on their own, do not link each to all and all to every line of each. Extrinsic traits, that is imputed ones, make of the discrete writings a single and continuous, uniform statement: one whole Torah in the mythic language of Judaism. The community of Judaism imputes those traits, sees commonalities, uniformities, deep harmonies: one Torah of one God. In secular language, that community expresses its system – its world view, its way of life, its sense of itself as a society – by these choices, and finds its definition in them. Hence, in the nature of things, the community of Judaism forms *a textual community.* That cogent community that forms a canon out of a selection of books therefore participates in the process of authorship, just as the books exist in at least two dimensions.

Let us turn to the problem of the community of texts. Since the present angle of vision may prove fresh, let me unpack its terms. I just now pointed to two dimensions, *autonomy*, on the one side, and *connection*, on the second. That is to say, a book enjoys its own autonomous standing, but it also situates itself in relationship to other books of the same classification. Each book bears its own statement and purpose, and each relates to others of the same classification. The community of texts therefore encompasses individuals who (singly or collectively) comprise (for the authorships: compose) books. But there is a set of facts that indicates how a book does not stand in isolation. These facts fall into several categories. and this brings us back to Morgan's and Gennette's reading of intertextuality. Books may go over the same ground or make use in some measure of the same materials. The linkages between and among them therefore connect them. Traits of rhetoric, logic, and topic may place into a single classification a number of diverse writings. Then, as I said, there is the larger consensus of members who see relationships between one book and another and so join them together on a list of authoritative writings. So, as is clear, a book exists in the dimensions formed of its own contents and covers, but it also takes its place in the second and third dimensions of relationship to other books.

If I finally may invoke the suggestive word, intertextuality, in the way in which I think the conception applies, we treat the relationships in which a given document stands as one expressed in the prepositions *between* and *among*. That is to say, in its intellectual traits a document bears relationship, to begin with, to some other, hence we describe relationships between two documents. These constitute formal and intrinsic matters: traits of grammar, arrangements of words and resonances as to their local meaning, structures of syntax of expression and thought. But in its social setting a document finds bonds among three or more documents, with all of which it is joined in the imagination and mind of a community. These range widely and freely, bound by limits not of form and language, but of public policy in behavior and belief. Documents because of their traits of rhetoric, logic, and topic form a community of texts. Documents because of their audience and authority express the intellect of a textual community.

The principal issue worked out in establishing a community of texts is hermeneutical, the chief outcome of defining a textual community, social and cultural. The former teaches us how to read the texts on their own. The latter tells us how to interpret texts in context. When we define and classify the relationships between texts, we learn how to read the components – words, cogent thoughts formed of phrases, sentences, paragraphs – of those texts in the broader context defined by shared conventions of intellect: rhetoric, logic, topic.   More concretely, hermeneutical principles tell me how, in light of like documents I have seen many times, to approach a document I have never before seen at all. Hermeneutics teaches me the grammar and syntax of thought.   Let me give one example of the role of hermeneutics in an inductive inquiry into form.   Memorizing a passage of a complex text will teach me the rhythms of expression and thought, for instance, that make of the sounds of some other document an intelligible music.   Not only so, but documents joined into a common classification may share specific contents, not only definitive traits of expression – meaning and not solely method.   So when I know how to assess the relationships between documents, I also come to a better way of sorting out the effects of those relationships: the intersections, the repetitions.   So much for the writings of "the rabbis." Now let us turn to the representations of those writings by the Jewish circle of hermeneutics.

VI. Geoffrey Hartman

Writing with Sanford Buddick, Geoffrey Hartman represents *midrash* (meaning, midrash-hermeneutics) in this way:

> a variety of "open" modes of interpretation, a life in literature or in scripture that is experienced in the shuttle space between the interpreter and the text. Abiding in the same intermediary space is a whole universe of allusive textuality...which lately goes by the name intertextuality. In this spacious scene of writing the interpreter's associative knowledge is invested with remarkably broad powers, including even the hermeneutical privilege of allowing questions to stand as parts of answers.[18]

In diverse ways, using what some may find excessive, even overripe, language, Hartman in that way represents both the hermeneutic and the literature, midrash-compilations, that presents the results thereof. Hartman and Buddick depict rabbinic interpretation as, in Green's précis, "unsystematic, serpentine, preoccupied with text and language. Its alleged salient and dominant characteristics are allusiveness, intertextuality, multiplexity, indeterminacy, and openness. These make it appear a harbinger of, or even coexistensive with, current dissenting theories of literature."[19] Hartman and Buddick appeal to Scripture as the

---

[18]*Midrash and Literature* (New Haven, 1986: Yale University Press), p. xi, quoted by William Scott Green, "Romancing the Tome: Rabbinic Hermeneutics and the Theory of Literature," *Semeia* 1987, 40:147-168, p. 147.
[19]Green, p. 150.

precipitant of thought and represent exegesis as a continuation of Scripture: "its [Midrash's] weaving together of prooftexts and commentary quickens our understanding of textual production and suggests a symbiosis of interpretive and creative writing." But what if, as I have shown, Scripture by itself does not play a central role in providing the program and agenda for the framers of rabbinic midrash-compilations? Then this representation of what happens in midrash-hermeneutics, which yield midrash-compilations, is not accurate at all. But Hartman is not a major player in the game, even though he is the only eminent literary critic on the field.

VII. Susan Handelman

It is Susan Handelman, who has provided the most ambitious theory of how rabbinic writings relate – but it is also the least informed account of the traits of the literature at hand.[20] Her principal position is readily summarized, as to intertextuality, as follows:

> ...all units are so closely interwoven and simultaneously present that none can be considered in separation from any other at any given moment; it is a world of "intertextuality'"...[21]

---

[20]Her discussion of "the development of the oral law," pp. 42-50, is breathtakingly uninformed. She grasps nothing of the scholarly issues and imperfectly understands the issues. What she does is merely recite in full guillibility the "Orthodox" doctrine, which itself has nothing to do with the diverse and interesting classical positions on the matter. She does not seem to realize, for example, that the heirs of the Mishnah took two conficting positions on the relationship of the laws of the Mishnah to Sinai. She reads the issue as a historical one, in terms of the origin of the law. But it was a question of *authority*, not origin – a matter critical to the work of mine that she cites. Evidence of her imperfect grasp of issues is easy to adduce from her botched report of my work. I am given the opinion "that the oral law is not a product of organic historical development from the written text but an entirely autonomous coexistent body of thought correlative to but independent of the written scriptures...." *I have no position*, what I am doing is outlining positions I claim to discover in a variety of continuator-documents of the Mishnah, e.g., Avot as against Sifra and Sifré to Numbers. That is a minor matter. But Handelman's larger theory of the literature in fact rests on unsound historical premises, and these historical premises are critical to her literary theory. I choose here to ignore that fact and discuss the theory of the literature solely in relationship to the traits and characteristics of the literature, as exemplified in the sizable sample in the reader's hands. Then people can decide on the basis of the literature Handelman claims to discuss whether or not her description and consequent theory are right. My sense is that much in the attitude of the circle at hand may be called racist, or, more generously, excessively ethnic, in its fundamental views of the Jews and their supposedly unitary and uniform "psyche."

[21]Susan A. Handelman, *The Slayers of Moses*, p.78.

....interpretation is not essentially separate from the text itself–an external act intruded upon it–but rather the extension of the text, the uncovering of the connective network of relations, a part of the continuous revelation of the text itself, at bottom, another aspect of the text.[22]

But intertextuality forms only part of what is at stake in Handelman's characterization of the rabbinic literature and its prevailing hermeneutic, and we had best dwell on her position and not just lay the entire weight of matters upon the sentences just now cited.

Handelman makes a variety of generalizations about the character of the rabbinic writings, e.g., "In Rabbinic thought...it is often the obverse– the particular and concrete take precedence over the general and abstract." Her larger theory of hermeneutics is not at issue just now, only her characterization of the relationships among documents and her reading of intertextuality as that interesting conception applies to those documents.

Handelman is the most explicit about the Jewish roots of the hermeneutic at hand:

There are striking and profound structural affinities between the work of some of our most influential (Jewish) thinkers like Freud, Derrida, and Bloom, and rabbinic models of interpretation.[23]

But this does not exhaust Handelman's position. Indeed, as Green lays matters out:

Her book posits a direct historical continuity from talmudic interpretation to some contemporary hermeneutical schools, particularly psychoanalysis and deconstruction....in Handelman's judgment "the Talmudic mode of thought became the ingrained model of the Jewish psyche."...She says, "It is my thesis...that psychoanalysis was the Jewish science in a far deeper way than has been recognized. Its founder, who affirmed a common psychic structure" with the Jews, created what might be called a secular version of the Talmud, and an interpretive science whose methodology was in its finest details deeply rabbinic.' For the record [Green continues] there is no evidence that Freud ever studied or knew any rabbinic literature...On this basis it is hard to understand how he can have produced a method "in its finest details deeply rabbinic." Since, in Handelman's view, talmudic thinking was "the ingrained model of the Jewish psyche," and since Freud shared a "common psychic structure with the Jews," simply being a Jew made him a necessary recipient and purveyor of rabbinic hermeneutics. The same presumably could be said of Derrida or, for that matter, each and every modern Jew. The disturbing implications of the very notion of "the Jewish psyche,"

---

[22]Ibid., p. 39.
[23]Cited by Green, p. 149.

and of the "us/them" dualism and Jewish triumphalism necessary to the book's argument, require no elaboration.[24]

What is particularly pertinent to the narrow issue of intertextuality now requires specification. In Handelman's view, as Green spells it out, "Interpretation operates within the language of the text; it moves from word to word and verse to verse...'the text is inseparable from its commentary.'" She claims that textual meaning is indeterminate, so that there is no "plain sense" of Scripture recognized by the sages who produced the Midrash-writings.[25] Handelman further claims "the endless multiple meanings which the Rabbinic traditions ascribed to each word and letter of the Torah," a position refuted by Green, "By providing multiple warrant for [a single] message, the form effectively restricts the interpretive options."[26] Green's claim in the specific passage at hand can be demonstrated in literally thousands of passages, in which the multiplicity of proofs for a single proposition forms the focus and center of discourse, particularly, but not only, in midrash-compilations. The importance of Handelman's formulation of matters lies in her explicit invocation of the matter of interpretation. When, however, she says that no document or unit of discourse can be considered on its own, she lays down a claim that she does not – and cannot – make stick.

Let us dwell on this matter. If all Handelman means to claim of the intertextual character of the rabbinic literature is that when a unit of discourse occurs in more than a single document, we cannot consider one version in isolation from another, then she has found a remarkably extreme way in which to express a perfectly routine fact of everyday observation. If she means more than that, I cannot say what she wishes to propose. My guess is that she wants to say we have to read everything in light of everything else. Indeed we do, when we propose to describe, analyze, and interpret a system whole and complete, in light of all its literature. But if we ignore the lines of structure and order that separate one text from another and that account for the sequence in which the textual canon unfolds, we invite chaos. Then how to sort things out and

---

[24]Green, n. 2, p. 165-6.

[25]Handelman not only does not exhibit a keen mastery of the sources, she also reveals somewhat disconcerting flaws in her knowledge of the scholarly literature on numerous points. And that is not always a trivial ignorance. In the present instance, for example, she does not appear to have taken into account Raphael Loewe's classic essay, "The 'Plain' Meaning of Scripture in Early Jewish Exegesis," in J. G. Weiss, ed., Papers of the Institute of Jewish Studies London (Jerusalem, 1964), I, pp. 140-185. It seems to me that every word in Loewe's paper calls into question Handelman's reading of "the rabbis'" reading of Scripture, so that she should surely have wanted to address and refute Loewe's characterization of matters, rather than merely ignoring it as she does.

[26]Green, p. 165.

find the rules of order? – That is the challenge to learning, which in time to come all parties to the debate will have to undertake. But Handelman's contribution is not only to set the terms for debate. As we have seen, it is she who introduces the issue of intertextuality.

VIII. Shaye J. D. Cohen and Lawrence Schiffman

Two less substantial figures play a minor but suggestive part in the intertextual reading of the rabbinic writings, Shaye J. D. Cohen, a historian, and Lawrence H. Schiffman, an exegete of ancient Jewish texts. Their positions complement that of Handelman in their introduction of the intertextualist hermeneutic. Shaye J. D. Cohen states very simply, "Synoptic texts must always be studied synoptically, even if one text is 'later' than another."[27] Schiffman introduces a somewhat different metaphor from the synoptic one, "This system, composed of interlocking and re-interlocking parts possessed of an organic connection one to another, is never really divisible."[28] This metaphor claims much more than the first. Now we are told that everything "interlocks" with everything else, and, in a hashing of the metaphor, we learn further that there is an "organic" connection, so that nothing is ever "really divisible" from anything else.

Cohen states, "Synoptic texts must always be studied synoptically, even if one text is 'later' than another." Schiffman says, "This system, composed of interlocking and re-interlocking parts possessed of an organic connection one to another, is never really divisible." Cohen is certainly right that we must take account of diverse versions of a given saying or story as these may occur in two or more documents in sequence. But if that is all he means, then he has not told us something anyone doubted. Since he borrows language from Gospels' research, he clearly intends something more than the admonition that we not ignore parallel versions of a single story or saying. But claiming to say more, he produces less than meets the eye. He errs, specifically, in invoking the metaphor of the Synoptic Gospels, or of synoptic relationships among some of the Gospels and Q. The metaphor does not pertain.

Schiffman is right that sayings and stories do recur in two or more documents. He is wrong to maintain that, on that account, documents are not divisible (as he says), and what he further may mean by "possessed of an organic connection to one another" I cannot say. The formulation,

---

[27]See his "Jacob Neusner, The Mishnah, and Counter-Rabbinics," *Conservative Judaism* 1984. I have dealt with his article in my "The Mishnah and the Smudgepots," *Midstream*, 1986, and further in my *Judaism: The Evidence of the Mishnah* (Atlanta: Scholars Press for Brown Judaic Studies, 1988), second edition.
[28]In his *Sectarian Law in the Dead Sea Scrolls* (Chico, 1983), p. 3.

so far as it pertains to literary and redactional traits, is murky, the sense unclear. My best guess is that Schiffman, like Cohen, refers to the mere fact that we have some sayings and stories occur in more than a single document. Cohen's and Schiffman's formulation of the issue of connection leads no where. My sense is that, despite Cohen's and Schiffman's rather portentous framing of matters, there is less than meets the eye.

We may now wonder whether, in Handelman's formulation, no writing can ever be considered in separation from any other, whether, in Schiffman's formulation, the documents cannot be read one by one because they are never really divisible, or, in Cohen's, whether (some of) the documents before us really do relate in a synoptic manner, a term to which we shall return so that when the documents interrelate, each must be read in light of the other. Cohen and Schiffman raise the issue of texts that clearly interrelate, Cohen invoking the analogy of the synoptic relationships among Matthew, Mark, and Q in Gospels' research, Schiffman phrasing matters still more broadly. I marvel at the certainty of Handelman, Schiffman, and Cohen, and of the broadly-held consensus that they represent. Let me spell out what I find puzzling. It is, specifically, why in the world we should ever have wondered how – on the basis of *intrinsic* and not imputed traits – one document connects to others. Seeing each document on its own or viewing all documents all together by reason of a social consensus poses no special problems of logic or interpretation. The one perspective derives from the very definitive trait of a book or a document: its uniqueness. The other constitutes a social, not a textual issue: why do people see as one what in fact are several? The answer derives not from documents and their traits but from communities and their choices. Common sense tells us that a given document should undergo examination within its own framework, and it is equally reasonable to ask how a number of discrete documents preserved by a single community related to the interests expressed by that community.

IX. Intertextuality and Metaphors of Connection: Genealogy through Dialectic versus Structural Taxonomy

This brings us back to the matter at hand, connection, which I propose to contribute to the discussion of the meanings and uses of the conception of intertextuality. By connection, as I said at the outset, I mean sharing like traits, including materials, and by the absence of connection I mean not sharing traits of plan and program. What is at issue is defining what we know as fact and avoiding what can come to us as mere impression. There are two appropriate metaphors, and we explore them both, genealogical and taxonomical.

Genealogy serves for the relationships among texts some call synoptic in relationship, and I regard as dialectical in relationship. Taxonomy serves for all of the writings all together. The successive connections between (not among!) the Mishnah, Tosefta, and the two Talmuds are dialectical, in that each succeeding document takes up and responds to the problems and program of its predecessor, hence a moving, or dialectical, relationship and connection characterizes the whole.

The taxonomic metaphor derives from natural history, and it sees things as connected when they fall into a single category, and as not connected when they do not. The notion of connection as an essentially taxonomic issue requires some explanation, since it is not the more familiar of the two connections. First to define the matter: the diverse species of a genus are connected by reason of their taxonomic traits, and two or more genera are not connected when they lack in common any taxonomic points. The metaphor that derives the sense of connection from taxonomy, that is, relationship of like and unlike traits, established through systematic classification, directs us to data that we can readily find for ourselves. Since the data prove congruent to the work, we invoke as our sole useful metaphor the taxonomic one: things are connected when they fall into a common classification, and taxonomic relationship – like, unlike – serves as the criterion for connection. The analysis of the relationships, hence of the connections, between and among the principal documents of the Judaism of the dual Torah therefore pursues a program of comparison and contrast among those documents. The results of comparing and contrasting documents tell us how documents are or are not connected with one another.

Documents that fall into a single genus therefore may exhibit relationships, for instance points of rhetoric, logic, or topic, in common, and the speciation of those documents then tells us aspects in which they do not relate, that is, points not in common. Accordingly, by "community of texts" – within the metaphor deriving from taxonomy – I mean texts that coalesce, form a community and in that way establish connections with one another, thus texts that are connected are writings that fall within a single classification. The same traits exhibited by two or more texts will then indicate that the two texts form a single genus, falling into a shared category or classification – one defined by the traits they have in common. The connection, then, between one text and the next is established by shared traits of form or program or fixed relationship to a single document to which, in common, the texts relate. Such common characteristics therefore indicate that two or more texts connect with one another in a taxonomic framework, which seems to me the sole genuinely objective basis for establishing connection at all.

We may now return to the more obvious metaphor, genealogical connection. The genealogical connection maintains the view that one thing is connected to some other because the one begat the other, a connection based on origin. One thing is not connected to another if there is no affinity based on genealogy. At issue, then, is how we may establish genealogy. It may derive from direct relationship or from indirect. A direct relationship requires that document B not only draw upon document A but also take shape in response to the contents of document A. An indirect relationship involves document A as proximate ancestor for documents B, C, and D, in that (necessarily) later writings draw upon an earlier source in common. An example of a direct relationship between documents comes from Kings and Chronicles, with the later drawing upon, and reworking, the former. An example of an indirect relationship, also of a genealogical character, would point to Genesis and Exodus, both of which draw heavily upon common materials, e.g., J, E, JE, and P, but neither of which draws upon the other. In either sort of relationship, we may establish a genealogical connection between two documents, direct or through a third document, as well as the same sort of connection among three or more documents, upon the same basis. The genealogical metaphor for connection invokes not taxonomic but human relationships, e.g., family, filiation, affinity, cousin, uncle, mother-in-law, and the like. In the anthropomorphic setting in which our thought goes forward, the conception of relationship invariably evokes the metaphor of family, surely a more "self-evidently" accessible category than mere classification.

In order to utilize the metaphor of genealogy, we should have to know that document A has generated document B. While more commonsensical and therefore attractive, the metaphor for connection provided by family invokes considerations of history and precedence, generations and offspring, that, at this stage in our knowledge, we cannot take up. For how shall I determine affinities, filiations, and the like? What objective and factual data can I adduce in evidence of the claim that two or more texts form a family, hence stand in relationship as mother and daughter, or that one text stands in a filial relationship to some other? The metaphor, filiation, draws in its wake the issues of history in the sense of temporal sequence, the conception, for example, that A begat B, so B represents a generation of A. That represents a quite different statement of what we mean by relationship from the one I have offered. But, except for the Mishnah, we do not know that document A's framers came prior to document B's, and our dates for the documents and the order we assign to them, if not wholly arbitrary, do not rest upon firm foundations. Everything is at best approximate and derives from impressions and guesses.

More weighty still, except for the Mishnah, Tosefta, and two Talmuds, we do not know that the authorship of B had access to the work of A and *as a matter of decision* adopted the model of A. Evidence to prove filiation must encompass demonstrations of points of contact and intersection. That is to say, connection as a direct and concrete category requires that we make judgments of a historical order: this first, then that. But I cannot demonstrate such connection as would have one set of authors meet with and make use of the work of another's writings. So that kind of connection lies beyond demonstration, and a different metaphor of connection will prove more useful.

True, we can show that some small portion of the materials of document A occur also in document B. That fact provides some variant readings of modest interest. But what fact flows from the sharing of a unit of discourse in common? The shared use of some materials in common, and proves that two sets of authorships drew upon a common corpus of materials. The connection then is common access to a third authorship – that alone. We cannot then posit direct relationship between group A and group B, but only indirect and adventitious relationship. And that sort of relationship hardly tells us the two groups, that is, the two documents, stand in a relationship of connection that we can exploit, e.g., for hermeneutical or historical purposes. It tells us the opposite. These and similar problems of demonstrating the presence of relationships comparable to families, filiations, and the like require us to look elsewhere for our notion of relationship. In place of connection, I posit a metaphor that rests on no more than demonstrated points of similarity and difference. Now that the metaphor and its rejected alternative have been fully exposed, let us turn to a clearer statement of connections between and among documents as I propose to investigate them.

The genealogical metaphor, which compares connection, a rather abstract category, to genealogical affinity therefore rests on an essentially historical premise. One thing is connected to some other because the one begat the other, a connection based on origin. One thing is not connected to another if there is no affinity based on genealogy. But that metaphor, while self-evidently illuminating, cannot serve most of our documents here. The reason is that the premise of the metaphor of connection as genealogy within families demands data we do not have. We do not know that the Mishnah begat Leviticus Rabbah or Genesis Rabbah, for instance (to take a silly example), so if materials occur in both documents, we cannot claim that the one document is connected in a relationship of filiation to its predecessor. I have already explained why we do not know the relationships, as to history, of documents, though we can classify documents in relationship to common points of origin and focus, Mishnah and Scripture, respectively. On the other hand, as I have suggested, there are clear relationships among documents that stand in a straight line, the later ones commenting on the earlier ones. Those relationships demand analysis, and they are the ones characteristic of the Mishnah, Tosefta, and two Talmuds. But for the literature as a whole we cannot show continuous unfolding out of a single, linear connection. The opposite is the case. Many of the documents stand quite independent of the generality of writings and intersect with the rest only casually and episodically.

X. Intertextuality or Merely a Community of Texts

Viewing the documents from the angle of their intrinsic traits, we find no single community of texts.[29] That position claims too much and finds no substantiation in the data. I see not only an absence of a collectivity, but a failure even of sustained imitation of later texts by earlier ones. Indeed I am struck by the independence of mind and the originality of those rabbinic authorships that did pretend to receive and transmit, but in fact imagined and invented. True, individual texts do relate to other individual texts, either in a sustained dialectical relationship, as in the case of Mishnah and its continuator-exegeses, or in a taxonomic relationship of connection, as in the case of Sifra and Sifré to Numbers and of Genesis Rabbah and Leviticus Rabbah, or in an episodic and anecdotal relationship, as in the case of documents that make use of sayings or stories in common.[30] But the received position, outlined by Hartman, Cohen, Schiffman, and Handelman, maintains far more and will not find satisfaction in the modest points of intersection and overlap that can be adduced in evidence. In fact, overall, there is no community of texts existence of which is proven by intrinsic traits.

Handelman's position now requires review at its central point, which is repeated in Hartman's and is critical to the matter before us:

> ...interpretation is not essentially separate from the text itself–an external act intruded upon it–but rather the extension of the text, the uncovering of the connective network of relations, a part of the continuous revelation of the text itself, at bottom, another aspect of the text.

I think matters are precisely the opposite: interpretation in every rabbinic writing is essential separate from the text that is interpreted, and the separation is both formal and conceptual and always explicit: the text that

---

[29]In my *Canon and Connection: Intertextuality in Judaism* (Lanham: University Press of America, 1987) I have conducted extensive and detailed studies, which validate the statements made here.

[30]The connection between these sayings or stories that occur in two or more documents scarcely requires analysis in the present context; what we have is simply diverse versions of given units of discourse.

is interpreted is cited verbatim. When we treat as indivisible the text and its later interpretation, what we describe is not the text and its author's meaning, but the community and its enduring values. These relate, but they are not one and the same thing. The "connective network of relations," in Handelman's formulation, therefore would correspond to that dimension of "continuity" in mine. For it is an extrinsic, not an intrinsic aspect of the document to which, in the nature of things, we speak when we ask about relations. People impute meanings to texts, and that too forms a dimension of interpretation. But when we speak of "intertextuality," that is hardly what we mean, as Morgan has already shown us.

As to genealogical connections, here it seems to me Handelman grossly confuses quite distinct categories. Specifically, in order to provide a literary theory on the heuristic and hermeneutic requirements of a text (or a set of texts), she has drawn upon a theological conception, namely God's giving of the one whole Torah, oral and written, to Moses at Sinai. It is true that the faithful impute the authorship to God. But I do not think literary scholarship of a descriptive and interpretive character has to invoke that fact of faith as a fact of literature. So Handelman seems to me guilty of confusing categories best kept apart. If we do not acknowledge as a matter of descriptive fact that "the text has a divine author," – thus One Authorship, Creator of not only this text, but, as it happens, heaven and earth, the fish in the sea, the birds in the sky, and you and me and all – then genealogical connections have, as a matter of fact, to emerge on their own. We have worked hard at showing the simplest genealogical connections. We have found some, between one document and another, but none among all the documents.

The distinctions between author and text, beginning, middle, and end, text and meaning, reader and interpretation, Handelman says are blurred in "Rabbinic thought." But, as we now recognize full well, the very category "Rabbinic thought" itself blurs distinctions among and between documents, so the blurring derives not from the data but from the category. If I knew to what court of facts and judgments she here appeals in speaking of "Rabbinic thought," I could propose modes of analyzing and evaluating her thesis as to that sort of genealogical connections that she wishes to evoke in showing "the unity of the text." Our inquiry into connections has sorted out a variety of possibilities.

I find a measure of pathos in Handelman's reading, because she has made every effort to master a theoretical literature in the service of a received and holy canon which, as a matter of fact, she seems to know only imperfectly. The work derives from piety, reverence for the received canon, as the imputation of the single authorship of God suggests. Certainly the givens of her thought, like those of Cohen and Schiffman, accord more comfortably with Orthodox Judaic than with secular literary or historical canons of inquiry. But good will and faith do not substitute for the hard work of learning, including mastery of not only the texts but also the scholarly debates that do, after all, circulate today. My sense is that Handelman's (to me) impressive mastery of contemporary critical thought finds no match in her (to me) rather limited knowledge of contemporary debates on the canon of Judaism in its formative age, which I doubt she has fully sorted out for herself. Joined to convictions of a profoundly theological character treated as matters of literary fact, these imbalances in learning produce propositions that prove somewhat awry.

XI. Theology or Hermeneutics: One or the Other, Not Both

Hartman, Cohen, Schiffman, and Handelman[31] correctly express the consequences of theology in their incorrect literary judgments of the character of the ancient rabbinic writings. This they do when they confuse theology with literary criticism, finding traits dictated by theological conviction in documents that, as a matter of fact, only occasionally exhibit the allegedly paramount traits. They therefore commit equivalent of creationism, confusing propositions of the faith with properties of the world out there. Creationism maintains that, since Scripture says God created the world this way, not that, therefore geology must be rejected. For hermeneutics the equivalent error is to maintain that, since the system joins the texts, therefore the texts were and are indivisible and have to be read each in the light of all, always all together and all at once. But the correct theological conviction has misled the faithful into insisting that, because everything is Torah, and Torah is everywhere, therefore, in hermeneutical terms, nothing may be read in its own setting. We could not demonstrate the presence of those connections that would as a matter of fact validate theological convictions. So, as hermeneutic, they do not apply. When Handelman, speaking for ages of faithful Judaists, says, "...interpretation is not essentially separate from the text itself – an external act intruded upon it – but rather the extension of the text, the uncovering of the connective network of relations, a part of the continuous revelation of the text itself, at bottom, another aspect of the text," as a matter of theology she speaks with accuracy. But it is solely from the aspect of theology, that is, of the canon. It is therefore a social judgment, extrinsic to the traits of the texts and intruded upon them. Once canonical texts then do participate in that common discourse, each contributes its component of the single, continuous discussion.

---

[31]And Kugel, as shown in the next chapter and in my *Midrash as Literature: The Primacy of Documentary Discourse*.

Let me account for the enormous error of imputing the traits of intertextuality to the canonical texts of Judaism: *We err when we seek to demonstrate that a system recapitulates its texts.* That is what leads us to impute to texts intrinsic traits of order, cogency, and unity. It is, further, what provokes us to postulate connection, rather than demonstrating it. The source of error flows from treating as literary facts what are, in fact, judgments of theology, that is, the reification of faith, the transformation of convictions of culture into facts of literature and – it must follow – a theory of hermeneutics. The fact is that the system not only does *not* recapitulate its texts, it selects and orders them, imputes to them as a whole cogency that their original authorships have not expressed in and through the parts, expresses through them its deepest logic, and – quite by the way – also dictates for them the appropriate and operative hermeneutics. The canon (so to speak) does not just happen after the fact, in the aftermath of the texts that make it up. The canon is the event that creates of documents holy texts before the fact: the canon is the fact. Since we cannot demonstrate connection, we must draw conclusions of a heuristic and hermeneutical character. These are readily stated. The simple rule may be laid down both negatively and positively. The documents do not (naturally, as a matter of fact) *coalesce* into a canon. They (supernaturally, as a gesture of faith) are *constructed* into a canon. In the context at hand, we may say, intertextuality, which forms the semiotic counterpart of the theological category of canon, is available for hermeneutics only post facto. Let me state my conclusion with appropriate emphasis:

The canon emerges not through recognition of mere facts, pre-existing unities, but of made up and imputed ones. The canon comes into being through a process not of post facto aggregation of like documents or connected ones drawn by a kind of unnatural magnetism to others of their kind, but of selection, choice, deliberation. The system does not recapitulate the canon. The canon recapitulates the system. In the beginning are not words of inner and intrinsic affinity, but the word: the system, all together, all at once, complete, whole, finished – the word awaiting only that labor of exposition and articulation that the faithful, for centuries to come, will lavish at the altar of the faith.[32]

---

[32]Many of the points made here are elaborated in my *Canon and Connection: Intertextuality in Judaism.* Lanham: University Press of America, 1986. *Studies in Judaism* Series.

Chapter Three

Wrong Ways in Literary Study [2]:
The Case of James Kugel's Joking Rabbis and
Other Serious Issues

> The basic unit of the Bible, for the midrashist, is the verse: this is what he seeks to expound, and it might be said that there simply is no boundary encountered beyond that of the verse until one comes to the borders of the canon itself.
>
> James Kugel

At issue is whether, and to what extent, we are to read and interpret a work of literature initially within a particular social and historical context. In our reading of the received writings of former times may we ignore questions of circumstance and context, setting and society? In my view, in introducing Midrash, Kugel commits an act of gross ahistoricism. That is, he purports to read Scripture-exegesis out of the determinate past. He instead treats Midrash as a statement both deriving from, and directed toward, an indeterminate and eternal present: nothing in particular to whom it may concern. Indeed, his proposed introduction to, and therefore definition of, midrash is so encompassing as to include pretty much everything about anything to do with Scripture and much else. The definition signals confusion generated by an ahistorical and anti-contextual approach to interpretation of midrash, in which documents make no difference, and knowledge of the particular time and place and condition of a given authorship contributes in no way to our understanding of the genre in all its specificity.

Let me specify the statements of Kugel subject to discussion here, so that an accurate representation of his views, in his own words, may define the issues for debate. As I see it, in his "Two Introductions to Midrash," he makes these five important points:[1]

---

[1]I shall stipulate that minor errors of the representation of the Hebrew texts, translation, major errors of interpretation and even description, will not impede discourse. It is not about details or misunderstandings or misinterpretations that I conceive a book-length debate to be appropriate, but about a position

1. *Midrash stands for Judaic biblical interpretation in general:*

> At bottom midrash is not a genre of interpretation but an interpretative stance, a way of reading the sacred text...The genres in which this way of reading has found expression include ...translations of the Bible such as the early Aramaic targumim; retellings of biblical passages and books such as the "Genesis Apocryphon"...; sermons, homilies, exegetical prayers and poems, and other synagogue pieces; and of course the great standard corpora of Jewish exegesis..., in short, almost all of what constitutes classical and much of medieval Jewish writing....for at heart midrash is nothing less than the foundation stone of rabbinic Judaism and it is as diverse as Jewish creativity itself.[2]

2. *Midrash is precipitated by the character of the verse subject to exegesis:*

> ...midrash's precise focus is most often what one might call surface irregularities in the text: a good deal of the time, it is concerned with...*problems.*[3]

3. *Midrash is an exegesis of biblical verses, not of books:*

> ...midrash is an exegesis of biblical verses, not of books. The basic unit of the Bible for the midrashist is the verse: this is what he seeks to expound, and it might be said that there simply is no boundary encountered beyond that of the verse until one comes to the borders of the canon itself.[4]

4. *The components of midrash-compositions are interchangeable:*

> Our midrashic compilations are in this sense potentially deceiving, since they seem to treat the whole text bit by bit; but with the exception of certain patterns, these "bits" are rather atomistic, and, as any student of rabbinic literature knows, interchangeable, modifiable, combinable – in short, not part of an overall exegesis at all.[5]

5. *Midrash is the way every Jew reads Scripture:*

> Forever after, one cannot think of the verse or hear it recited without also recalling the solution to its problematic irritant–indeed, remembering it in the study-house or synagogue, one would certainly pass it along to others present, and together appreciate its cleverness and erudition. And so midrashic explications of individual verses no doubt circulated on their own, independent of any larger exegetical context. Perhaps in this sense it would not be inappropriate to compare their manner of circulating to that of jokes in modern society; indeed, they were a kind of

---

fundamental to his entire position and, as I shall show, utterly in contradiction to the character of the literature Kugel claims to describe, analyze, and interpret.
[2]Op. cit. pp. 91-2.
[3]P. 92.
[4]P. 93.
[5]P. 95

joking, a learned and sophisticated play about the biblical text, and like jokes they were passed on, modified, and improved as they went, until a great many of them eventually entered into the common inheritance of every Jew, passed on in learning with the text of the Bible itself.[6]

We shall pass by in silence the sleight of hand that transforms the *no doubt* of the middle of the paragraph into the factual historical statement at the end, that "a great many of them *eventually entered....*" These minor slips need not detain us; we may stipulate up front that Kugel is an honest scholar.

Before we enter the debate, however, I have to specify what is at stake. Why should anyone not in a rabbinical school or a synagogue pulpit care about introducing midrash, on the one side, and assessing the literary traits of the documents subject to description, on the other?[7] The stakes in fact are high. They concern whether and how we see literature in context, and what we may mean by the appropriate arena for discourse. Kugel is a Jewish species of the genus, literary critic, and he stands for a whole school of contemporary literary criticism, one which treats the critic as creator, not merely interpreter, of literature.

Let me spell out the issue, first in its particularity, then in more general terms. I maintain that midrash-exegesis of Scripture reaches us in distinctive documents, and the first (though not the last) point of entry into the reading and interpretation of midrash-exegesis finds location in the document: hence, documentary discourse. As he says explicitly and repeatedly in his "Two Definitions," Kugel treats documentary lines as null, just as he treats all data, deriving from all times and all places, as equally valid and wholly undifferentiated evidence for the genre he claims to define. That is how and why the very broad issue comes to concrete debate. If Kugel is right about the Midrash-documents, then, I am inclined to think, we may generalize as follows.

First, we may reasonably ignore the documentary limits pertaining to the very particular literature at hand. Second, even though the midrash-exegeses were formed into compilations of exegesis in circumstances we may identify, for a social group we may describe in detail, in response to issues we may define and describe, we may – so the argument runs – turn directly to the contents of all the books of midrash-exegesis, without paying any attention to the context of any one of them.

---

[6]P. 95.

[7]Felicities of style do not comprise one of the reasons to read the literary critical essays at hand. The papers assembled in the volume edited by Hartman and Buddick seem to me remarkably prolix and verbose, using a great many fancy words to say a few simple things, most of them wrong. But we shall not dwell on trivialities, though, admittedly, it is no joy to read the circle represented by Kugel. Still, his paper is by no means the worst of the lot.

And, second, it must follow, then we surely may do so when we read literature not so definitively circumscribed by time, circumstance, and social setting. That conclusion will then permit us to maintain as a general principle of hermeneutics an essentially ahistorical, anti-contextual, and formal reading. In interpreting all literature we may treat as null those considerations of society and history, particular sensibility and distinctive circumstance, to which documents in all their particularity and specificity point.

But it is the documentary definition of discourse – *this* particular compilation or book and its traits, *that* book and its aesthetic, its plan and its program – that to the present have guided us in our reading of the received classics of our culture in the West. It will no longer matter, in our understanding of the heritage of the West, that an author lived in one time, rather than some other, and addressed one situation, rather than a different one. Everything is the same as everything else, and no work of writing speaks to anyone in particular. The stakes therefore are high. It is probably unfair to Kugel to impute to him the confusion between mishmash and midrash, but in the approach to midrash exemplified in his circle, there does surface a tendency to put in one's thumb and pull out a plum, with slight regard to the ingredients or even the flavor of the pudding at hand.

Let me now broaden discourse and introduce the still larger issue, one of general intelligibility signaled by the contrast between mishmash and midrash. It concerns the textuality of a text: whether or not a document has integrity. Kugel's position rests on the prevailing, and theologically correct but descriptively wrong, notion that all the canonical writings of Judaism are to be read as a single document: "the one whole Torah of Moses, our rabbi." That hermeneutic derives from the theological conviction that at Sinai God gave the Torah, in two media, oral and written, to Our Rabbi, Moses, and, furthermore, everything that a great prophet or sage later on would say forms part of that one and seamless Torah. As believing Jews, Kugel and his Orthodox-religious colleagues (most of his circle, in *Prooftexts*, are Orthodox or Reversioners to "Tradition") maintain these convictions, and, as a believing and practicing but not Orthodox Jew, so do I. But for the inductive construction of intrinsic evidence, such a theological premise makes no contribution to hermeneutics.

When I systematically tested the claims framed within the literary-critical category known as that of "intertextuality," as these theological-literary claims are advanced by Shaye J. D. Cohen, Lawrence Schiffman, and Susan Handelman, I found no sustaining evidence in the canonical literature of Judaism in its formative age, down through the seventh century. Each test that I devised in support of each claim and definition of intertextuality produced negative results.[8] Kugel's treatment of midrash in particular rests upon the same deeply flawed construction of the Judaic canon in general and measured against the limns of actual documents, is equally groundless. It derives as much as do the misconstructions of Schiffman, Cohen, and others, from the received, Orthodox-Judaic reading of the holy books of Judaism. I state the Orthodox-Judaic position, represented in both the State of Israel and in Jewish seminaries in this country, as well as in the few universities possessed or controlled by the Orthodox, e.g., Yeshiva University and Harvard University. *That reading is ahistorical, ignoring all issues of specific time, place, and context; unitary, homogenizing all documents into a single Torah (as Kugel says, reaching out to the limits of the canon); linear and incremental, seeing a single Judaism, in a straight line from Sinai, and, therefore, triumphalist.*

It also is – as a matter of fact – wrong. A debate such as this one, with its large and abstract issues, therefore involves real people, exchanging views (where they choose to address one another and not to debate – as they persist in doing – through *Todschweigen*) on deeply held

---

[8] *Canon and Connection: Intertextuality in Judaism* (Lanham: University Press of America, 1987). That book forms the third in the sequence from *The Integrity of Leviticus Rabbah. The Problem of the Autonomy of a Rabbinic Document* (Chico: Scholars Press for Brown Judaic Studies, 1985), then *Comparative Midrash: The Plan and Program of Genesis Rabbah and Leviticus Rabbah* (Atlanta: Scholars Press for Brown Judaic Studies, 1986). But these two books just applied to the documents at hand the findings of my *History of the Mishnaic Law of Purities. VII. Negaim. Sifra* (Leiden: E. J. Brill, 1976), which demonstrated the documentary definition of Sifra. The next chapter spells out the main points pertinent to the argument with Kugel, Handelman, and that circle in general. None of these books has been reviewed in the journal of the circle at hand, *Prooftexts*. Kugel simply declines to consider the facts and arguments of those books. When in autumn, 1984, I asked him why he passed in utter silence by my work on many of the problems and texts he deals with in the section on the rabbinic literature of his work in his book on the parallelism of biblical poetry, he stated, "Your name is not on the canon of scholarship, and I do not have to pay attention to your work." Geoffrey Hartman just now, in a personal letter, took the same position. I cannot take it personally.

[9] I look in vain in an article purportedly defining midrash for debate with Gary G. Porton, "Defining Midrash," or to Porton's *Understanding Rabbinic Midrash. Text and Commentary* (New York: Ktav Publishing House, 1985) as noted elsewhere in this book. In Kugel's defense I note that his essay originally appeared in 1983, so was completed in 1982. But in presenting his published paper at the conference of which the Hartman volume is the report, he does not appear to have updated his original paper, nor has he tried to come abreast with current literature. Still, even as of 1983, Kugel appears to have learned very little from a very long list of scholars, whose books he does not cite or dismisses casually and routinely. The same traits of sectarianism characterize other writers in the book edited by Hartman and Buddick, and call into question the effectiveness of the referee-

convictions. So we must ask, *cui bono?* Why is the issue raised as it is?
Profound theological convictions intervene, and as I said, the issues are
not literary nor even religious but narrowly theological. That explains
why evidence and rigorous argument play so slight a role in the debate; it
explains why episodic citation of self-evidently probative proof texts takes
the place of rigorous reasoning; and it accounts for the deplorable fact
that books and articles of the other side are not answered but
ostentatiously ignored as though they did not exist. The viewpoint
represented by Kugel proves particularly attractive to Orthodox Jews and
formerly-non-Jewish Jews who have become reversioners to Judaism in
what they imagine to be its "traditional" form. A sound theological reason
yields that preference.

From the classical perspective of the theology of Judaism the entire
canon of Judaism ("the one whole Torah of Moses, our rabbi") equally
and at every point testifies to the entirety of Judaism. All documents in the
end form components of a single system. Each makes its contribution to
the whole. If, therefore, we wish to know what "Judaism" or, more
accurately, "the Torah," teaches on any subject, we are able to draw freely
on sayings relevant to that subject wherever they occur in the entire canon
of Judaism. Guided only by the taste and judgment of the great sages of
the Torah, as they have addressed the question at hand, we thereby
describe "Judaism." And that same theological conviction explains why
we may rip a passage out of its redactional context and compare it with
another passage, also seized from its redactional setting. In the same way
Kugel and his friends wish to move freely across the boundaries of
documents alike, that is to say, ignoring all questions of time and
condition in pursuit of the episodes of Torah, one by one, all alike, all
equal on a single plane of circumstance and context: the one whole Torah
of Moses, our rabbi, timeless and ubiquitous. But the theological
apologia for doing so has yet to reach expression; and there can be no
other than a theological *apologia.* In logic I see none; epistemologically
there never was one.

Let me lay out the alternative to the theological reading of the canon.
These are three dimensions to a document within the canon of the
Judaism of the dual Torah. Documents stand in three relationships to one
another and to the system of which they form canonical parts, that is, to
Judaism, as a whole. The specification of these relationships constitutes
the principal premise of my position and validates the approach to *the*

---

system of Yale University Press.   Scholarly responsibility requires all of us to
debate with those with whom we disagree, not to pretend the other side does not
exist and to assassinate through silence entire viewpoints and positions. That is
not scholarship, except among orthodoxies, and, in the Judaic setting, within
Orthodox Judaism.

primacy of documentary discourse in the study of midrash that I offer here.

1. Each document is to be seen all by itself, that is, as autonomous of all others.

2. Each document is to be examined for its relationships with other documents universally regarded as falling into the same classification, as Torah.

3. And, finally, in the theology of Judaism (or, in another context, of Christianity) each document is to be allowed to take its place as part of the undifferentiated aggregation of documents that, all together, constitute the canon of, in the case of Judaism, the "one whole Torah revealed by God to Moses at Mount Sinai."

Simple logic makes self-evident the proposition that, if a document comes down to us within its own framework, as a complete book with a beginning, middle, and end, in preserving that book, the canon presents us with a document on its own and not solely as part of a larger composition or construct. So we too see the document as it reaches us, that is, as autonomous.

If, second, a document contains materials shared verbatim or in substantial content with other documents of its classification, or if one document refers to the contents of other documents, then the several documents that clearly wish to engage in conversation with one another have to address one another. That is to say, we have to seek for the marks of connectedness, asking for the meaning of those connections. For the purpose of definition, as much as of comparison, is to tell us what is like something else, what is unlike something else. We know what something is only when we also know what it is not, hence comparison and definition form twin-procedures. To begin with, we can declare something unlike something else only if we know that it is like that other thing. Otherwise the original judgment bears no sense whatsoever. So, once more, canon defines context, or, in descriptive language, the first classification for the labor of definition as well as for comparative study is the document, brought into juxtaposition with, and contrast to, another document.

Finally – and this is the correct entry for theological discourse, whether in the philosophical or historical or literary idiom – we take the measure of the dimension of continuity, in which we see all documents together in a single statement. The community of the faithful of Judaism, in all of the contemporary expressions of Judaism, concur that documents held to be authoritative constitute one whole, seamless "Torah," that is, a complete and exhaustive statement of God's will for Israel and humanity. We take as a further appropriate task, if one not to be done here, the description of the whole out of the undifferentiated testimony of all of its parts. These components in the theological context are viewed, as is clear, as equally authoritative for the composition of the whole: one, continuous system. In taking up such a question, we address a problem not of theology alone, though it is a correct theological conviction, but one of description, analysis, and interpretation of an entirely historical order. It is at this third point of entry that Kugel and his associates join discourse.

Were they theologians, they would have chosen the right door. But if they propose to interpret the literature as literary scholars, they should have come in through the first entry. For, in my view the various documents of the canon of Judaism produced in late antiquity demand a hermeneutic altogether different from the one of homogenization and harmonization, the ahistorical and anti-contextual one represented by Kugel. It is one that does not harmonize but that differentiates. It is a hermeneutic shaped to teach us how to read the compilations of exegeses first of all one by one and in a particular context, and second, in comparison with one another.

Now back to Kugel's propositions. Is it the fact that, as he maintains, *Midrash is precipitated by the character of the verse subject to exegesis:*

> ...midrash's precise focus is most often what one might call surface irregularities in the text: a good deal of the time, it is concerned with...*problems.*[10]

In detail, Kugel may well be right. That is to say, once an exegete has chosen the verse and knows what he wishes, in general, to prove, then a set of the properties of a given verse may attract attention. Why one type of property, rather than some other, why one issue, not another – these are questions to which the discrete exegesis of a verse on its own does not respond. In the comparison of such midrash-compilations as the two families we have examined, Sifra and Sifré to Numbers, on the one side, Genesis Rabbah, Leviticus Rabbah, and Pesiqta deRab Kahana, on the other, we can propose theses in response to those questions – the ones of *why this, not that?* – and we can test those theses against the traits of rhetoric, logic, and even topic. Accordingly, I do not register a one-sided disagreement with the position represented by Kugel that the traits of a given verse register in the formation of an exegesis of that verse. I am certain that the received exegetical literature, the thousand-year tradition of reading the midrash-exegeses precisely the way Kugel and others wish to read them, enjoys ample proof in result in detail. But it begs the question to conclude *post hoc, ergo propter hoc,* as Kugel and his friends

---

[10]P. 92.

do. So his position is not necessarily wrong, merely lacking in rigorous logic.

Next case: *Midrash is an exegesis of biblical verses, not of books:*

> ...midrash is an exegesis of biblical verses, not of books. The basic unit
> of the Bible for the midrashist is the verse: this is what he seeks to
> expound, and it might be said that there simply is no boundary
> encountered beyond that of the verse until one comes to the borders of
> the canon itself.[11]

It is simply false to claim that there is no boundary between midrash-exegesis of a single verse and the entirety of the canon of Judaism. The opposite is the fact. Most documents exhibit a well-conceived program and plan, with clearly defined principles of rhetoric, logic, and topic, guiding compositors in shaping and framing the document as a whole. The principles may be uncovered through inductive inquiry into the forms and logic of cogent discourse exhibited in a given document, then through the analytical comparison of the plan and program of one document with those of another. I have done so for Genesis Rabbah and Leviticus Rabbah, for Pesiqta deRab Kahana and Pesiqta Rabbati, and many other rabbinic compilations and compositions. Kugel has yet to publish a line in support of his position.

And yet here too, Kugel is not completely wrong. Some materials do travel freely from document to document, though apart from verses of Scripture, nothing known to me appears in every document of the dual Torah in its repertoire of late antiquity, through the Talmud of Babylonia. Hyman's *Torah hekketubah vehammesurah*, which lists pretty much all places in the corpus in which a given verse comes under discussion, sustains that judgment, as a rapid survey will show. Nonetheless, the peripatetic sayings and stories do journey hither and yon. So Kugel is talking about facts, if not (in proportion to the whole) a great many, and if not (in weight of evidence) probative ones.

But why they are accepted here and not there (where – to argue imaginatively, as Kugel and his friends do so elegantly – they *might have* appeared), what a given authorship has chosen to accomplish through citing a passage they have found in an earlier document, we cannot explain for the documents of late antiquity merely by saying things move from here to there. If a document's authorship exhibits a cogent program, then we should be able to explain why they have used a peripatetic saying or story or exegesis of a verse of Scripture in the way they have. Or, we should be able to state, we do not know what, if anything, they proposed to accomplish in resorting to the passage at

---

[11]P. 93.

hand. Or we should ask about the history of a composite unit of materials prior to the authorship's selecting it, for at least some travelling materials were composed into a larger conglomerate prior to their insertion in some of the several documents in which they occur. So the reason a given midrash-exegesis recurs may well be found in the history of the larger composite of which it forms a part. That proposition is fairly easy to demonstrate, as a matter of fact. And it calls into question the notion that authorships compose their documents essentially through free association.[12]

On to the critical issue: *The components of midrash-compositions are interchangeable:*

> Our midrashic compilations are in this sense potentially deceiving, since they seem to treat the whole text bit by bit; but with the exception of certain patterns, these "bits" are rather atomistic, and, as any student of rabbinic literature knows, interchangeable, modifiable, combinable – in short, not part of an overall exegesis at all.[13]

Kugel is stupefyingly wrong – totally, completely, utterly uninformed. He does not demonstrate that the components of midrash-exegesis are mere atoms, readily interchanged, modified, combined in diverse ways. In his defense, I point to what I said at the third proposition. Some (few) midrash-exegeses do occur in a number of passages. Characterizing all of them as Kugel does, however, simply violates the facts of something on the order of 80-90 percent of the midrash-exegeses in the documents that in fact have been examined. Perhaps Kugel has facts in hand to prove his allegation correct, but he does not present them, and my suspicion is that he is talking off the top of his head or just making things up on the basis of impressions.

But there is another line of argument in support of Kugel's contention. The midrash-documents of medieval times are highly imitative, borrowing and arranging and rearranging whole tracts of received materials. The authorships intervene in various ways, in some cases

---

[12]The conception that authorships play an active role in the formation of what they include in their documents is not new to me or particular to my school. It is in fact a routine inquiry, one that has produced interesting results for diverse scholars. I call attention, for example, to Steven Fraade, "Sifré Deuteronomy 26 (ad Deut. 3:23): How Conscious the Composition," *Hebrew Union College Annual* 1983, 54:245-302. Despite his certainty on these matters, I can find in Kugel's notes no reference to, or argument with, Fraade and his important work. My own debate with Fraade is in my *Religious Studies of Judaism. Description, Analysis, and Interpretation* (Lanham: University Press of America, 1986 *Studies in Judaism* Series) I:93-128, in particular, pp. 104-108, "Fraade vs. Fraade." But Fraade in his HUCA paper is certainly on the right track.

[13]p. 95

making up exegeses and assigning them to named authorities of a thousand years earlier. They succeed because of their power of imitation. Now if Kugel wishes to propose that the pseudepigraphic character of the midrash-compilations of medieval and early modern times – the making of collections/*yalquts* continued into the nineteenth century! – demonstrates the interchangeable character of the received materials, I believe he can make a solid case. But that case testifies to the taste of the imitators and pseudepigraphs, rather than to the historical setting and point of origin of the earlier documents. Usefulness to later authorships tells us about the enduring appeal of the creations of earlier ones. It does not tell us that everything is everywhere interchangeable – unless as our premise we take the facticity of attributions, on the one side,[14] and the fundamental irrelevance of context and circumstance of the original formation of the document, on the other. But, as a matter of fact, Kugel and his friends build on both of these premises.

We come now to a triviality: *Midrash is the way every Jew reads Scripture:*

> Forever after, one cannot think of the verse or hear it recited without also recalling the solution to its problematic irritant–indeed, remembering it in the study-house or synagogue, one would certainly pass it along to others present, and together appreciate its cleverness and erudition. And so midrashic explications of individual verses no doubt circulated on their own, independent of any larger exegetical context. Perhaps in this sense it would not be inappropriate to compare their manner of circulating to that of jokes in modern society; indeed, they were a kind of joking, a learned and sophisticated play about the biblical text, and like jokes they were passed on, modified, and improved as they went, until a great many of them eventually entered into the common inheritance of every Jew, passed on in learning with the text of the Bible itself.[15]

Kugel does not prove that "every Jew" has received this "common inheritance," though as a matter of religious faith he may hold that every Jew should accept it. He does not demonstrate that we deal with "a kind of joking," and nothing in the propositions and syllogisms I have laid out in my researches justifies his rather jejune characterization of this literature. How this literary judgment, which I regard as unproved and probably groundless, accords with the theological position at hand I cannot say. What I find stunning in the midrash-compilations as well as in their contents, the midrash-exegeses is the urgency and immediacy of matters, not the cleverness and erudition demonstrated therein. Israel, the people of God, turned to with deep anxieties about salvation to Genesis, Leviticus, and the sacred calendar. I find nothing amusing, merely

---

[14]I shall refer to Kugel's history of midrash in a moment.
[15]P. 95.

clever, or particularly erudite in what the sages found there. In my description, analysis, and interpretation of the midrash-compilations, I find messages of self-evident truth in response to questions of life and death.

As a believing and practicing Jew, I too have a position to express. In this judgment of Kugel's I find no merit, since it treats as trivial and merely personal what is in fact a monumental theological statement of the founders of Judaism. Our sages were not scholars, mere clever erudites. They were holy men and they gave God's judgment, through the Torah, oral and written, to suffering Israel – then and now. As a religious Jew, that is my deepest conviction, on account of which I cannot find redeeming arguments in behalf of Kugel's amazing judgment.

Taking *midrash-meaning-exegesis* out of the documentary context, that is, *midrash-meaning-a-document* that organizes and presents midrash turns *midrash* into *mishmash*. That is not because of errors of judgment about trivialities, let alone because he does not know what he is talking about, but because of a fundamental error in the reading of the literature. Since, as I said, Kugel has evidently read the documents atomistically, he claims that they are made up only of atoms. When he works his way through complete compilations of midrash-exegeses and gives us his judgment on whether or not they form mere scrapbooks or purposely statements, documents of integrity, as I have done, we shall see whether or not he maintains the view he announces in the statement under discussion here.

Still, before concluding, I hasten to say a word in Kugel's defense. It would be an altogether too harsh judgment to conclude that Kugel is merely making things up as he goes along, though a certain distance does appear to have opened up between Kugel's allegations about the literature he purports to interpret and the actual character of documents of that same literature. I believe he has conscientiously done his best to represent things he has studied as well as he can. But it would be a bit generous to concede that he has done his homework awfully well. Since my description of the documents is accurate and available for all to study if they wish, and since that literary judgment on matters of rhetoric, logic, and topic stands at complete variance with Kugel's premises, I think we shall have to conclude that he has some considerable gaps in his mastery of the sources. And yet, by stating in a forthright and unabashed way the convictions of Orthodox Judaism as well as a fair part of ethnic Judaic scholarship concerning midrash, Kugel deserves our thanks for precipitating a fruitful debate. We in the academic sector of Judaic studies welcome that debate and intend to pursue it most vigorously.

In conclusion let us turn to the upshot of the matter, Kugel's claim to give us "two introductions to midrash." Kugel's two introductions yield not even one definition. Midrash in his definition is pretty much the same thing as "Jewish creativity itself." Let us return to Kugel's most general statement of the matter:

> At bottom midrash is not a genre of interpretation but an interpretative stance, a way of reading the sacred text...The genres in which this way of reading has found expression include...translations of the Bible such as the early Aramaic targumim; retellings of biblical passages and books such as the "Genesis Apocryphon"...; sermons, homilies, exegetical prayers and poems, and other synagogue pieces; and of course the great standard corpora of Jewish exegesis..., in short, almost all of what constitutes classical and much of medieval Jewish writing....for at heart midrash is nothing less than the foundation stone of rabbinic Judaism and it is as diverse as Jewish creativity itself.[16]

Kugel does not tell us what midrash is, when he says it is "a way of reading the sacred text." For until he explains precisely what *way* it is – *and what way it is not* – he has clarified nothing. And definition requires comparison, for when we define we exclude just as we include. But in this statement, Kugel encompasses everything Jews wrote as midrash. To me in this definition, Midrash is pretty much a mishmash.

And it is a mishmash of Judaisms, in the sense that "Jewish creativity" encompasses everything any Jew wrote anywhere (at least, within the canon of contemporary Orthodox Jewish scholarship). In making this bizarre judgment, Kugel not only declines to define midrash. He also fails to differentiate among the different groups behind the writings to which he makes reference. The Genesis Apocryphon is not a document produced and preserved by the same people who wrote and handed on Genesis Rabbah ("rabbinic Judaism indeed!"), for example, and no one has demonstrated the rabbinic provenience of the Targumim (except for Onqelos). Many have shown the opposite. So I do not exaggerate in concluding that Kugel homogenizes everything every Jew every wrote, so to speak, into one Judaism.

A further aspect of his "Two Definitions of Midrash" requires passing attention at this point, his history of midrash[17]. In that history, Kugel takes at face value all attributions of sayings and most of books, so that if a given figure, rabbinical or otherwise, is assigned a statement, Kugel takes as fact that the man made that statement at the time at which he is supposed to have lived. Kugel furthermore invokes for his history of interpretation of Scripture works that rest upon the same gullible position, e.g., p. 100, n. 6: "For the historical setting of this transition and parallels

---

[16]Op. cit. pp. 91-2.
[17]See pp. 80-90, which I have neglected, and, especially, the repertoire of scholarly authorities cited in those pages. This is the connection to my *Reading and Believing: Ancient Judaism and Contemporary Gullibility*.

to the inspired interpreter outside the rabbinic tradition see D. Patte, *Early Jewish Hermeneutic in Palestine.*" Patte at that stage in his work took for granted and at face value pretty much everything he read in the rabbinic literature, so presenting a picture of the fourth century B.C. out of writings of the fifth century A.D., a mere nine hundred years later. On that basis Kugel presents us with his linear, incremental, and unitary picture of the history of midrash within Judaism: everything everybody ever wrote, more or less. That introduces nothing.

Accordingly, I believe that the authorships of the actual Midrash-documents will have found puzzling many aspects of Kugel's introduction and description of their work. The source of his misrepresentation of the literature is not trivial, and he has not made minor mistakes to be blown up out of all proportion into an indictment of the integrity of the man and his scholarship. On the contrary, no one doubts his scholarly ethics, his learning, his character, commitment, and conscience – only his critical judgment *on the issue at hand.* And the issue is not one of orthodoxy or heresy, but merely one of introduction: the accurate description, analysis, and interpretation of some old books. I think he has not accomplished an accurate description, because he read the parts but not the whole. I think he has not accomplished a rigorous analysis because he has read acutely but has not undertaken a program of comparison and contrast. I think he has not given us a plausible interpretation – that is, an introduction, a definition – because he has thought deeply but not worked inductively on the basis of intrinsic evidence and, alas, also has brought a set of convictions, I have shown of a theological character, that are inappropriate to the secular work of literary analysis.

Since Kugel clearly has worked hard on the study of Midrash-exegeses, readily invoking what everybody knows as proof for his premises or positions ("as any student of rabbinic literature knows"), we must conclude that – as in the case of all mortals – his strength is his weakness. What he knows he knows in one way, rather than in some other. Having spent a great deal of effort to explain how a given verse has precipitated a received exegesis, he quite reasonably concluded that exegeses begin with the problems of verses. Having reached that position, furthermore, he appears not to have spent a great deal of time in the analysis of rhetoric, on the one side, or in the inquiry into the principles of logical cogency and intelligible discourse, on the other. This has further discouraged him from asking whether a document as a whole proposes to make a point or to register a syllogism or a set of syllogisms. I suppose that, if you work in a pickle factory all day long, everything you eat for supper will taste like pickles.

And yet, I think there is a deeper premise than the one defined by scholarly habits, both bad and good. The clue lies in Kugel's explicit recognition of the category of canon: "there simply is no boundary encountered beyond that of the verse until one comes to the borders of the canon itself." That is another way of saying that the Torah is one and seamless, or that Judaism is Judaism. And so it is – at the end. But the problem of how diverse documents, with their premises and their distinct syllogisms, fit together is not solved merely by saying it is solved. Precisely how the diverse documents constitute a canon, where, when, and why a given document and its message made its way into the canon – these are questions Kugel and those he represents do not address. They treat as the premise of their literary critical reading of midrash-exegeses what in fact defines the most profound and difficult problem in the reading of all of the documents that, today, after the fact, constitute the canon, or the Torah.

In the academy we do not frame our hypotheses out of the detritus of theological conviction. In the sectarian world of seminary and yeshiva (and Harvard and Yale), people do just that. Kugel stands for a position – not limited to Orthodox Judaism by any means – that everything is one thing and bounded only at the outer limits. That is correct theology. But it is bad scholarship. The reason is not merely that, as a matter of fact, it is wrong. Bad scholarship treats as a premise what is in fact the issue; it begs the question. Kugel is a man of intelligence, sensibility, learning and industry. I am confident that, as he reflects on the case made here, he will learn to construct his argument and introduce midrash by framing hypotheses and testing them, crafting well-composed questions and exploring them, rather than, as he does here, by defining axioms and repeatedly *illustrating* them in the medieval-Yeshiva manner. Then, I am certain, he will find greater motivation than he has exhibited to date to study the work of others who have pursued the same inquiries – and to study the texts not bit by bit but as a whole. When he does, I do not think he will maintain that our sages of blessed memory were joking.

Chapter Four

Right Ways in Literary Study [1]:
Seeing Documents Whole:
The Case of Sifra's Critique of Mishnaic Logic

If, as I maintain, documents are to be read whole, not only in their discrete parts, how shall I show that that is the right way of framing our inquiry? The answer is to demonstrate that one document differs from another not in mere detail but in its most fundamental traits of intellect. For that purpose I turn directly to the question of the logic of intelligible discourse, which tells an authorship how to frame its data into cogent propositions and form of the whole a single, intelligible statement. I shall now show that two authorships, one of the Mishnah, the other of Sifra, made quite distinct judgments as to the matter of the logic of cogent argument and intelligible discourse. There, on the face of it, we see evidence in favor of my view that the right way of reading a document, to begin with, is whole and complete, not only in this detail or that.

The authorship of Sifra undertook a vast polemic against the logic of classification that forms the foundation of the system of the Mishnah. This they did two ways. The first, and less important, was to demonstrate that the Mishnah's rules required exegetical foundations. The second, and paramount way was to attack the very logic by which the Mishnah's authorship developed its points. To understand the polemic of Sifra, therefore, we have to grasp the fundamental logical basis for the workings of the Mishnah. Then we shall see in its polemical context the recurrent statement of the authorship of Sifra: *classification does not work, because there is no genus, but only species.* Therefore the Mishnah's Listenwissenschaft, its insistence that things are either like one another, therefore follow the same rule, or opposite to one another, therefore follow the opposite rule – these fundamental building blocks of Mishnaic thought prove deeply flawed. For if nothing is ever really like something else, then we cannot classify different things together, as the same thing. And, it follows, we also can make no lists of things that, whether in a polythetic or a monothetic framework, follow the same rule and therefore generate a generalization. Since, as we shall now see, the logic of the

Mishnah begins with the premise that diverse species form a single genus, so can be subjected to comparison and contrast, that dogged insistence, time and again, upon the incomparability of species, forms a fundamental critique of the practical reason of the Mishnah. A full appreciation of matters now requires that we dwell at some length upon the system of the Mishnah.

I. The System of the Mishnah and its Logic of Classification

The Mishnah's authorship invariably invokes the philosophical logic of syllogism, the rule-making logic of lists. Like good Aristotelians, they would uncover the components of the rules by comparison and contrast, showing the rule for one thing by finding out how it compared with like things and contrasted with the unlike.[1] Then, in their view, the unknown would become known, conforming to the rule of the like thing, also to the opposite of the rule governing the unlike thing. That purpose is accomplished, in particular, though list-making, which places on display the data of the like and the unlike and implicitly (ordinarily, not explicitly) then conveys the rule. That is why, in exposing the interior logic of its authorship's intellect, the Mishnah had to be a book of lists, with the implicit order, the nomothetic traits, dictating the ordinarily unstated general and encompassing rule. And all this why? It is in order to make a single statement, endless times over, and to repeat in a mass of tangled detail precisely the same fundamental judgment. The Mishnah in its way is as blatantly repetitious in its fundamental statement as is the Pentateuch. But the power of the Pentateuchal authorship, denied to that of the Mishnah, lies in their capacity always to be heard, to create sound by resonance of the surfaces of things. The Pentateuch is a fundamentally popular and accessible piece of writing. By contrast, the Mishnah's writers spoke into the depths, anticipating a more acute hearing than they ever would receive. So the repetitions of Scripture reenforce the message, while the endlessly repeated paradigm of the Mishnah sits too deep in the structure of the system to gain hearing from the ear that lacks acuity or to attain visibility to the untutored eye. So much for the logic. What of the systemic message? Given the subtlety of intellect of the Mishnah's authorship, we cannot find surprising that the message speaks not only in what is said, but in what is omitted.

When we listen to the silences of the system of the Mishnah, as much as to its points of stress, we hear a single message. It is a message of a

---

[1]Compare G. E. R. Lloyd, *Polarity and Analogy. Two Types of Argumentation in Early Greek Thought* (Cambridge: Cambridge University Press, 1966). But the core-logic of *Listenwissenschaft* extends back to Sumerian times.

system that answered a single encompassing question, and the question formed a stunning counterpart to that of the sixth century B.C. The Pentateuchal system addressed one reading of the events of the sixth century, highlighted by the destruction of the Jerusalem temple in 586 B.C. At stake was how Israel as defined by that system related to its land, represented by its temple, and the message may be simply stated: what appears to be the given is in fact a gift, subject to stipulations. The precipitating event for the Mishnaic system was the destruction of the Jerusalem temple in A.D. 70, but at stake now was a quite fresh issue. It was, specifically, this: what, in the aftermath of the destruction of the holy place and holy cult, remained of the sanctity of the holy caste, the priesthood, the holy land, and, above all, the holy people and its holy way of life? The answer was that sanctity persists, indelibly, in Israel, the people, in its way of life, in its land, in its priesthood, in its food, in its mode of sustaining life, in its manner of procreating and so sustaining the nation. The Mishnah's system therefore focused upon the holiness of the life of Israel, the people, a holiness that had formerly centered on the Temple. The logically consequent question was, what is the meaning of sanctity, and how shall Israel attain, or give evidence of, sanctification. The answer to the question derived from the original creation, the end of the temple directing attention to the beginning of the natural world that the temple had (and would again) embodied. For the meaning of sanctity the framers therefore turned to that first act of sanctification, the one in creation. It came about when, all things in array, in place, each with its proper name, God blessed and sanctified the seventh day on the eve of the first Sabbath. Creation was made ready for the blessing and the sanctification when all things were very good, that is to say, in their rightful order, called by their rightful name. An orderly nature was a sanctified and blessed nature, so dictated Scripture in the name of the Supernatural. So to receive the blessing and to be made holy, all things in nature and society were to be set in right array. Given the condition of Israel, the people, in its land, in the aftermath of the catastrophe war against Rome led by Bar Kokhba in 132-135, putting things in order was no easy task. But that is why, after all, the question pressed, the answer proving inexorable and obvious. The condition of society corresponded to the critical question that obsessed the system-builders.[2]

---

[2]That is not to suggest no other questions can have precipitated system-making, either in the sixth century B.C. or in the second A.D. I cannot think of a less likely proposition. We recognize, after all, that the Pentateuchal Judaism formed the answer to the question selected by the temple priesthood that sponsored the making of the Torah and that, institutionally, then formed its political class. Along these same lines, the Mishnaic Judaism emerged in a coalition of interests of priesthood, householders, and scribes. We do not know what other Judaisms came into being, nor can we identify the urgent questions and self-evidently valid

Once we discern that message, we shall also understand the logic necessary for its construction and inner structure. For the inner structure set forth by a logic of classification alone could sustain the system of ordering all things in proper place and under the proper rule. The like belongs with the like and conforms to the rule governing the like, the unlike goes over to the opposite and conforms to the opposite rule. When we make lists of the like, we also know the rule governing all the items on those lists, respectively. We know that and one other thing, namely, the opposite rule, governing all items sufficiently like to belong on those lists, but sufficiently unlike to be placed on other lists. That rigorously philosophical logic of analysis, comparison and contrast, served because it was the only logic that could serve a system that proposed to make the statement concerning order and right array that the Mishnah's authorship wished to set forth. To the urgent question, what of the holiness of Israel after the destruction of the temple in A.D. 70, therefore, the system of the Mishnah provided the self-evidently valid answer and gave that answer in ineluctable and compelling logical form. That sanctification, as a matter of fact, from the viewpoint of the system now endured and transcended the physical destruction of the building and the cessation of sacrifices. For Israel the people was holy, enduring as the medium and the instrument of God's sanctification. The system then instructed Israel so to act as to express the holiness that inhered in the people. This Israel would accomplish by the right ordering, in accord with a single encompassing principle, of all details of the common life of the village and the home, matching the temple and the cult.

The diverse topical program of the Mishnah, time and again making the same points on the centrality of order, works itself out in a single logic of cogent discourse, one which seeks the rule that governs diverse cases. And, as we now see, that logic states within its interior structure the fundamental point of the document as a whole. The correspondence of logic to system here, as in the Pentateuch viewed overall, hardly presents surprises. Seeing how the logic does its work within the document therefore need not detain us for very long. Let us take up two pericopes of the Mishnah and determine the logic that joins fact to fact, sentence to sentence, in a cogent proposition, that is, in our terms, a paragraph that makes a statement. To see how this intellect does its work we turn first to Mishnah-tractate Berakhot, Chapter Eight, to see list-making in its

---

answers represented by the world view, way of life, and social entity, invented by those other Judaic systems. All I mean to underline is the congruence between the social world and the systemic construction, not that the system formed the only, or the best possible, statement not only to that social world, but also *of* that social condition. That forms a distinct proposition, and one I reject as, if plausible, unproven.

simplest form, and then to Mishnah-tractate Sanhedrin, Chapter Two, to see the more subtle way in which list-making yields a powerfully-argued philosophical theorem.

In the first of our two abstracts we have a list, carefully formulated, in which the announcement at the outset tells us what is catalogued, and in which careful mnemonic devices so arrange matters that we may readily remember the conflicting opinions. So in formal terms, we have a list that means to facilitate memorization. But in substantive terms, the purpose of the list and its message(s) are not set forth, and only ample exegesis will succeed in spelling out what is at stake. Here is an instance of a Mishnah-passage which demands an exegesis not supplied by the Mishnah's authorship.

Mishnah-tractate Berakhot Chapter Eight

	8:1.	A.	These are the things which are between the House of Shammai and the House of Hillel in [regard to] the meal:
[1]		B.	The House of Shammai say, "One blesses over the day, and afterward one blesses over the wine." And the House of Hillel say, "One blesses over the wine, and afterward one blesses over the day."
[2]	8.2.	A.	The House of Shammai say, "They wash the hands and afterward mix the cup." And the House of Hillel say, "They mix the cup and afterward wash the hands."
[3]	8:3.	A.	The House of Shammai say, "He dries his hands on the cloth and lays it on the table." And the House of Hillel say, "On the pillow."
[4]	8:4.	A.	The House of Shammai say, "They clean the house, and afterward they wash the hands." And the House of Hillel say, "They wash the hands, and afterward they clean the house."
[5]	8:5.	A.	The House of Shammai say, "Light, and food, and spices, and *Havdalah*." And the House of Hillel say, "'Light, and spices, and food, and *Havdalah*."
[6]		B.	The House of Shammai say, "'Who created the light of the fire.'" And the House of Hillel say, "'Who creates the lights of the fire.'"

The mnemonic serving the list does its work by the simple reversal of items. If authority A has the order 1, 2, then authority B will give 2, 1. Only entry [3] breaks that pattern. What is at stake in the making of the list is hardly transparent, and why day/wine vs. wine/day, with a parallel, e.g., clean/wash versus wash/clean, yields a general principle the authorship does not indicate. All we know at this point, therefore, is that we deal with list-makers. But how lists work to communicate principles awaits exemplification.

The next abstract allows us much more explicitly to identify the *and* and the *equal* of Mishnaic discourse, showing us through the making of connections and the drawing of conclusions the propositional and essentially philosophical mind that animates the Mishnah. In the following passage, drawn from Mishnah-tractate Sanhedrin Chapter Two, the authorship wishes to say that Israel has two heads, one of state, the other of cult, the king and the high priest, respectively, and that these two offices are nearly wholly congruent with one another, with a few differences based on the particular traits of each. Broadly speaking, therefore, our exercise is one of setting forth the genus and the species. The genus is head of holy Israel. The species are king and high priest. Here are the traits in common and those not shared, and the exercise is fully exposed for what it is, an inquiry into the rules that govern, the points of regularity and order, in this minor matter, of political structure. My outline, imposed in bold-face type, makes the point important in this setting.

Mishnah-tractate Sanhedrin Chapter Two

1. The rules of the high priest: subject to the law, marital rites, conduct in bereavement

2:1   A.   A high priest judges, and [others] judge him;
     B.   gives testimony, and [others] give testimony about him;
     C.   performs the rite of removing the shoe [Deut. 25:7-9], and [others] perform the rite of removing the shoe with his wife.
     D.   [Others] enter levirate marriage with his wife, but he does not enter into levirate marriage,
     E.   because he is prohibited to marry a widow.
     F.   [If] he suffers a death [in his family], he does not follow the bier.
     G.   "But when [the bearers of the bier] are not visible, he is visible; when they are visible, he is not.
     H.   "And he goes with them to the city gate," the words of R. Meir.
     I.   R. Judah says, "He never leaves the sanctuary,
     J.   "since it says, *'Nor shall he go out of the* sanctuary' (Lev. 21:12)."
     K.   And when he gives comfort to others
     L.   the accepted practice is for all the people to pass one after another, and the appointed [prefect of the priests] stands between him and the people.
     M.   And when he receives consolation from others,
     N.   all the people say to him, "Let us be your atonement."
     O.   And he says to them, "May you be blessed by Heaven."
     P.   And when they provide him with the funeral meal,
     Q.   all the people sit on the ground, while he sits on a stool.

2. The rules of the king: not subject to the law, marital rites, conduct in bereavement

2:2   A.   The king does not judge, and [others] do not judge him;

B. does not give testimony, and [others] do not give testimony about him;

C. does not perform the rite of removing the shoe, and others do not perform the rite of removing the shoe with his wife;

D. does not enter into levirate marriage, nor [do his brother] enter levirate marriage with his wife.

E. R. Judah says, "If he wanted to perform the rite of removing the shoe or to enter into levirate marriage, his memory is a blessing."

F. They said to him, "They pay no attention to him [if he expressed the wish to do so]."

G. [Others] do not marry his widow.

H. R. Judah says, "A king may marry the widow of a king.

I. "For so we find in the case of David, that he married the widow of Saul,

J. "For it is said, *'And I gave you your master's house and your master's wives into your embrace'* (II Sam. 12:8)."

2:3 A. [If] [the king] suffers a death in his family, he does not leave the gate of his palace.

B. R. Judah says, "If he wants to go out after the bier, he goes out,

C. "for thus we find in the case of David, that he went out after the bier of Abner,

D. "since it is said, *'And King David followed the bier'* (2 Sam. 3:31)."

E. They said to him, "This action was only to appease the people."

F. And when they provide him with the funeral meal, all the people sit on the ground, while he sits on a couch.

3. Special rules pertinent to the king because of his calling

2:4 A. [The king] calls out [the army to wage] a war fought by choice on the instructions of a court of seventy-one.

B. He [may exercise the right to] open a road for himself, and [others] may not stop him.

C. The royal road has no required measure.

D. All the people plunder and lay before him [what they have grabbed], and he takes the first portion.

E. *"He should not multiply wives to himself"* (Deut. 17:17) – only eighteen.

F. R Judah says, "He may have as many as he wants, so long as they *do not entice him* [to abandon the Lord (Deut. 7:4)]."

G. R. Simeon says, "Even if there is only one who entices him [to abandon the Lord] – lo, this one should not marry her."

H. If so, why is it said, "He should not multiply wives to himself"?

I. Even though they should be like Abigail [1 Sam. 25:3].

J. *"He should not multiply horses to himself"* (Deut. 17:16) – only enough for his chariot.

K. *"Neither shall he greatly multiply to himself silver and gold"* (Deut. 17:16) – only enough to pay his army.

L. *"And he writes out a scroll of the Torah for himself"* (Deut. 17:17)

M. When he goes to war, he takes it out with him; when he comes back, he brings it back with him; when he is in session in court, it is with him; when he is reclining, it is before him,

N. as it is said, *"And it shall be with him, and he shall read in it all the days of his life"* (Deut. 17:19).

2:5 A. [Others may] not ride on his horse, sit on his throne, handle his sceptre.

B.   And [others may] not watch him while he is getting a haircut, or while he
is nude, or in the bath-house,

C.   since it is said, *"You shall surely set him as king over you"* (Deut. 17:15)
– that reverence for him will be upon you.

The Mishnah's authorship's philosophical cast of mind is amply
revealed in this essay, which in concrete terms effects a taxonomy, a study
of the genus, national leader, and its two species, [1] king, [2] high priest:
how are they alike, how are they not alike, and what accounts for the
differences. The premise is that national leaders are alike and follow the
same rule, except where they differ and follow the opposite rule from one
another. But that premise also is subject to the proof effected by the
survey of the data consisting of concrete rules, those systemically inert
facts that here come to life for the purposes of establishing a proposition.
By itself, the fact that, e.g., others may not ride on his horse, bears the
burden of no systemic proposition. In the context of an argument
constructed for nomothetic, taxonomic purposes, the same fact is active
and weighty.

No natural historian can find the discourse and mode of thought at
hand unfamiliar; it forms the foundation of all disposition of data in quest
of meaning, of making connections, drawing conclusions. For if I had to
specify a single mode of thought that established connections between
one fact and another, it is in the search for points in common and
therefore also points of contrast. We seek connection between fact and
fact, sentence and sentence in the subtle and balanced rhetoric of the
Mishnah, by comparing and contrasting two things that are like and not
alike. At the logical level, too, the Mishnah falls into the category of
familiar philosophical thought. Once we seek regularities, we propose
rules. What is like another thing falls under its rule, and what is not like the
other falls under the opposite rule. Accordingly, as to the species of the
genus, so far as they are alike, they share the same rule. So far as they are
not alike, each follows a rule contrary to that governing the other. So the
work of analysis is what produces connection, and therefore the drawing
of conclusions derives from comparison and contrast: the *and,* the
equal. The proposition then that forms the conclusion concerns the
essential likeness of the two offices, except where they are different, but
the subterranean premise is that we can explain both likeness and
difference by appeal to a principle of fundamental order and unity. To
make these observations concrete, we turn to the case at hand. The
important contrast comes at the outset. The high priest and king fall into a
single genus, but speciation, based on traits particular to the king, then
distinguishes the one from the other. In a treatise on government,
organizing details into unifying rules, the propositions of the present
passage will have been stated differently. But the mode of thought, the

manner of reaching conclusions, above all, the mind-set that sees connections in one way, rather than some other, that draws conclusions in this wise, not in that – these will have found an equally familiar place in the mind of both philosophy, of Aristotle's kind in particular, and the Jewish intellect represented by the Mishnah.

But comparing the intellect of the Mishnah's system-builders to that of Aristotle diverts our gaze from the still more apt likeness, the one with which we commenced. Like the authorship of the Pentateuch, the framers of the Mishnah have drawn together diverse materials in a single, nearly seamless fabric. And in them they have made a single statement, many times over, in the setting of an extraordinarily vast range of topics. Once authorship has registered the statement it wishes to make, it finds possible the expression of that same statement through what seems to me an unlimited range of topical media. Not only so, but just as in the Pentateuch a single logic of cogent discourse joins fact to fact and sentence to sentence into proposition and paragraph respectively, the same takes place in the Mishnah. That logic of list-making, which brings to the surface a deeper intellectual structure formed of comparison and contrast, classification and exclusion, predominates throughout. Accordingly, a single logic serves to make a single statement, in behalf of both the authorship of the Pentateuch and the framers of the Mishnah.

Speaking anonymously, collectively, and authoritatively, each set of system-builders has followed precisely the same rules of intellect, which, stated very simply, require a logic of a single taxon to make a statement of a singular character. And, as in the Pentateuch, so in the Mishnah, the form of the logic must fit the framework of the statement: teleology for a statement made up of connections between events and lessons drawn from events, philosophical syllogism for a statement made up of rules governing (or deriving from) a variety of cases. And that brings us to the final issue of systemic analysis in quest of insight into intellect: both authorships leave open the question of tradition, since, as we see with great clarity, each group of system-builders has chosen to do one thing only: set forth a system, without laying claim to the authority of tradition. And that is surely a trait of intellect of system-builders, so persuaded of the compelling character of their statement as to deny need to invoke the authority of tradition. Logic takes the place of tradition, argument and powerful rhetoric, of the argument of precedent and an authoritative past. It is one thing to claim God said it all to Moses, who wrote it down. It is another to say that the unbroken chain of tradition from Sinai stands behind the document, and the Pentateuchal Judaism affirms the one and rejects the other. The Pentateuchal compositors claimed their system came not through tradition but from Sinai, dictated whole and complete by God to Moses. Given their extraordinary achievement, as I said, we need hardly find surprising the claim that, with enormous but entirely ordinate pride, they made in behalf of that achievement.

But the Mishnah's authorship claimed no less. For, in the very face of the Torah of God revealed to Moses at Sinai, they built and set forth a system resting wholly on the foundations of logic and order set forth within the systemic statement itself. That is to say, their's was a statement standing on the firm two feet of the systemic authorship itself. The authorship of the Pentateuch appealed to Sinai for authority. The framers of the Mishnah kept silent about why people should keep the rules of their document and so construct out of an inchoate and chaotic world that system that they set forth. The systemic statement contained its own authority. That, at any rate, is what they seem to me implicitly to have said through those inviting silences that invite us, in the end, to join in the conversation they inaugurated. Logic, compelling and uncompromising, sustained the system; an appeal to tradition would have contradicted that proud claim of the system-makers of the Mishnah, and it is a claim that they did not deign to put forth. True, others alleged in their behalf that their authority, if not their exact positions, set them into a chain of tradition commencing with Moses at Sinai. But that claim came only in the context of debates following the closure of the Mishnah and made necessary by the character of the Mishnah. To state the upshot simply, the framers of the Mishnah set forth a system that, in its very nature, demanded to be transformed into a tradition.

II. Sifra's Critique of the Logic of the Mishnah

Now the intellectual labor of relating system to tradition and also of finding an appropriate logic of cogent discourse for the composition of a system could be accomplished in more than one way. And that brings us to the position of the authorship of Sifra. To state matters simply, what we shall now see in Sifra is a two-pronged polemic against the Mishnah, one a mere feint, the other the main attack.

[1] The authorship of Sifra, as we already know, commonly invokes the exact language of the Mishnah or the Tosefta, asks whether the position presented in that language, lacking all proof-texts drawn from Scripture, is not a matter of mere logic, and proves that it is not. That shows that what is required is law resting on scriptural proof.

[2] The authorship of Sifra, as we shall see time and again, systematically demonstrates the futility of the logic of Listenwissenschaft, classification or taxonomy, comparison and contrast. This it does in a very simple way. It shows that species that look as though they form a common genus do not in fact form such a genus. Therefore it is not possible to compare and contrast two species to find the law common to

the two of them, if they compare, or the law that differentiates one from the other, if they contrast.

A systemic statement could be woven into the cloak of tradition by its presentation as (mere) exegesis of a received text. The urgent question and self-evidently valid answer, not stated openly as a proposition for demonstration and argument, but merely repeated endlessly in the form of commentary, bore its own power of persuasion. Repeating the point gains for the message a self-evident proposition that argument and therefore counterargument can deny it. And that is the first of the two attacks of Sifra's authorship on the Mishnah, the feint. What about the other? While I should claim that the whole of the document is composed as a sustained demonstration of the improbability of the logic of classification, let me give two examples, the first from the opening pages of the document. It suffices to make the point at hand.

I:I

1. A. "The Lord called [to Moses] and spoke [to him from the tent of meeting, saying, 'Speak to the Israelite people and say to them']" (Lev. 1:1):
   B. He gave priority to the calling over the speaking.
   C. That is in line with the usage of Scripture.
   D. Here there is an act of speaking, and in connection with the encounter at the bush [Ex. 3:4: "God called to him out of the bush, 'Moses, Moses'"], there is an act of speaking.
   E. Just as in the latter occasion, the act of calling is given priority over the act of speaking [even though the actual word, "speaking" does not occur, it is implicit in the framing of the verse], so here, with respect to the act of speaking, the the act of calling is given priority over the act of speaking.

2. A. No [you cannot generalize on the basis of that case,] for if you invoke the case of the act of speaking at the bush, which is the first in the sequence of acts of speech [on which account, there had to be a call prior to entry into discourse],
   B. will you say the same of the act of speech in the tent of meeting, which assuredly is not the first in a sequence of acts of speech [so there was no need for a preliminary entry into discourse through a call]?
   C. The act of speech at Mount Sinai [Ex. 19:3] will prove to the contrary, for it is assuredly not the first in a sequence of acts of speech, yet, in that case, there was an act of calling prior to the act of speech.

3. A. No, [the exception proves nothing,] for if you invoke in evidence the act of speech at Mount Sinai, which pertained to all the Israelites, will you represent it as parallel to the act of speech in the tent of meeting, which is not pertinent to all Israel?
   B. Lo, you may sort matters out by appeal to comparison and contrast, specifically:
   C. The act of speech at the bush, which is the first of the acts of speech, is not of the same classification as the act of speech at Sinai, which is not the first act of speech.

D.   And the act of speech at Sinai, which is addressed to all Israel, is not in the same classification as the act of speech at the bush, which is not addressed to all Israel.

4.   A.   What they have in common, however, is that both of them are acts of speech, deriving from the mouth of the Holy One, addressed to Moses, in which case, the act of calling comes prior to the act of speech,

     B.   so that, by way of generalization, we may maintain that every act of speech which comes from the mouth of the Holy One to Moses will be preceded by an act of calling.

5.   A.   Now if what the several occasions have in common is that all involve an act of speech, accompanied by fire, from the mouth of the Holy One, addressed to Moses, so that the act of calling was given priority over the act of speaking, then in every case in which there is an act of speech, involving fire, from the mouth of the Holy One, addressed to Moses, should involve an act of calling prior to the act of speech.

     B.   But then an exception is presented by the act of speech at the tent of meeting, in which there was no fire.

     C.   [That is why it was necessary for Scripture on this occasion to state explicitly,] "The Lord called [to Moses and spoke to him from the tent of meeting, saying, 'Speak to the Israelite people and say to them']" (Lev. 1:1).

     D.   That explicit statement shows that, on the occasion at hand, priority was given to the act of calling over the act of speaking.

I:II

1.   A.   ["The Lord called to Moses and spoke to him from the tent of meeting, saying, 'Speak to the Israelite people and say to them'" (Lev. 1:1)]: Might one suppose that the act of calling applied only to this act of speaking alone?

     B.   And how on the basis of Scripture do we know that on the occasion of all acts of speaking that are mentioned in the Torah, [there was a prior act of calling]?

     C.   Scripture specifies, "from the tent of meeting,"

     D.   which bears the sense that on every occasion on which it was an act of speaking from the tent of meeting, there was an act of calling prior to the act of speaking.

2.   A.   Might one suppose that there was an act of calling only prior to the acts of speech alone?

     B.   How on the basis of Scripture do I know that the same practice accompanied acts of saying and also acts of commanding?

     C.   Said R. Simeon, "Scripture says not only, '...spoke,...,' but '...and he spoke,' [with the inclusion of the *and*] meant to encompass also acts of telling and also acts of commanding."

The exercise of generalization addresses the character of God's meeting with Moses. The point of special interest is the comparison of the meeting at the bush and the meeting at the tent of meeting. And at stake is asking whether all acts of God's calling and talking with, or speaking to, the prophet are the same, or whether some of these acts are of a different classification from others. In point of fact, we are able to come to a generalization, worked out at **I:I.5.A.** And that permits us to explain why there is a different usage at Lev. 1:1 from what characterizes parallel cases. **I:II.1-2** proceeds to generalize from the case at hand to other usages entirely, a very satisfying conclusion to the whole. I separate **I:II** from **I:I** because had **I:I** ended at **5**, it could have stood complete and on its own, and therefore I see **I:II** as a brief appendix.

My second example derives from Parashat Vayyiqra Dibura Denedabah Parashah 9. It shows how in the context of defining norms, the same polemic is carried forward.

XVI:I

3. A. "[and present it to Aaron's sons,] the priests. The priest shall scoop out of it a handful [of its choice flour and oil]:"

   B. **This teaches that the taking up of a handful of meal-offering requires the action of a priest [and may not be done by an outsider] (T. Men. 1:2G).**

   C. Is that not [the contrary proposition] a matter of logic? [Proof of the foregoing requires scriptural demonstration, since logic cannot have produced that result.]

   D. If the slaughter of a beast for sacrifice, which is assigned a place at the northern side of the altar, is not assigned the services of a priest, the act of taking the handful, which is not assigned a place at the north side of the altar, surely should not be assigned the services of a priest?

   E. The act of pinching the nerve will prove the contrary, for it has not been assigned a place at the northern side of the altar, but it has been assigned the requirement that only a priest do it.

   F. No, if you have stated such a rule with reference to the pinching of a bird's neck, which is assigned a position at the altar itself, will you so state of the taking of a handful of meal offering, which is not assigned a position at the altar [but may be done anywhere in the courtyard]?

   G. Since it has not been assigned a place at the altar, it also should not be assigned the action of an officiating priest.

   H. [Because logic proves the opposite of the fact, it was necessary for Scripture to state matters explicitly, as follows:] "[and present it to Aaron's sons,] the priests. The priest shall scoop out of it a handful [of its choice flour and oil]:"

   I. **This teaches that the taking up of a handful of meal-offering requires the action of a priest [and may not be done by an outsider] (T. Men. 1:2G).**

4. A. Might one suppose that while taking up a handful of meal offering requires the action of a priest, if it is done by an outsider, it should be acceptable?

   B. Scripture says, "The priest shall scoop out."

   C. Scripture has so ordained matters that if a non-priest should scoop out the handful, the offering is invalid.

The polemic of No. 3 is against logic, not merely against the ascriptural presentation of the law by the authorship of Tosefta. That is a secondary consideration. The minor clarification at No. 4 of course is tacked on.   Now we shall see a handsome demonstration of the impossibility of relying upon the logic of *Listenwissenschaft,* precisely the logic of the Mishnah, as we have seen:

XVIII:II

1.   A.   "The priest shall scoop out of it a handful:"

     B.   Is the rule that a single handful suffices not only for a single tenth-ephah of the offering, but a single handful also suffices for sixty tenth-ephahs?

     C.   Or is the rule that a single handful serves only a single tenth-ephah, while there must be sixty handfuls taken up out of sixty tenth-ephahs?

     D.   Lo, I reason as follows:

     E.   The meal offering requires the taking up of a handful, and it also requires frankincense. Just as in the case of frankincense, a single handful serves for a single tenth-ephah, and a single handful serves also for sixty tenth-ephahs, so in the case of the taking up of the handful, a single handful serves for one tenth-ephah, and a single handful serves for sixty tenth-ephahs.

     F.   Or try taking this route:

     G.   The meal offering requires the taking up of a handful, an it also requires oil. Just as in the case of the oil, a single log of oil serves for a single tenth-ephah, while sixty logs of oil are required for sixty tenth-ephahs, so in the case of a handful, the taking up of a handful serves a single tenth-ephah, while for sixty tenth-ephahs, there must be sixty taking ups of handfuls.

     H.   Let us then see to the correct analogy:

     I.   We should establish an analogy from something which is wholly offered up on the altar fire to something that is wholly offered up on the altar fire, but oil should not then enter the picture, since it is not wholly burned up on the altar fire.

     J.   Or take this route:

     K.   We should establish an analogy from something in which the smaller portion is indispensable to the validity of the entire portion [for instance, if any of the required fine flour or oil is lacking, the entire meal offering is null], but let us not propose proof from the example of frankincense, in which the lack of a smaller portion of the whole is not indispensable to the validity of the entire portion.

     L.   [Accordingly, we appeal to Scripture to settle matters, as it does when it says:] "The priest shall scoop out of it a handful:"

     M.   It is the rule that a single handful suffices not only for a single tenth-ephah of the offering, but a single handful also suffices for sixty tenth-ephahs.

This elegant exercise once more proves the falsity of appealing to classification for settling a moot point, because taxonomy yields contradictory results.

Let me give yet another example, because it shows a much more subtle critique of the logic of classification. It indicates that Sifra's authorship was prepared to concede the possibility of polythetic, not merely monothetic, classification – and to destroy that possibility as well!

We proceed directly to the immediately following pericope, because it goes through the same process and then reverts to the more familiar attack on the very possibilities of classificatory or taxonomic logic. I present Parashat Vayyiqra Dibura Denedabah Pereq 13:

XXIII:I

1.   A.   [Continuing the foregoing: R. Simeon says, "'When you present to the Lord a meal offering that is made in any of these ways, *it shall be brought* [to the priest who shall take it up to the altar' – that statement serves to encompass under the rule of waving also the sheaf of first grain, for it is said, 'When you come into the land which I give you and reap its harvest, *you shall bring* the sheaf of the first fruits of your harvest to the priest, [and he shall wave the sheaf before the Lord, that you may find acceptance]' (Lev. 23:10), '...who shall take it up to the altar' serves to encompass the meal offering of the wife accused of adultery, that that too requires being brought near: 'who shall take it up to the altar' [parallel to Num. 5:25]:"

      B.   is that proposition not a matter of logic?

      C.   If the meal offering brought by a sinner, which does not require waving, does require drawing near, the meal offering of a wife accused of adultery, which does require waving, surely should require drawing near.

      D.   No, if you have invoked that rule in the case of the sinner's meal offering, which derives from wheat, will you invoke the same rule in the case of the meal offering of an accused wife, which does not derive from wheat [but from barley, and therefore falls into a different genus]?

      E.   The meal offering of the sheaf of first grain will prove the contrary, for it too does not derive from wheat [but rather from barley] and yet it does require being brought near!

      F.   No, if you have invoked that rule in the case of the meal offering of the sheaf of first grain, which requires also oil and frankincense, will you place into that same category and subject to that same rule the meal offering of an accused wife, which does not require oil and frankincense?

      G.   Lo, you must therefore reason by appeal to a polythetic analogy [in which not all traits pertain to all components of the category, but some traits apply to them all in common]:

      H.   The sinner's meal offering, which derives from wheat, is not in all respects equivalent to the meal offering of the sheaf of first grain, which after all does not derive from wheat, nor is the meal offering of the sheaf of first grain, which requires oil and frankincense, equivalent in all respects to the meal offering of the sinner, which does not require oil and frankincense. But the common trait that pertains to them both is that they both require the taking up of a handful, and, furthermore, they both require being brought near.

      I.   So I shall invoke the case of the meal offering of an accused wife, which is equivalent to them in that the taking up of a handful is required. It should also be equivalent to them in being brought near.

J.   Or perhaps what they have in common is that they are not valid if they derive from coarse meal and they require drawing near. Then that would exclude the meal offering of the accused wife, which indeed is valid when it derives from coarse meal, and which, therefore, should not require drawing near.

K.   [Accordingly, Scripture is required to settle the matter, which it does when it states,]"..who shall take it up to the altar,"

L.   which then serves to encompass the meal offering of the wife accused of adultery, and indicates that that too requires being brought near.

Precisely the same mode of argument worked out in **XXII:I** now applies to Simeon's proposition, with the same satisfactory result. I need hardly repeat the point that is already familiar.

III. Conclusion

Conducting a sustained and brilliant polemic against the Mishnah, the authorship of Sifra presents, in a systemic and orderly way, an amazing, subtle demonstration that there is no such thing as a genus, but only species. Then, it follows for our authorship, Scripture serves as the sole source for rules governing otherwise incomprehensible, because incomparable, species. A critical corollary is that the Mishnah not only rests upon false logic, but in failing to tie its propositions to Scripture, its authorship has set the law of the Torah upon unreliable foundations. The framers of Sifra then correct the errors of logic, on the one side, and set forth solid foundations in revelation, there alone, on the other. All of this they do while working their way through what will seem, on the surface, somewhat remote facts indeed. My hope is that the reader will find as compelling as I do the powerful, sustained, and amazingly cogent argument our authorship sets forth only in the minutia of cultic law.

The authors of Sifra, working on the book of Leviticus, have given us a mélange of materials, some of them exegetical in a narrow sense, others more broadly speculative Since all named authorities are supposed to have lived before the publication of the Mishnah in ca. A.D. 200, the work is assigned to the same period as the formation of the Mishnah. But passages in the Sifra cite verbatim both the Mishnah and the Tosefta, so the document as we have it certainly reached closure some time after ca. A.D. 200. It is an Amoraic text as much as the Tosefta and the Talmud of the Land of Israel. That fact is shown not only by the document's citing the Mishnah verbatim and pursuing an exegetical program vis-à-vis the Mishnah. There is a still more telling consideration. The polemic of the work takes account of the character of the Mishnah as a piece of writing essentially autonomous of Scripture and repeatedly claims one thing. It is that the rules of the Mishnah demand scriptural support, through exegesis. They cannot stand on their own as the result of a mere exercise in logic and reason. Accordingly, one principal purpose in the formation of the document addresses the issue of the standing of the Mishnah in relationship to Scripture (in theological terms: the Oral Torah in relationship to the Written Torah).   It must follow that the document in its fundamental focus and stress derives from the period from ca. 200 to ca. 400.   That is the age that also yielded the Tosefta, supplements to the Mishnah; the commentaries to Genesis and Leviticus called Genesis Rabbah and Leviticus Rabbah; the Talmud of the Land of Israel; and some of the formative layers of the Talmud of Babylonia.

Sifra has its own, strikingly polemical, purposes, for which the laws pertinent to, and even shared with, the Mishnah and the Tosefta are reshaped.   Sifra proposes to present a kind of gemara, that is, an essay, worked out dialectically through questions and answers, rapidly and with great economy of expression and thought, moving from point to point within discrete thematic structures.   While it often enough simply cites a verse and adds a few words about its interpretation, it much more commonly then goes on to raise a series of logical questions about that primary citation and original interpretation.   These questions may vary, but predominant among them, the common one is, Might one think the opposite? How do we know that the original interpretation may withstand the test of reason, the consideration of different, mostly contrary, propositions?   This, I think is the definitive characteristic of gemara and justifies our calling Sifra a sort of the Bavli, or Babylonian Talmud, in its own right.   But I should claim that our authorship has given us a far more engaging statement than did the framers of the Bavli, because of the stunning coherence of their recurrent and methodical exercise.

One critical polemic, fundamental to Sifra's purpose, is to demonstrate the inadequacy of reason unaided by revelation.   Time and again Sifra asks, Does this proposition, offered with a proof-text, really require the stated proof of revelation?   Will it not stand firmly upon the basis of autonomous reason, unaided by Scripture?   Sometimes Scripture will show that the opposite of the conclusion of reason is the result of exegesis.   Therefore the truth is to be discovered solely through exegesis. At other times Sifra will show that reason by itself is flawed and fallible, not definitive.   At important points it will seek to prove not only a given proposition, but also that that proposition is to be demonstrated solely through revelation, through exegesis of Scripture.   In all it is difficult to avoid the impression that the primary purpose of the compilers of Sifra is to criticize the Mishnah and the Tosefta, documents notoriously uninterested in the exegetical foundations of their laws.

We address the result of the formation of a consensus, that is, the work not of an individual author but of an authorship, a textual community. Received in a canonical process of transmission under the auspices of a religious system, specifically, the system of the Judaism of the dual Torah,

Sifra enjoys authority and status within that canon and system. Hence it is deemed to speak for a community and to contribute to the consensus of that community. Not only so, but the most superficial trait of all tells us that Sifra itself constitutes the statement of a consensus. Sifra has no named author. Accordingly, it is represented, on the surface, as the statement of a consensus. That consensus, the anonymous authorities behind the document as we have it, I call an authorship. The purpose of this fresh translation and analysis of Sifra therefore is to identify the world view expressed by the authorship of the document at hand.

Part Three

HISTORY:

WRONG WAYS AND RIGHT WAYS IN THE
HISTORICAL STUDY OF FORMATIVE JUDAISM

Chapter Five

Wrong Ways in Historical Study [1]: Positivism, Gullibility, and the History of Formative Judaism

In historical debate, we gain access to no knowledge *a priori.*[1] All facts derive from sources correctly situated, e.g., classified, comprehensively and completely described, dispassionately analyzed, and evaluated. Nothing can be taken for granted. What we cannot show, we do not know. These simple dogmas of all historical learning derive not from this writer but go back to the very beginnings of Western critical historical scholarship, to the age of the Renaissance. When the Donation of Constantine proved false, all received facts of a historical character stood at risk. These same principles – *"it ain't necessarily so, /it ain't necessarily so, /the things that you're liable /to read in the Bible – /it ain't necessarily so"* – emerged with new sharpness from the mind of Spinoza, who founded modern critical biblical scholarship. They passed through the purifying skepticism of the Enlightenment, which learned – because it had to – how to laugh. But gullibility suffered a still further blow in the nineteenth century's refounding of historical science. Systematic skepticism illuminated the founders of historical sciences in the nineteenth century. They serve as commonplace models in the twentieth. Anyone who claims to tell us what happened a long time ago obeys these simple rules, and no one who ignores them can properly use the past tense. At issue is not personal conviction – fundamentalism in a theological sense, of which I accuse no one in this article – but public principles of professional inquiry. In raising doubts about the findings of those to be cited shortly, I wonder about their professionalism. At issue are matters of public inquiry, not available for idiosyncratic and private apologia through a mere: "I believe." When the fundamentalist states, "I believe," he makes a statement of profound consequence. When – as we shall see in *ipsissima verba* – a gullible scholar claims that the "burden of

---

[1]This essay is a reprise and précis of my *Reading and Believing: Ancient Judaism and Contemporary Gullibility* (Atlanta: Scholars Press for Brown Judaic Studies, 1986).

proof is on the doubter," and frames questions we can ask only if we assume the sources contain factual information about what people really said and did – he violates the language-rules of his professed field and says something that is merely silly.

The credulity characteristic of the traditional settings of Judaic studies, Yeshivot and Jewish universities and seminaries in the diaspora and in the State of Israel, leads scholars in those places to take not only as fact but at face value everything in the holy books. "Judaism" is special and need not undergo description, analysis, and interpretation in accord with a shared and public canon of rules of criticism. "We all know" how to do the work, and "we" do not have to explain to "outsiders" either what the work is or why it is important. It is a self-evidently important enterprise in the rehearsal of information. Knowing these things the way "we" know them explains the value of knowing these things. That is the mentality of a ghetto, a closed circle, and the generality of Jewish scholars of Judaism in late antiquity have not left the ghetto, nor do they even admit to themselves that they presently reside therein. People who are gullible generically believe everything they hear, and gullibility as generic generates belief in whatever the holy books say. If, therefore, a canonical ("holy") book says a holy man said something, he really said it, and if the book says he did something, he really did it. That is gullibility.

Scholarship in the service of gullibility frames questions that implicitly affirm the accuracy of the holy books, asking questions, for example, that can only be answered in the assumption that the inerrant Scriptures contain the answers – therefore, as a matter of process, do not err. By extension holy books that tell stories produce history through the paraphrase of stories into historical language: this is what happened, this is how it happened, and here are the reasons why it happened. Scholarship of a credulous character need not serve God, it may serve Satan. Lives of Jesus may portray him as son of God or as magician. Both statements are equally fundamentalist in scholarly premise, the one white, the other black gullibility, the one positive, the other negative. There is no methodological or epistemological difference. The gullibility of which I speak, moreover, characterizes not solely Orthodox believers, from whom one can ask no better, but, deplorably, Conservative, Reform, and national-secular Israeli scholars, who claim to be "critical" and who probably believe they are, as well as among non-Jewish scholars, in the New Testament in particular, who approach the same sources for their own purposes. Nearly all scholars work on the premise that if the Talmud says someone said something, he really said it, then and there. That premise moreover dictates their scholarly program, for it permits them to describe, analyze and interpret events or ideas held in the time in which that person lived. Some of these would deny the charge, and all of them would surely point, in their writing, to evidence of a critical approach. But the questions they frame to begin with rest on the assumption that the sources respond. The assumption that, if a story refers to a second century rabbi, then the story tells us about the second century, proves routine. And that complete reliance merely on the allegations of sayings and stories constitutes gullibility: perfect faith in the facticity of fairy-tales. That is gullibility, not a new kind but a very old kind. The only difference is that the current generation of scholars claims to know better – and should know better. The results, furthermore, attract the interest of scholars in adjacent fields, New Testament, early Christianity, ancient history and classics, for instance. But the newest practitioners of gullibility *redivivus* cannot work on the subjects of their choice if they confront the critical program of the day. So they generally pretend to accept that program, while in fact ignoring it. In this respect the old fundamentalists showed greater candor. These judgments cannot make any reader happy; they do not give me joy in writing them. But the scholars' words themselves in every case prove my judgment accurate, indeed moderate. The judgments invariably pertain to what people say, not who or what they are, which is not at issue. My interior intent therefore is to restate the question of method in one aspect alone. Let me state it as emphatically as I can:

How do you know exactly what was said and done, that is, the history that you claim to report about what happened long ago? Specifically, how do you know he really said it? And if you do not know that he really said it, how can you ask the question that you ask, which has as its premise the claim that you can say what happened or did not happen?

The generality of these scholarly writings rests on false premises as to the character of the evidence and therefore asks the wrong questions and produces worthless answers. The burden of my indictment is that total gullibility about what ancient sources tell us, incapacity critically to analyze those sources, presently characterize the use, for historical purposes, of the documents of Judaism in late antiquity. Believing Jews of Orthodox or Conservative or Reform, or secular origin, whether young or old, use these sources in ways in which no reputable scholar of the Old or New Testaments would condone in the scholarly reading of the biblical writings. Eminent scholars take for granted that we may ignore the entire critical program of biblical learning. So the study of ancient Judaism in its formative centuries produces results in no way based on the principles of scholarship universally honored.

Can we draw an analogy to how things would be done in biblical studies if the same epistemological premise governed? Indeed we can. Working along the same lines, in like manner Old Testament scholars would analyze tales of conversations between Moses and Aaron or Pharaoh as if they really took place, and not as the imaginary compositions of great writers of religious fiction. The scholars, young and old, from whom we shall hear at some length, invoke arguments from the *plausibility* of the contents of a statement for the veracity of that statement. New Testament scholars following that program would tell us that Jesus really made such-and-such a statement, because it sounds like something he would say. So the *"if-I-were-a-horse,-I'd-like-to-eat-oats-too"* school of anthropology finds company in the great stables of Jewish scholarship. The scholars under discussion furthermore invoke the claim that they can identify the point of origin of a statement, without also telling us how we would know if we were wrong. The works of scholarship under discussion recapitulate the mode of historical thought of the Talmud – "since this statement uses this language, it must have been said before such and such a point, after which such language cannot have been used." So they blunder into minefields of pure guesswork. An analogy in biblical studies? In like manner, biblical scholars would tell us that such and such a proposition has the ring of truth; or "if such and such a proposition is true, then we can solve a further problem," or, "since text X knows nothing of the rule in text Y, therefore text X must come before text Y." That may be so – but not on the basis of argument alone. At some point, evidence must make its contribution, not to mention tests of falsification and verification. Otherwise we shall never know whether we are right. Deductive logic untested by evidence and unchallenged by skeptical analysis rules supreme.

To state matters simply: if biblical history were written the way the history of the Jews and Judaism in late antiquity (which used to be called "Talmudic history") is written today, the histories of ancient Israel would begin with the creation of the world – in six days, of course. If complete indifference to the history of the writings in hand were to characterize New Testament scholarship, as that indifference governs Talmudic-historical scholarship, we should be reading more and more harmonies of the Gospels. For the recognition that the four Evangelists preserve viewpoints distinctive to themselves should never have shaped the interpretation of the Gospels, and we should be left with ever more complicated restatements of the Diatesseron. New Testament scholars know full well that when they come to the rabbinic sources, they tend to use it in ways in which they do not utilize the New Testament. But, as I shall now show, they may take comfort in the simple fact that since the specialists in the Talmudic writings read the documents in a fundamentalist way, the New Testament scholars do no worse. Nonetheless, both Old and New Testament scholarship, with its keen interest in questions of formulation and transmission of sayings, composition of sayings into documents, preservation of documents, and other critical issues must find primitive and alien the traits of mind to which I shall now point. In contemporary Judaic studies, we routinely deal with premises last found plausible in biblical studies more than one hundred and fifty years ago. The prevalent scholarly premise is this: if a source says Rabbi X said something, he really said it. Without that premise, not a single paragraph I shall present can have been conceived and written. If we did not know in advance that whatever is assigned to an authority represents a view held by that person in the time in which, in general, we assume that person lived, none of the scholars at hand can have formulated and asked the questions that they ask and provided the answers they give. Since that premise is manifestly unacceptable as the starting point of historical scholarship, which always starts by asking *how* ancient writers know what they tell us and analyzes sources and their usefulness prior to framing questions, for instance, reporting what really happened, it must follow that all of the work of the sample I shall survey is, from a critical-historical viewpoint, a mere curiosity.

I. Gullibility in New Testament Scholarship on Judaism

Let me rapidly restate what I mean by gullibility in the academic context. Two traits of mind define academic gullibility. One is believing everything you read. The second is free-associating about what you read, without the control of a test of right or wrong. If I believe without asking how does the author of this text knows that the things he imputes to an authority really were said by that authority, hence at the time that that authority lived, I am a fundamentalist. In the setting of the rabbinic writings of late antiquity, if I take for granted that what is attributed to a given rabbi really was said by him, in his day, when he lived, and recorded verbatim from that day until it was written down, and if – and this proves the premise on which I work – on that basis I say what happened in that rabbi's time, then I am credulous. And if not, then I am not. Helmut Koester, *Introduction to the New Testament*. I. *History, Culture, and Religion of the Hellenistic Age* (Philadelphia: Fortress Press, 1982, and Berlin and New York: Walter DeGruyter, 1982. Translated from the German *Einfuehrung in das Neue Testament,* Berlin: Walter de Gruyter, 1980) I, p. 406, states:

> **Hillel.** What would give to later rabbinic Judaism its characteristic mark was the practice of legal interpretation in the Babylonian synagogue. Hillel (who lived until about 20 CE) came from Babylon. He may have also studied in Jerusalem, but his exegetical principles, which together with his humaneness became determinative for rabbinic Judaism, reveal the diaspora situation, for which legislation related to the temple cult and to living conditions in an overwhelmingly Jewish country were of only academic interest. This perspective as well as his great gifts as a teacher made Hillel the father of rabbinic Judaism – much more so than his

famous exegetical rules, like the conclusion *a minore ad maius* and the conclusion from analogy. In contrast, his often-quoted opponent Shammai represents a branch of Pharisaism which was closely related to the temple. Shammai is aristocratic, severe, and nationalistic. But Gamaliel I, Hillel's successor as the head of his school (probably a son of Hillel) had also become a member of the Jerusalem aristocracy. He was a member of the Jerusalem sanhedrin who became famous for his wisdom (and as such he appears in Acts 5:34-39), though he may have distanced himself sometimes from the prevailing opinion of that institution, as is indicated by the report of the Book of Acts. However, Gamaliel's son Simeon became the leader of the Pharisaic war party and was associated with the first government of the revolutionaries, although he later had to make room for a more radical leadership. This Pharisaic war party can be largely identified with the Shammaites with whom Simeon, grandson of Hillel, perished in the chaos of the Jewish war.

Koester presents a pastiche of allusions to references to Hillel in a diverse body of writings, some of them separated from the time in which Hillel lived by only two hundred years, others by much longer. For example, "Hillel the Babylonian" and merely "Hillel" do not occur side by side. Should we not ask whether, overall, "Hillel-the-Babylonian" references present a viewpoint about Hillel different from the "merely-Hillel" sources? "His" exegetical principles are assigned to him only in sources of the fourth century and beyond – four hundred years later. Does Koester describe the life of Jesus on the basis of statements of fourth century Church fathers? I think not. The conclusion *a minore ad maius*, for example, is a commonplace in Scripture and not Hillel's invention. I can direct him to chapter and verse, both in Scripture and in the later rabbinic exegesis of Scripture. For more than a few passages in the canon of Judaism recognize that fact. Koester is copying what he read somewhere. Koester even favors us with the gentle and humane Hillel, in the tradition of the stories, obviously partisan, that contrast the humane Hillel and the captious Shammai – stories that, in the main, circulated only in the latest parts of the canon, redacted at ca. A.D. 500-600, for instance. Then, with "But Gamaliel...," we jump into a different body of sources, now drawing on Josephus and Acts for the rest of the tale. So we mix up a rather diverse group of sources, some from the first century, some from the seventh, believing whatever we find in any one of them, and forming the whole into a harmonious statement: pure gullibility.

II. Example of Gullibility
in the Study of the History of the Jews

Shaye J. D. Cohen, "The Significance of Yavneh: Pharisees, Rabbis, and the End of Jewish Sectarianism," *Hebrew Union College Annual* 55, 1984, pp. 27-53 presents an important thesis. In order to make certain he is represented accurately, I cite his own précis of his article, which is as follows:

> After the destruction of the second temple in 70 C.E. the rabbis gathered in Yavneh and launched the process which yielded the Mishnah approximately one hundred years later. Most modern scholars see these rabbis as Pharisees triumphant, who define "orthodoxy," expel Christians and other heretics, and purge the canon of "dangerous" books. The evidence for this reconstruction is inadequate. In all likelihood most of the rabbis were Pharisees, but there is no indication that the rabbis of the Yavnean period were motivated by a Pharisaic self-consciousness (contrast the Babylonian Talmud and the medieval polemics against the Karaites) or were dominated by an exclusivistic ethic. In contrast the major goal of the Yavnean rabbis seems to have been not the expulsion of those with whom they disagreed but the cessation of sectarianism and the creation of a society which tolerated, even encouraged, vigorous debate among members of the fold. The Mishnah is the first work of Jewish antiquity which ascribes conflicting legal opinions to named individuals who, in spite of their disagreements, belong to the same fraternity. This mutual tolerance is the enduring legacy of Yavneh.

Now what is important is not Cohen's theory, with which I do not undertake an argument, but whether or not to formulate and prove his theory, he has exhibited that gullibility that seems to characterize pretty much everyone else. To answer that question let us proceed to ask how Cohen uses the evidence, investigating the theory of the character of the sources that leads him to frame his questions in one way and not in some other. What we shall see, first of all, is that Cohen takes at face value the historical allegation of a source that a given rabbi made the statement attributed to him. At pp. 32-33 Cohen states:

> The text narrates a story about a Sadducee and a high priest, and concludes with the words of the wife of the Sadducee:
>
> A. Although they [= we] are wives of Sadducees, they [= we] fear the Pharisees and show their [= our] menstrual blood to the sages."
>
> B. R. Yosi says, "We are more expert in them [Sadducean women] than anyone else. They show (menstrual) blood to the sages, except for one woman who was in our neighborhood, who did not show her (menstrual blood to the sages, and she died [immediately]" (Bab. Niddah 33b).

Cohen forthwith states, "In this text there is chronological tension between parts A and B. A clearly refers to a woman who lived during second temple times, while B has R. Yosé derive his expertise about Sadducean women from personal acquaintance." Why Cohen regards that "tension" as probative or even pertinent I cannot say. Now we may wonder whether Cohen believes Yosé really made the statement attributed to him. We note that Cohen does not specify the point at which "the text" was redacted. The fact that the Babylonian Talmud reached closure in the sixth or seventh century makes no difference. *If the text refers to Yosé, then it testifies to the second century, not to the seventh.* We shall now hear Cohen treat the text as an accurate report of views held in the time of which it speaks. How does he know? Because the text says so: it refers to this, it refers to that. What we have is a newspaper reporter, writing down things really said and giving them over to the National Archives for preservation until some later reporter chooses to add to the file: gullibility of a vulgar order indeed. Here is Cohen again, in the same passage, starting with the pretense of a critical exercise of analysis:

> In this text there is chronological tension between parts A and B. A clearly refers to a woman who lived during second temple times, while B has R. Yosi derive his expertise about Saducean women from personal acquaintance. He recalls a Saducean woman who lived in his neighborhood and died prematurely because (R. Yosi said) she did not accept the authority of the sages to determine her menstrual status.

To this point Cohen simply paraphrases the text, and now he will verify the story. It seems to me that Cohen takes for granted Yosé really made the saying attributed to him, and, moreover, that saying is not only Yosé's view of matters, but how matters really were. He says so in so many words: "This baraita clearly implies that R. Yosi is referring to contemporary Saducean women. If this is correct, R. Yosi's statement shows that some Saducees still existed in the mid-second century but that their power had declined to the extent that the rabbis could assume that most Saducees follow rabbinic norms." It seems to me beyond doubt that Cohen takes for granted that what is attributed to Yosé really was said by him, and, more interestingly, Yosé testifies to how things were not in one place but everywhere in the country. "If this is correct" Cohen concludes not that Yosé *thought* there were still a few Saducees around, but that there *were* still a few Saducees around. There is a difference. Cohen does not tell us what conclusions he draws *if this is not correct,* because, in point of fact, that possibility he declines to explore. Nonetheless, he wants to verify the story. How? By finding another text that tells the same story. He states:

> The version of the Tosefta is similar:
>
> A.   "Although we are Saducean women, we all consult a sage."
>
> B.   R. Yosi says, "We are more expert in Saducean women that anyone else: they all consult a sage except for one who was among them, and she died" (Tosefta Niddah 5:3).
>
> The Tosefta does not identify Pharisees with sages, a point to which we shall return below, and omits the phrase "who was in our neighborhood." Otherwise, it is basically, the same as the Babylonian version.

Now the reader may rightly wonder, perhaps Cohen intends something other than historical narrative about views Yosé held or opinions he taught. Cohen leaves no doubt as to his intention. Let us listen as he tells us what *really* happened: since Yosé made his statement, Yosé's statement tells us about the second century. Then Yosé's statement proves that there were Sadducees in the mid-second century but they had no power. I find no evidence whatsoever that Cohen grasps the critical problem of evaluating the allegations of sources. He looks into a source and comes up with a fact. If he finds two versions of the same story, the fact is still more factual. Gullibility, pure and simple! And, if that were not enough, he gives us the "proof" of "according to rabbinic tradition." That tradition suffices: "They always failed, of course, but they resisted; by the second century they stopped resisting." Let us review those clear statements of his:

> This baraita clearly implies that R. Yosi is referring to contemporary Sadducean women. If this is correct, R. Yosi's statement shows that some Sadducees still existed in the mid-second century but that their power had declined to the extent that the rabbis could assume that most Sadducees follow rabbinic norms. Contrast the Sadducees of the second temple period who, according to rabbinic tradition, tried to resist rabbinic hegemony (see below). They always failed, of course, but they resisted: by the second century they stopped resisting. This is the perspective of R. Yosi.

The "if this is correct" changes nothing. As soon as the "if" has been said, it is treated as a "then." "Then" it is correct, so Cohen here tells us the story of the Sadducees in the first and second centuries. In the first century they resisted "rabbinic norms," whatever they were, but in the second century, they gave up. This is Cohen's conclusion, based on his failure to ask how the Bavli and the Tosefta's compilers or the author of the story at hand knew the facts of the matter. The sole undisputed fact is that they represent the facts one way, rather than some other. But that does not suffice. Thus far we have seen a use of evidence entirely as gullible as that of Koester. Now, again, let us give Cohen his due. Any fair-minded reader may claim that what we have is a mere lapse. Cohen may have made a minor lapse that we should forgive. So let us see how he analyzes sources. At p. 42 he says:

> Rabbinic tradition is aware of opposition faced by Yohanan ben Zakkai at Yavneh but knows nothing of any expulsion of these opponents (Bab. Rosh Hashanah 2b). Yohanan ben Zakkai was even careful to avoid a confrontation with the priests (Mishnah 'Eduyyot 8:3).

Now what have we here? "Rabbinic tradition" indeed. What can that possibly mean? All rabbis at all times? A particular rabbi at a given time? Church historians these days rarely base their historical facts on "the tradition of the Church." Would that we could write a life of Jesus based on the tradition of the Church, how many problems we could solve. Cohen does not favor us with an exercise in differentiation among the sources. His is an undifferentiated harmony of the Jewish Gospels. Indeed, to the opposite, he looks into "rabbinic tradition," undifferentiated, unanalyzed, and gives us a fact: *Bab. Rosh Hashanah 2b*. What can that be? It is a story about someone. What does the story tell us? Is it true? Why should we think so? Cohen does not ask these questions. He alludes to a page in the Talmud, and that constitutes his fact, on which, it goes without saying, he proposes to build quite an edifice. So the Talmud is a kind of telephone book, giving us numbers through which we make our connections. In no way does he establish a critical method which tells us why he believes what he believes and disbelieves what he rejects.

But he does have a clear theory of matters. Where sources concur with Cohen's thesis, he accepts them, and where not, not. Cohen wants to prove that earlier there were disputes, later on disputes ended. Now some sources say that earlier there were no disputes, later on there were disputes. *So Cohen rejects the historicity of the sources that say there were no disputes earlier and accepts that of the ones that say there were no disputes later.* This sleight of hand I find on p. 48. Here he cites T. Hagigah 2:9, "At first there was no dispute in Israel." He proceeds to point to an "irenic trend," Mishnah Yevamot 1:4 and Eduyyot 4:8, which alleges that while the Houses disputed various matters, they still intermarried and respected each other's conformity to the purity rules. Then Cohen: "But this wishful thinking cannot disguise the truth. The two Talmudim find it almost impossible to understand this statement. The Houses could not marry or sup with each other. They were virtually sects – kitot the Palestinian Talmud calls them (Yer. Hagigah 2:2). At Yavneh sectarian exclusiveness was replaced by rabbinic pluralism, collective authority was replaced by individual authority."

What Cohen has done is to reject the statements in *earlier* sources – Mishnah, Tosefta – and adopt those in *later* ones (the Palestinian Talmud). He has done so simply by fiat. He cites what they say, and then he calls it wishful thinking. The truth, he discovers, is in the judgment of the Palestinian Talmud. I find this strange, for two reasons. First, it is odd to reject the testimony of the earlier source, closer to the situation under discussion, in favor of the later. Second, it is not entirely clear why and how Cohen knows that the Mishnah's and Tosefta's statements represent wishful thinking at all. Had he cited the talmudic discussions of the passage, readers would have found that the problem confronting the later exegetes is not quite what Cohen says it was. The Talmuds do not say that the parties were "virtually sects." That statement, it is true, occurs where Cohen says it does – but that is not on the passage of M. Yevamot 1:4 etc.

that Cohen is discussing. It is on another passage entirely. The talmudic discussion on the Mishnah-passage and its Tosefta-parallel is a legal one; the sages are troubled by the statement that people who disagree on laws of marriage and of purity can ignore those laws. The Talmudic discussion in no way sustains Cohen's statement. If now we reread the sequence of sentences, we find an interesting juxtaposition:

1. The two Talmudim find it almost impossible to understand this statement.

2. The Houses could not marry or sup with each other. They were virtually sects – kitot the Palestinian Talmud calls them.

3. At Yavneh sectarian exclusiveness was replaced by rabbinic pluralism, collective authority was replaced by individual authority.

Now sentence three does not follow from sentence two, unless sentence two has had something to do with "sectarian exclusiveness" replaced by "rabbinic pluralism." But the passage cited by Cohen does not say that, it has no bearing on that proposition. Cohen writes as though the evidence supports his thesis, when, in fact, the evidence has no bearing on that thesis. The sentences in fact do not follow from one another. No. 1 is factually inaccurate. No. 2 makes the valid point that the Yerushalmi calls the sects *kitot*. That is an undisputed fact. It however bears no consequences for the statements fore or aft. And no. 3 is parachuted down, Cohen's own judgment. So, to repeat, he believes what he wishes to believe, the *later* sources' allegations, disbelieves what he does not wish to believe, the *earlier* sources' statements, finds in a source not related to anything a statement he wishes to believe, cites that, then repeats – as though it had been proved – the fundamental thesis of his paper. I find this confusing.

It follows that Cohen's reading of the source begins with a generous view of the *a priori* accuracy of his own convictions about what the source is saying. Yohanan's "care" in avoiding a confrontation is Cohen's allegation, for the source does not quite say that. It says, in point of fact, not that he avoided confrontation, but that he did not think he could force the priests to do what they refused to do. Cohen simply cites the tractate and its chapter and paragraph number, and lo, another fact, another proof. I shall now show that Cohen can tell us "the truth," because *he* knows which source is giving us facts and which source is giving us fancies. That explains why what gets a question -mark "(at Yavneh?)" half a dozen lines later loses the question-mark and becomes a fact: "At Yavneh sectarian exclusiveness was replaced by rabbinic pluralism." On what basis? Let us hear. For this purpose we review the materials just now set forth. At pp. 48-49 he says:

Some of the rabbis were aware that their ideology of pluralism did not exist before 70. "At first there was no dispute (mahloqet) in Israel" (Tos. Hagigah 2:9 and Sanhedrin 7:1). How did disputes begin? According to one view in the Tosefta, disputes were avoided by the adjudication of the great court which sat in the temple precincts and determined either by vote or by tradition the status of all doubtful matters. In this view, when the great court was destroyed in 70, disputes could no longer be resolved in an orderly way and mahloqot proliferated. According to another view, "once the disciples of Hillel and Shammai became numerous who did not serve [their masters] adequately, they multiplied disputes in Israel and became as two Torahs." In this view Jewish (i.e., rabbinic) unanimity was upset by the malfeasance of the disciples of Hillel and Shammai, a confession which would later be exploited by the Karaites. What happened to the disputes between the Houses? They ceased at Yavneh, how we do not know. Amoraic tradition (Yer. Yevamot 1:6 [3b] and parallels) tells of a heavenly voice which declared at Yavneh, "Both these [House of Hillel] and these [House of Shammai] are the words of the living God, but the halakha always follows the House of Hillel." As part of this irenic trend someone (at Yavneh?) even asserted that the disputes between the Houses did not prevent them from intermarrying or from respecting each other's purities (Mishnah Yevamot 1:4 and 'Eduyyot 4:8; Tos. Yevamot 1:10-12) but this wishful thinking cannot disguise the truth. The two Talmudim find it almost impossible to understand this statement. The Houses could not marry or sup with each other. They were virtually sects – *kitot* the Palestinian Talmud calls them (Yer. Hagigah 2:2 [77d]). At Yavneh sectarian exclusiveness was replaced by rabbinic pluralism, collective authority was replaced by individual authority. The new ideal was the sage who was ready not to insist upon the rectitude of ("stand upon") his opinions. The creation of the Mishnah could now begin.

When Cohen says, "...were aware," he treats the thesis of his article as the fact of the matter. Who were these rabbis? And how do we know of what they were, or were not, aware? Did they live at Yavneh, in 70? Or did they live in the early third century, when the Mishnah had reached closure, or did they live a hundred years later, when the Tosefta was coming to conclusion? Cohen does not tell us. But he clearly thinks that their awareness is evidence of historical fact. Now these in the aggregate constitute historical statements, e.g., "the Houses were virtually sects." Why Cohen valorizes Y. Hag. 2:2 – a late source – and dismisses the evidence of the Mishnah and Tosefta is something that causes a measure of surprise. In fact he has set out to prove at the end of his paragraph the very point he takes for granted at the outset of his paragraph. Philosophers call that begging the question.

Cohen's review of the stories makes a feint toward criticism. He cites diverse views, balancing one view against another. But from Cohen we do not have a history of peoples' opinions, we have facts. "What happened to the disputes between the Houses? They ceased at Yavneh, how we do not know." Materials deriving from the period after the Bar Kokhba War are particularly rich in allusions to Houses' disputes that take up moot principles otherwise debated entirely in the age beyond Bar Kokhba's war. We clearly have mid-second century literary conventions. I do not mean to suggest that the names of the Houses served as more than literary conventions; I demonstrated that they served at least as literary conventions. Why? Were there "Houses of Shammai and Houses of Hillel" in the time of Yosé, in the mid-second century? Is that why so many sayings about the relationships among the Houses are assigned, in fact, to mid-second century authorities? But the assignments of those sayings occur in documents edited only in the third century, at which point (some stories have it) the patriarch, Judah, discovered that he descended from Hillel. So perhaps the disputes of the Houses served a polemical purpose of the patriarchate, since the ancestor of the patriarchate – everyone knew – kept winning the disputes. These are only possibilities. In answering the question as Cohen phrases it, all we have are possibilities, few of them subject to tests of falsification or validation.

Cohen knows facts, the unbelieving among the rest of us, only possibilities. But why in particular much more than half a century beyond the point at which Cohen knows the Houses went out of business: "They ceased at Yavneh, how we do not know." Well, just what ceased at Yavneh, if the names of the Houses persisted as literary conventions and points of polemic for a hundred years and more. It must follow that Cohen's claim of knowledge of an "irenic trend" rests on nothing more than two things, first, the source's claim of such a trend. second, Cohen's opinion as to the facts. This is proved by the stories cited from M. Yeb. 1:4 and M. Ed. 4:8 and so on.

Let us review in sequence Cohen's statements:

1. But this wishful thinking cannot disguise the truth

2. At Yavneh sectarian exclusiveness was replaced by rabbinic pluralism, collective authority was replaced by individual authority

3. The new ideal was the sage who was ready not to insist upon the rectitude of his opinions.

4. The creation of the Mishnah could now begin.

All of these statements may well be true. But in the paragraph I have cited, in which these statements occur, not a single source, not a single piece of evidence, proves any such thing. I cite No. 1 to prove that Cohen claims to make a historical statement. No. 2 then tells us he sees a movement from sect to church (though he does not appear to have read Max Weber, who saw much the same movement). Cohen has not proved that the "new ideal" of the sage antedates the Mishnah, in which it is said that that is the

ideal. But he has ignored the fact that the Mishnah imputes that irenic
position to none other than the House of Hillel – who lived long before
"Yavneh." And what all this has to do with "the creation of the Mishnah"
only Cohen knows. So, in a climax of total confusion, if a passage in the
Mishnah refers to the time of the Houses, but Cohen thinks that the fact
does *not* apply to the time of the Houses, he ignores the allegation of the
Mishnah's passage. If a passage in the Yerushalmi, two hundred years
later, refers to the earlier period and says what Cohen thinks was the fact,
then that later passage is true while the earlier one is not. What does he do
in the case at hand? He assigns that allegation neither to the context of the
age of the Mishnah itself, as, to begin with, I would find plausible, nor to
the age of which the passage itself speaks, namely, the time of the Houses
(before 70, so Cohen), as other believers, consistent in their gullibility,
would insist. In Cohen's mind, the passage testifies to an age of which it
does not speak, and also in which the document that contains the passage
was not redacted. This is pure confusion, and I can find, in the rest of
Cohen's article, still more utter chaos. But Cohen is consistent: if he does
not think something happened, then he also will not believe sources that
say it happened, even though they are early sources. We already have
noticed that if a passage in a later rabbinic document refers to an earlier
time and Cohen does think the fact applies to that early time, then he of
course produces the source to prove the point that, to begin with, he
wishes to make. So he prefers the later source that conforms to his thesis
over the earlier one that does not. Let us not forget where we started.
Does Cohen believe that if the source says someone said something, then
he really said it? Well, yes, on the one side Cohen does believe it, when
the source says something Cohen thinks the source should have said the
man said, as in the case of Yosé. But no, on the other side Cohen does
not believe it, when the source says something Cohen thinks the source
should not have said the man (or group) said, as in the case of the Houses
when they are represented in an irenic mode. So Cohen's scholarship
emerges as rather credulous except when he is confused. And let us at the
end not miss the simple point that his thesis to begin with rests on the
conviction that the sources as we have them present us with the facts we
require to test – and prove – a thesis of that order and not some other.
That framing of the question attests to a profound gullibility indeed.

III. Example of Gullibility as Omniscience:
Steven T. Katz on Yavneh

Steven T. Katz, "Issues in the Separation of Judaism and Christianity
after 70 C.E.: A Reconsideration," *Journal of Biblical Literature* 103,
1984, pp. 43-76 provides a fine example of historical naiveté – knowing

even more than the sources claim to tell us. On pp. 46-7 of his article, Katz states:

> In addition, the leading Palestinian Tannaim were frequent travelers. The Talmud records a journey of R. Gamaliel, R. Eliezer ben Azariah, R. Akiba, and R. Joshua to Rome, as well as the travels of many other sages throughout Palestine and its environs and also to Babylonia and points west.

Katz's footnote is not to a source at all, but to W. D. Davies, *Setting of the Sermon on the Mount*, pp. 295-6. So we do not know how Katz proposes to read the stories about the "leading Tannaim" as "frequent travelers." We do not know what sources Katz has in mind. The "frequent travels" may in fact be the same story told a number of times. But, it is clear, Katz does believe these trips took place . Without further discussion of why he thinks so, he presents us with just another example of gullibility. He does not know the rather sizable literature on the stories, going back three quarters of a century. Katz, not knowing or even resorting to the sources, can tell us what the rabbis had to say on their "historical" journeys:

> No doubt during such travels the criticism of Jewish Christianity voiced at Yavneh was discussed and propagated among the Jewish communities of the Diaspora.

But why no doubt? How does Katz know? He does not let us in on his secret.

> Further, there is no reason to doubt that much unofficial decrying of Jesus and Christianity occurred orally.

How does Katz know this? What evidence does he have of the folk oral tradition? How does he know that *Toledot Yeshu* goes back (the gist? the wording too?) to the period at hand? He tells us, then, that "there is no reason to doubt," which is true. But there also is no reason to think so either, except for Katz's allegation. Very soon the "no doubt" and "no reason to doubt" turns into a fact. Here is how an "it would not be surprising," one sentence later turns into a fact:

> It would also not be surprising if the folk, oral tradition, which was later embellished and codified as the Toledot Yeshu, also had its start in these circumstances. If Jews were to accept the Christian account of the virgin birth or the resurrection they would be on their way to becoming Christians. From the Jewish perspective such claims were "unbelievable" and thus open to caricature and lampooning. However, it needs to be emphasized that vulgar and popular criticism, while not surprising, should not be confused with any "official" letter of condemnation from Yavneh or elsewhere. For the latter there is no evidence in rabbinic sources.

So we wonder why go to all this trouble to make up history, conversations, motives, distinctions between gossip and doctrine, and the rest. What is at stake for Katz? In fact he undertakes an exercise in Judaic theological apologetics. He wants to oppose the views that the Jews told really nasty stories about Jesus. Here is what he says:

> The excesses of Harnack, repeated most recently by Frend, concerning the nature of "official Jewish communications, compared with casual, if negative," gossip, need to be noted if only to be rejected as unfounded.

Katz appears to be saying: Harnack and Frend hold that there were official Jewish *communications*. But Katz holds there was only casual, if negative, *gossip*. I am not sure why Katz thinks this makes things nice. If this is his sense, then Katz has turned his gullibility into an argument of history bearing significant theological implications. That is, he believes the story that rabbis made trips. He wants to turn these trips into something other than propaganda missions, organized to oppose Christianity. How does he do it? It is enchanting: with a few well placed "no doubts" and "there is no reason to doubt" and "it would also not be surprising," Katz has invented not only the subject matter of the rabbis' discourse with the Jews in distant places but the exact content. He knows what they told the other Jews, and he even tells us that the Jews found these beliefs "unbelievable," thus open to caricature and lampooning. He does not have a footnote to point to first century evidence of this kind of caricature and lampooning. But he knows that it was vulgar and popular criticism. Then he has told us that it would not be surprising if the sages at hand told nasty stories when they made their trip. But this is not really "official" and it is only casual. But that makes it nice, or, at least, nicer. All of this fantasy on the basis of what? Exactly nothing. *Not a single primary source is cited, let alone analyzed.* The entire vision derives from Katz's arguments from, and with, secondary scholarship. The argument at hand is based on what is mostly Katz's own made-up doctrine of what the rabbis said on their frequent travels..

IV. The Pseudocritical Method,
or Why Yosé by Any Other Name Still Lived
in the Second Century:
Rosalie Gershenzon and Elieser Slomovic

Let us now turn to the one new methodological development in the past quarter-century, which I call pseudocriticsm: the evasion of the critical problem, along with a claim to have solved it. In their article, "A Second Century Jewish-Gnostic Debate: Rabbi Jose ben Halafta and the Matrona," *Journal for the Study of Judaism* 16, 1984, pp. 1-41, Rosalie Gershenzon and Elieser Slomovic introduce the rhetoric of a critical approach to learning, but not the substance of that approach. In fact they evade the question while pretending to answer it. It is the wave of the future. Let me explain. Gershenzon and Slomovic carry forward and illustrate the now-familiar gullibility, but their current article advances the discussion. They show most vividly how the younger generation tries to exhibit the stigmata of the critical approach, while, in point of fact, trying to talk their way around it. That is what I would call "pseudocriticism," as I shall explain. But first, let us consider the evidence that they are, in fact, gullible. For otherwise, the charge of pseudocriticism bears no relevance. If they do not pretend to be critical, why accuse them of the pretense? But if they are gullible and then pose as something else, it is another matter. So what makes me classify them with the others? There are two reasons.

First, one mark of gullibility is to translate theological conviction into literary and historical fact. A principal conviction of Judaism is that God revealed one whole Torah, in diverse media, to Moses at Sinai. Consequently, all components of that one whole Torah contribute equally, and with slight differentiation, along with all others. For the fundamentalist historian, the upshot is simple. We ignore the point of origin of all stories and sayings. Anything in the canon bears equal weight with anything else, and that without the slightest regard for the particular document in which a saying or story makes its appearance. The received theology states, "There is no consideration of priority or anachronism in the Torah," and so, for the fundamentalists, the same applies. The two authors cite a broad range of stories about a second century rabbi, in no way, at no point differentiating among those stories by the criterion of their point of documentary origin. For example, they do not tell us that story A appears in a document closed in the second century, story B, in one in the third, story C, in one in the fourth, and so on. Everything is the same as everything else.

Second, the more familiar side of gullibility – credulity about attributions – requires only brief restatement. In fairness, I hasten to say they explicitly deny that that is their view. But the two authors insist that all the stories at hand not only speak *about* the second century rabbi but also testify to ideas *held at the time he lived.* The basis for that insistence marks them as fundamentalists. They invoke the contents of the stories to justify the second-century dating of the stories, just like Schiffman. They argue that at the time Yosé lived Gnosticism flourished, so (even though they do not allege he *really* said them) Yosé's statements require interpretation in the context of debates between Gnostics and rabbis. But if Yosé did not make the sayings attributed to him, then why the second century in particular? We should not have turned to the second century to the exclusion of the third or fourth if the name of Yosé did not appear in those sayings – and if in our mind the appearance of that name did not carry *prima facie* weight that he really made those statements.

The authors go on: in fact, – so their circular argument goes – [1] when we read these stories knowing that Yosé was arguing with Gnosticism, [2] sure enough, he is arguing with Gnosticism. The fact about Gnosticism is established. But, as I shall ask, is that the only possibility? Where are the others? The two authors do not rigorously examine other possibilities, so they rest their case on the argument from content: it sounds right, so it is right, and the old "ring of truth" sounds loud and clear. We come back to the original observation, that the two authors ignore the time of the appearance of the documents that contain the stories they cite, paying attention only to the contents of the stories but not to their provenance. On that basis, as I said, they immediately leap into the second century – when Yosé lived. So two distinct strands of gullibility intertwine, first, the argument from contents, second, the argument that it does not matter where the saying in his name now is preserved.

Now I wonder, why to begin with should we invoke only second-century Gnosticism in the interpretation of the stories, and ignore whatever other issues or dispute flourished at the time of the composition of the documents that contain the stories? In fact, I have noticed that Genesis Rabbah, universally assigned to the fourth century, contains a systematic refutation of positions we know were held by Gnostics, particularly concerning Creation, the Creator-God, the knowability of the unknown or Most High God, the goodness or evil of Creation, and on and on. Most of these stories, moreover, occur in the name of later third and fourth century authorities. So here we have a quite different setting for a dispute between sages and Gnostics – after the triumph of Christianity. Now the document at hand may be shown to address issues burning in the Jewish community in particular. It is quite plausible to wonder whether within Jewry people held the positions so vigorously refuted by the exegetes. We are not required therefore to read the stories in relationship to debates between Jews and outsiders. So the second century need not present us with our own hermeneutical option, nor do debates between Jews and gentiles tell us the only setting to which such stories refer. I do not suggest I have proved anything. I mean only to make a simple point.

First, we see an egregious error. The authors ignore the age *in* which the document that contains a story was closed, but immediately introduce the traits of the age *to* which the story refers. Second, the authors announce a thesis but do not test their thesis against contrary possibilities. They are enormously pleased with their thesis, and that is that. And why not? For the contents of the stories conform to the requirements of their thesis. So here is a fresh and complex version of gullibility, in four aspects: first, second-level gullibility about attributions ("he did not really say it but someone in his day did"), second, indifference to the differentiation among documents and insistence that everything is pretty much the same as everything else, third, appeal to the contents of a story in validation of its historicity (which is the first again), and fourth, failure to validate a theory by constructing a test of falsification.

None of this presents us with anything genuinely new. But Gershenzon and Slomovic pretend to deal with problems, while in fact ignoring them. That is what makes the article by Gershenzon and Slomovic uncommonly interesting. And that is the center of my indictment of that article: pseudocriticism. The pseudocritical method is to acknowledge the problem and to pretend it has been faced, when in fact no clear solution has been proposed at all. So, as I said, the question is raised and then evaded. Now to the evidence, on pp. 1-3 of their article:

> Of the many encounters between Jews and non-Jews recorded in rabbinic literature, surely the most elusive and provocative are the epigrammatic discussions between sages and upper class Roman women during the Imperial Period. In eighteen passages found in various midrashim, R. Jose Ben Halafta, head of the academy in Sepphoris in the second half of the second century C.E., confronts an anonymous "matrona." In the following study, we have identified all of the pertinent passages, and propose to examine the entire corpus afresh, with due attention to its historical and religious background....

So far, so good. The authors take an interest in narrow historical questions. After reviewing earlier approaches and explaining why, in drawing together all of the pertinent passages and treating the whole and not only bits and pieces, they will advance the question, they go on to the critical issue (pp. 2-3):

> Two anticipatory questions arise: can the midrashim in question, embedded in contextual layers which cannot themselves be reliably dated, be ascribed with any certainty to R. Jose? Can the entire polemic be regarded as a historical encounter between two actual antagonists, rather than as a conventional literary vehicle in which the ostensible literary opponent is merely a fiction mouthing widely known arguments?

I give the answer whole and complete, and then come back and analyze its parts:

> After all, many of the questions raised by the matrona were regarded as legitimate exegetical problems within the rabbinic schools. Our proposal that these midrashim be treated as a unit does not depend on a demonstration – obviously impossible – that they reflect actual encounters between specific individuals. Whatever the historical and literary impetus for enclosing their contents in this unusual polemical frame work, we believe that they record the major arguments in the second century Gnostic-Jewish debate, as preserved by Jewish

spokesmen. Later redactors may no longer have recognized Rabbi Jose's opponent as a Gnostic, but they recognized and preserved the language of religious polemic and the second century Galilean provenance.

There are several a priori reasons for treating this group of midrashim as a unit. First, although a wide variety of encounters between sages and matronas is reported in the literature, both in Palestine and in Rome itself, the passages involving R. Jose are unique. They are the only ones which present a straight forward religious polemic in query-answer format. The polemical approach is almost invariably exegetical, a pattern which appears to be characteristic of early refutations of heretical doctrine. All the other passages are anecdotal or episodic, and some have cautionary or legendary overtones. Second, the passages under consideration share distinctive features of style and tone, most notably the homely, almost banal illustrations utilized by R. Jose, and the surprisingly friendly mood of the argument. These features will become apparent upon closer acquaintance. Finally, a brief examination of religious, social and political conditions in second century Galilee suggests that at that time and place an encounter between a leading Jewish sage and an educated Roman aristocrat with Gnostic leanings was, if not routine, quite plausible. Indeed, almost no other time and place could have been more suitable. Let us briefly examine some of these contributing factors.

Now let us review these paragraphs. First the question:

1. Can the entire polemic be regarded as a historical encounter between two actual antagonists, rather than as a conventional literary vehicle in which the ostensible literary opponent is merely a fiction mouthing widely known arguments?

2. After all, many of the questions raised by the matrona were regarded as legitimate exegetical problems within the rabbinic schools.

Second the answer:

3. Our proposal that these midrashim be treated as a unit does not depend on a demonstration – obviously impossible – that they reflect actual encounters between specific individuals.

Clearly, the authors see a connection between the question and the answer:

1. *Can the entire polemic be regarded....*

2. *After all, many of the questions...*

Then comes:

3. *Our proposal....*

But what, exactly, is the connection between sentences 1 and 2 and sentence 3? I see none at all. The authors win our trust by asking the critical question, how do we know the stories really took place in the second century, involving Yosé in particular? But then they make a statement that has no bearing whatsoever on the question. Let me unpack this matter with some care. First they say that they do not attribute the stories to Yosé in particular. Then they talk, rather, about grouping the stories. What connection between the one (1, 2) and the other (3), the question and the answer? The question has not been answered by the answer, because the answer has nothing to do with the question. The answer evades the question, denying its relevance. But there is the implicit premise, denied by the evasion at hand. I can expose the implicit premise simply by a question of my own: why leap into the second century? It is because, as they explicitly say, "We believe that they record the major arguments in the second century Gnostic-Jewish debate." But why the second century in particular, *if not because Yosé is their protagonist?* For if not Yosé, then I should think that the third or the fourth centuries offer themselves as candidates. And, again, if not the second century, then why Gnostic-Jewish debate in particular? Why not a debate within the Jewish community? We could as well interpret the stories as evidence of opinions held within the Jewish community as outside of its borders. My point should not be lost in a cloud of rhetorical questions. It is very simple. I maintain that Gershenzon and Slomovic fail to answer the question that they ask. To review:

First of all, they deny that the historical question matters. Then, in the very next sentence, they assume the historical question has been settled.

They tell us it does not matter that Yosé in particular made these statements. But they tell us that the stories record the major arguments *in the second century Gnostic-Jewish debate as preserved by Jewish spokesmen.* The upshot may be stated very simply, but requires emphasis:

If it is not the historical Yosé in particular, then it is another Jewish spokesman whose name just happened to be Yosé.

We have once more crossed the border into the land of make-believe. But, failing to read carefully and ask how one sentence logically produces the next, and how a concluding sentence flows logically from the preceding sentences, we are supposed to concede the authors have taken up the critical agenda. They have not even touched it. Let us now reread the concluding paragraph, and see: (1) arguments from content, and (2) the prevailing, but denied, premise that, after all, Yosé really said these things, because (3) other things Yosé said (not: imputed to Yosé) "share distinctive features of style and tone" with these sayings, and, anyhow, (4) in second century Galilee, Gnostics and sages kept meeting, so "almost no other time and place could have been more suitable." So we once more examine *ipsissima verba*:

> There are several a priori reasons for treating this group of midrashim as a unit. First, although a wide variety of encounters between sages and matronas is reported in the literature, both in Palestine and in Rome itself, the passages involving R. Jose are unique. They are the only ones which present a straight forward religious polemic in query-answer format. The polemical approach is almost invariably exegetical, a pattern which appears to be characteristic of early refutations of heretical doctrine. All the other passages are anecdotal or episodic, and some have cautionary or legendary overtones. Second, the passages under consideration share distinctive features of style and tone, most notably the homely, almost banal illustrations utilized by R. Jose, and the surprisingly friendly mood of the argument. These features will become apparent upon closer acquaintance. Finally, a brief examination of religious, social and political conditions in second century Galilee suggests that at that time and place an encounter between a leading Jewish sage and an educated Roman aristocrat with Gnostic leanings was, if not routine, quite plausible. Indeed, almost no other time and place could have been more suitable. Let us briefly examine some of these contributing factors.

The charge of closet-gullibility rests on this basis:

1.   The fact that a number of similar *stories* occur in a number of documents is turned into "a wide variety of *encounters* between sages and matronas is reported in the literature." That is not the fact. The fact is that the similar stories occur a number of times. If we turn that fact into "a wide variety of *encounters*," we are making things up, just as the sages of the Talmud turned two versions of a saying into two stages in Yohanan ben Zakkai's career. The stories may speak of a number of different events. Or they may speak of only one event, told in a number of different ways. Or they may speak of nothing that really happened, but only of something that someone imagines happened.

2.   The argument from style is this: the stories share distinctive features of style. But what else does that fact prove? I am baffled. If now the authors do not wish to suggest Yosé really said these things, then what historical fact do they hope to demonstrate by showing that fixed and shared literary conventions characterize the genre of story at hand? I imagine they can show a literary fact – like Cohen, recognizing a convention of genre, but I do not know what *historical* event they therefore allege they have uncovered.

3. The argument from content: this is how we imagine things should have taken place anyhow, so "quite plausible," generates: "no other time and place could have been more suitable." But how do we know unless we compare one proposed context with some other? In fact this is no more than part of the large-scale evasion. I look in vain for any sustained investigation of other times and places. If Gershenzon and Slomovic imagine such possibilities, they do not take them up and show they do not serve, or do not serve so plausibly, as the one at hand.

So to the indictment: the critical agendum makes its appearance, but the authors in the end prove incapable of responding to it at all. They rehearse the argument from content, they appeal to style, they tell us what is plausible – the usual gullibility. The mark of pseudocritical method I find in the obscurities of a sequence of sentences which, as I read them, have no logical connection from one to the next: gibberish. To conclude: Gershenzon and Slomovic in their article hardly show the connection between the question:

Can the entire polemic be regarded as a historical encounter

and the answer,

Our proposal...does not depend on a demonstration–obviously impossible–that they reflect actual encounters.

There once again is considerably less here than meets the eye. They choose to evade the question, rather than to answer it. The evasion consists in three facts. They evade the historical question (1) by reintroducing what they have just denied:

we believe that they record the major arguments in the second century Gnostic Jewish debate, as preserved by Jewish spokesmen.

So, as I said, it was not the historical Yosé, but someone else named Yosé (or: many other spokesmen, who as a matter of literary convention all are called Yosé?). They evade the historical question (2) by confusing the issue through introducing irrelevant facts of literary convention, treating those facts as if they had a bearing on the historical question, when, in fact, they do not. They evade the historical question (3) by introducing arguments from content: it *sounds* right.

V. The Future of Gullibility *Redivivus*

Those whom I have cited (and numerous others, not cited) had reason to know better. I have raised the issues in work after work for fifteen years. the methodological issues have been presented in sustained and widely circulated books and articles. Not only so, but a fresh range of questions, deriving from a different perception of the evidence and what it tells us, has been explored in the past fifteen years. The historical gullibility of Wissenschaft des Judenthums, its positivism and naive notion that we know exactly what happened have found an honorable place in a museum for ancient notions. But the younger fundamentalists have paid no attention (from their elders, we could expect nothing). They need not have concurred with my answers, but they did face the responsibility of explaining in a reasoned and public way, in light of my critical program concerning the character and historical usefulness of the texts they cite, why they take for granted that if a source assigns a saying to a given rabbi, he really said that saying. The scholars I have cited have evaded that responsibility. All therefore fall into the category of gullibility, if not fundamentalism: they believe whatever they hear, or (as we have seen) whatever they choose to believe within what they hear. The former treat everything as self-evidently true, and the latter make things up as they go along and call the result scholarship.[2]

Gullibility will continue flourish as a political force in the ghetto-sector of the Jewish scholarly world. It has no future at all outside of the institutions of that world, since, without the walls of ghettos to protect it, the scholarly equivalent of belief that the world is flat and that the sun goes around the earth cannot sustain itself. Gullibility invokes its own self-evidence. Where people find self-evident the convictions and propositions of scholarly gullibility, they will write articles and even books like those we have examined. Where people find self-evident the methods and principles of critical learning in the Western humanities, they will write articles and books like mine – or, I hope, better ones: more abstract, more encompassing, more venturesome and imaginative. That is the future: two worlds, each in its orbit, never to meet, except to collide.

It remains to ask, what price gullibility? The cost to the study of the texts at hand – which the believers claim to prize – is incalculable. For the believers insist on asking questions the holy books do not answer, and they also do not wish to listen to the answers the holy books give to questions the holy books do take up. So the Orthodox, the religious fundamentalists, the credulous, the Israeli talmudic historians, and the

---

[2] But the truth is that the gullibles produce few, if any books in the field they call "Talmudic history," or "the period of the Mishnah and the Talmud. Out of Jerusalem, world capital of credulity in this field, we have not had a major work on a historical problem since Urbach's *Hazal* (1969). Cohen, Katz, and the others cited here have not written books (beyond the dissertation, in Cohen's case) in this area. When a paradigm dies, a sure sign is that those who propose to sustain it run out of ideas, things they want to know, research they find urgent. So: no books. Our side is not troubled by that problem.

other believers whatever their belief reject what the sources at hand wish to teach and impose a program of inquiries for which the sources scarcely serve. We cannot ask religious texts that by no reasonable standard can tell us what really happened on a given day long before the texts' own redaction to report to us about "that day." Nor can we demand that that authorship record what Yosé really thought, or about how "the rabbis" said this or did that or changed their policy in such and such a way. Texts written down centuries beyond the point purportedly under discussion cannot have much information on those matters. We can and should ask the texts to give us their messages and to convey their meanings. But the believers do not want to listen to those messages, and that is a loss – to the holy books. For the true believers do not want to pay attention to the convictions important to the authorship of the holy books. The victim of the sin of gullibility is the canon that the believers claim to hold dear. They want what the sources do not give, and they do not want what the sources provide in abundance. And that is the principal cost.

Chapter Six

Wrong Ways in Historical Study [2]: "The Sermon on the Mount and the Sermon on the Plain" in Ancient Judaism

The Conception of "The Original Tradition," Dating Stories through their Contents, and Making Up Traditions-History in Contemporary Studies of Formative Judaism

One of the now-abandoned curiosities of New Testament exegesis posited that, because of the duplicate versions of the Sermon on the Mount, Jesus really preached two sermons, one on the mount, the other on the plain. A further now-uncommon premise is that behind a variety of versions of a saying is a single, original and authentic version. In what follows we shall see the persistence of the search for "the original tradition," as well as acutely contemporary examples of precisely the same mode of thought that, for so long, invented the duplication of "the sermon of the mount" on the plain. That is why, in calling attention to the present state of method in the study of ancient Judaism, I invoke as the model for future work the well-established achievements of the critical study of the Gospels.

I. The Quest for the Original Tradition

One mode of explaining the presence of diverse versions of a single event is to claim that behind several versions of a saying or story lies (1) an "original", (2) "tradition," handed on in linear fashion. I place quotation marks around both words, not because I wish to impute to the words meanings other than those commonly assigned to them. Rather, the reason is that, in context here, I do not know what they mean. By "original" one may mean the original version of a tradition later on elaborated. But one may also mean the original saying, as the person to whom it is attributed really said it. These represent quite different claims.

By "tradition" people commonly mean a story that has been made up and handed on in linear succession over a period of time. Hence if we refer to a "tradition" in the Mishnah or in the Bavli, we are properly understood to claim that a saying or story, made up earlier, has reached the Mishnah or the Bavli through a continuous, linear process of handing on, or tradition. But I am not at all sure that that has ever been demonstrated.

Until we know more than we now do about the origins of materials now found in written form in the documents at hand, we cannot claim that they are traditions, in the ordinary sense of the word. We can only allege that they are stories or sayings now found in the documents at hand. These stories or sayings may in fact prove to be traditions. How so? They may be shown to have undergone a long process of handing on, from one generation to the next, prior to being written down in the document at hand. But we cannot impute the status of "tradition" to what is in fact only a story or a saying. We have to prove that the pre-history of the story or saying permits us to classify it in that other category, namely, a story of a saying that has been handed on for a long time prior to reaching written form in the document at hand.

Providing an example of how the "tradition"-theory of the multiplicity of versions demands attention to the thesis that an "original" "tradition" was handed on. For without the claim that a given version stands close(st) to an "original" "tradition," the point that a version falls into the classification of tradition is difficult to discern. That is to say, I do not see that we have gained very much if we claim that people have handed a story or saying on over a period of time, if we do not also claim that one version of that "tradition" leads us closer to the "original" than some other. If alongside the theory of "tradition" we do not find a theory of "originality," perhaps even a claim of historicity made in behalf of the "original" "tradition," then the theory of tradition yields trivial observations. More important, the theory by itself never becomes susceptible to verification or falsification. We never know when we are wrong, therefore we cannot know that we are right. Making up a long "pre-history" of "tradition" back to an "original" version of the tradition therefore leads us deep into the imagination of the scholar who makes up the theory. As with Halperin, it is a study of the contemporary imagination, that alone.

Accordingly, the allegation of "tradition" ordinarily bears in its wake the claim of "original." The claim of the language at hand is this: something happened that has been put into permanent verbal formulas through oral formulation and then oral transmission and handed on for some time. Then, if we have a number of versions of a given saying or story, these several versions permit us to speculate, as we move backward from the latest tradition to an earlier one and finally to the first, the "original(s)," about the character and wording even of the "original(s)" of the "tradition." In this framework we may speak of the original tradition (now no longer needing quotation-marks).

In order to deal with the present theory on how to interpret thrice-told tales, I wish to lay out the three versions of sayings assigned to lists of recurrent names, or, as these versions are conventionally called, the "chains of Pharisaic tradition." That is to say, in what follows we look for what is original to closely related, yet distinct, versions of a given list. We shall find that, when we have recovered what appears to be the original version of the tradition, hence, the original tradition, we have not gained very much. We know, in point of fact, little more than that there was, at some point, a list that people used for lining up sets of quite diverse sayings about topics in no way related to one another. That is the upshot of the theory at hand when brought to bear on the sources best suited to receive that theory. We have three "chains of Pharisaic tradition," listing authorities of the party and assigning to them either moral apophthegms, purity decrees, or rulings on a minor aspect of the conduct of the sacrificial cult. These chains follow in probable order.

1. To Lay on Hands

A. Yosé b. Yoezer says [on a Festival-day] not to lay [hands on the offering before it is slaughtered]. Yosé b. Yohanan says to lay [hands].

B. Joshua b. Perahiah says not to lay [hands]. Nittai the Arbelite says to lay [hands].

C. Judah b. Tabbai says not to lay [hands]. Simeon b. Shetah says to lay [hands].

D. Shemaiah says to lay [hands]. Abtalion says not to lay [hands].

E. Hillel and Menahem did not differ, but Menahem went forth, and Shammai entered in.

F. Shammai says not to lay [hands]. Hillel says to lay [hands].

G. The former were *nasis*, and the later fathers of the court [M. Hagigah 2:2].

The opinions are in indirect discourse, "says to lay," "says not to lay." Normally "says" is followed by direct discourse. Someone has supplied the subscription (G) that the first-named were *nasis*, the second-named, heads of the court, considerations which do not figure in the body of the pericope and are irrelevant to its contents. But the pattern is not exact; the first-named always should say, not to lay on hands. Yet while Yosé b. Yoezer, Joshua b. Perahiah, and Judah b. Tabbai, say not to do so, Shemaiah has the wrong opinion for his position in the list. The little group at the end, Hillel-Menahem, then Shammai-Hillel, is also difficult. Hillel-Menahem break the pattern; the lemma is a later insertion. In fact, Hillel should say not to lay on hands, since he was supposed to have been *nasi.* We have already seen a story on this very point, in which Hillel is represented as following Shammai's practice.

Clearly, in the pericope before us Hillel is presumed to be *nasi,* despite the wrong opinion. But if we drop the interpolation of Hillel-Menahem, we find what the form calls for, merely: Shammai/Hillel: not to lay/lay, and that is surely the authentic reading according to the foregoing pattern. Therefore the original list had Shammai as *nasi,* Hillel as head of the court. The switch with Menahem (otherwise unknown) permits placing Hillel first, therefore makes him *nasi,* according to the subscription, so it becomes Hillel-Menahem-Shammai-Hillel. I cannot guess why Shemaiah's opinion has been reversed.

In Tos. Hag., R. Meir provides a far better solution to the problem of making Hillel *nasi* in traditions which originally have him as father of the court. Tos. Hag. 2:8 (ed. Lieberman, p. 382-3, lines 40-44) is as follows:

> They differed only on the laying of hands.
> "They are five pairs. The three of the first pairs who said not to lay on hands, and the two of the last pairs who said to lay on hands were *nasis.* The second ones [mentioned] were heads of the court," so R. Meir.
> R. Judah said, "Simeon b. Shetah [was] *nasi.* Judah b. Tabbai [was] head of the court."

Meir thus has five pairs:

1. *Nasi* (not to lay) + head of court (to lay)
2. *Nasi* (not to lay) + head of court (to lay)
3. *Nasi* (not to lay) + head of court (to lay)
4. *Nasi* (to lay)   + head of court (not to lay)
5. *Nasi* (to lay)   + head of court (not to lay)

Meir's list is the same as M. Hag. 2:2 as far as Shemaiah and Abtalion. He presumably had no mention of Hillel-Menahem, for that would have made Hillel-Shammai a sixth pair. But for the last pair he had a "to lay"-*Nasi* in first place. Was it Shammai or Hillel? Probably Hillel, since the 'not to lay"/"to lay" antithesis is primary to the tradition, and there seems no strong reason for changing the attributions.

So we have two forms of the list, one which can be reconstructed from M. Hag. 2:2, the other from Meir's report. They agree for the first four pairs; for the first, the form behind M. Hag. 2:2 had Shammai not, Hillel to; while Meir had Hillel to, Shammai not. Meir's tradition can be explained as a secondary development from the other, motivated by the desire of the Hillelites to represent Hillel as head of the government, *nasi.* What was done to the M. Hag. tradition by inserting the Hillel-Menahem pair before Shammai and Hillel was done in Meir's tradition by simply reversing the customary order and putting Hillel before Shammai. This is neat and may be correct, but it leaves us with a second, unanswered problem: who was Menahem and how did he get in? The possibility that the last of Meir's pairs may have been, Hillel said to lay, Menahem said not to lay, and there may have been no reference at all to Shammai – which would be understandable if we had an old list from the House of Hillel – cannot be wholly excluded. In that event Meir's list would be older and M. Hag. would represent a post-70 revision, when the Shammaites and the Hillelites, for survival's sake, combined their forces, the terms of the compromise (here) being that Shammai's name would have precedence, but the law would in general follow Hillel. Judah [b. Ilai] differs only with reference to Judah b. Tabbai and Simeon b. Shetah. The latter, he says, was *nasi*.

The list of M. Hag., excluding Menahem and the subscription, could not have been shaped later than the time of Meir and Judah, since both refer to it. Judah the Patriarch follows Meir, therefore has a *nasi* Yosé b. Yoezer, Joshua, Judah, Shemaiah, and Hillel. Since he thought he descended from Hillel and referred to the Bene Bathyrans' giving up their position to Hillel and making him *nasi*, it was natural to explain matters as he did in the subscription. But the subscription in M. Hag. 2:2 cannot come before Meir-Judah, who do not cite it verbatim. It looks like Judah the Patriarch's summary of Meir's comment.

2. Decrees

1. The Yerushalmi's version:

> Did not R. Zeira b. Abuna in the name of R. Jeremiah say, "Yoséf b. Yoezer of Seredah and Yosé b. Yohanan of Jerusalem decreed uncleanness upon the land of the peoples and upon glass utensils."
>
> R. Yonah [Var.: Yuda] said, "Rabbi Judah b. Tabbai."
>
> R. Yosé said, "Rabbi Judah b. Tabbai and Simeon b. Shetah decreed uncleanness on metal utensils.
>
> "Hillel and Shammai decreed concerning the cleanness of the hands" (Y. Shab. 1:4 = Y. Pes. 1:6, Y. Ket. 8:11).

2. The Bavli's version:

DTNY':

1. Yosé b. Yoezer of Seredah and Yosé b. Yohanan of Jerusalem decreed (GZR) [the capacity to receive] uncleanness upon the land of the people and on glassware.

2. Simeon b. Shetah obtained (TQN) a marriage-contract for the wife and decreed (GZR) [the capacity to receive] uncleanness upon metal utensils.

3. Shammai and Hillel decreed (GZR) uncleanness on hands (B. Shab. 14b).

The Babylonian version is a list of decrees. I assume Simeon b. Shetah's saying has been contaminated by the reference to the ordinance (TQN) about the marriage-contract, missing in Y., which is out of place here, for all are decrees and concern uncleanness. Judah b. Tabbai is absent – thus following Judah b. Ilai – and the Palestinian version supplies his name, making the list Yosé + Yosé, Judah + Simeon, and Hillel + Shammai, in all three instances with the *nasi* first, hence following Meir in Tos. Hag., and (of course) placing Hillel in the nasi's position. The absence of Joshua b. Perahiah-Nittai the Arbelite is curious. The addition of the places of origin of the Yosé's suggests that this might come after M. Hag., so I should also have expected the inclusion of the absent masters. Perhaps no one had traditions on uncleanness-decrees to attribute to the men. That guess depends upon the presumption that without considerable motivation people did not make up what they did not have. But often they did, as we have observed time and again.

The representation of Shammai as *nasi,* Hillel second to him, is congruent to the stories of the (temporary) predominance of the House of Shammai and of the (later) rise of the House of Hillel to power. It also explains why the Houses-form nearly always puts the Shammaite House ahead of the Hillelite one, in conformity with the order of M. Hag. The later masters, coming long after the Hillelite hegemony had been well established by the patriarchate, appropriately doctored the earlier materials in the ways that have become evident. This explanation however takes for granted two allegations of the later Tannaim, first, that Yohanan b. Zakkai took over from Shammai and Hillel and was Hillel's heir; second, that the Yavnean patriarch Gamaliel was descended from Hillel. But the allegation that Yohanan b. Zakkai was Hillel's continuator first occurs in M. Avot, which, as we shall see, comes later than the M. Hag.-chain. No Tannaitic or early Amoraic authority refers to Yohanan b. Zakkai as Hillel's disciple, and it is primarily in the highly developed traditions of The Fathers According to Rabbi Nathan that Yohanan's discipleship to Hillel plays a considerable role.

More strikingly still, in all the Gamaliel-traditions – pertaining either to the first or the second one – we find not the slightest allusion to the familial relationship between Gamaliel and Hillel. To the contrary, Gamaliel II-materials persistently allege that Simeon b. Gamaliel I followed Shammaite rules, certainly an extraordinary state of affairs for the "grandson" (or great-grandson) of Hillel himself. It is moreover remarkable that Simeon b. Gamaliel and Gamaliel I never occur in he Houses-materials. The heirs of Hillel (Yohanan b. Zakkai, Gamaliel) and the House of Hillel on the face of it have nothing whatever to do with one another. It may therefore be anachronistic to suppose that the Hillelites predominated because Yohanan b. Zakkai and Gamaliel II were the greatest student and the great-grandson of Hillel, respectively. It looks as if things were the other way around. They were given a relationship to Hillel because they came to power at a point at which the Hillelite House predominated, and the allegation that both were Hillelites was the condition of their leadership at Yavneh. Strikingly, while that allegation later was important, no one took the trouble to invent stories in which either authority ever cited "my master" or "my father" Hillel. As I said, no named authority from Hillel to Yavneh ever quotes Hillel. But the predominance of Hillelites at Yavneh is very well attested and may be regarded as an axiom. Nothing in the Tannaitic stratum of Yohanan b. Zakkai-materials places him into relationship with either the House of Shammai or the House of Hillel. Yohanan cites "my teachers" back to Moses, but never mentions Hillel (M. Yad. 4:3). This seems to me probative that the circles of Yohanan's immediate disciples had no traditions relating Yohanan to Hillel. Similarly, Gamaliel II repeatedly is given references to "the house of father," meaning Simeon b. Gamaliel I, but none to Hillel, directly or inferentially.

3. Moral Apophthegms

1. A. Moses received the Torah from Sinai and handed it on to Joshua, Joshua to the Elders, the Elders to the Prophets; and the Prophets handed it on to the men of the Great Assembly (KNST).

   B. They said three things, "Be deliberate in judgment, raise up many disciples, and make a fence around the Torah."

2. Simeon the Just was of the remnants of the Great Assembly. He used to say, "On three things the world stands: on the Torah, on the [Temple-] service, and on deeds of loving kindness."

3. Antigonus of Sokho received from Simeon the Just. He used to say, "Be not like slaves that minister to the master for the sake of receiving a reward, but be like slaves that minister to the master not for the sake of receiving a reward; and let the fear of heaven be upon you."

4. Yosé b. Yoezer of Seredah and Yosé b. Yohanan of Jerusalem received from them [sic].
   Yosé b. Yoezer says, "Let your house be a meeting-house for the Sages, and sit amid the dust of their feet, and thirstily drink in their words."

5. A. Yosé b. Yohanan of Jerusalem says, "Let your house be opened wide; and let the needy be members of your house; and do not talk much with a woman."

   B. They said this of a man's own wife: how much more of his fellow's wife! Hence the Sages have said, "He that talks much with women brings evil upon himself, and neglects the study of the Law, and at the end he inherits Gehenna."

6. Joshua b. Perahiah and Nittai the Arbelite received from them.
   Joshua b. Perahiah says, "Make for yourself a master (RB), and get a fellow (HBR) [-disciple]; and judge any man with the balance in his favor."

7.   Nittai the Arbelite says, "Keep far from an evil neighbor, and do not consort with a wicked neighbor, and do not despair of retribution."

8.   Judah b. Tabbai and Simeon b. Shetah received from them. Judah b. Tabbai says, "Make not yourself like them that would influence the judges; and when the suitors stand before you, let them be in your eyes as wicked men; and when they have departed from before you, let them be in your eyes as innocent, as soon as they have accepted the judgment."

9.   Simeon b. Shetah says, "Abundantly examine the witnesses; and be cautious in your words, lest from them they learn to swear falsely."

10.   Shemaiah and Abtalyon received from them. Shemaiah says, "Love work; and hate mastery (RBNWT), and seek not acquaintance with the ruling power (RSWT)."

11.   Abtalyon says, "Sages, give heed to your words, lest you incur the penalty of exile, and be exulted to a place of evil waters, and the disciples that come after you drink and die, and the name of Heaven be profaned."

12.   Hillel and Shammai received from them.
       Hillel says, "Be of the disciples of Aaron, loving peace, and pursuing peace, loving mankind, and bringing them near to the Torah."

13.   He used to say, "A name made great is a name destroyed, and he that increases not decreases, and he that learns not is worthy of death, and he that makes worldly use of the crown perishes."

14.   He used to say, "If I am not for myself who is for me? And being for mine own self, what am I? And if not now, when?"

15.   Shammai says, "Make your [study of] Torah [a] fixed [habit]. Say little and do much. And receive all men with a cheerful countenance."

16.   Rabban Gamaliel says, "Make for yourself a master (RB) [=Joshua b. Perahiah's saying, above]; and keep distant from doubt; and do not tithe by guesswork."

17.   Simeon his son says, "All my days I have grown up among the sages, and I have found nothing better for the person (GWP) than silence; and the expounding is not the principle, but the doing; and he that multiplies words occasions sin."

18.   Rabban Simeon b. Gamaliel says, "On three things the world stands: on truth, on judgment, and on peace, as it is written, Execute the judgment of truth and peace (Zech. 8:16)" (M. Avot. 1:1-18).

The form from no. 4 to no. 12 is fixed: the names of the two who received the Torah from the foregoing, then apophthegms assigned to each, in order. The apophthegms are always triplicates; each says ('WMR) three things. The list is heavily glossed. In no. 5, for example, we are given a *qal vehomer,* which then produces a saying of the sages. In no. 8, as soon as they have accepted makes specific what has already been presupposed by when they have departed. Its purpose is to rule out the possible objection, "What if they have not accepted the judgment?" – a typical sort of Talmudic quibble. Abtalyon's saying is not a triplicate, but the three evil consequences make up for the absence of three separate sayings. No. 3 is expanded by the affirmative revision and the gloss, thus three. Nos.

13 and 14 are added to Hillel's saying, not a gloss but a considerable interpolation of materials, some in Aramaic, occurring elsewhere. Now it is used to say (HYH 'WMR) as in nos. 2-3.

Strikingly, with Hillel and Shammai the pairs cease. Also Gamaliel, standing alone, is not said to "receive" from Hillel/Shammai, nor Simeon from Gamaliel. Gamaliel's saying follows the earlier form. Simeon's does not, for it is glossed by all my days ... I have found, making an apophthegm, "There is naught better" into an autobiographical comment. But the rest of the saying conforms to the earlier pattern. Then in no. 18, Simeon his son becomes Rabban Simeon b. Gamaliel and is given a statement incongruent to the foregoing form. That saying is a counterpart of Simeon the Just's, though the specification of the "three things" changes, and is glossed with a scriptural proof-text. What is striking is the persistence of the "three things" form in the sayings that come in-between. No. 18 has been tacked on to the foregoing list to close with a parallel to no. 2.

Simeon the Just's saying is parallel to Simeon b. Gamaliel's, which clearly represents a post-135 revision of no. 2: the Torah now is truth, a philosophizing tendency; the temple service is now replaced by justice; and deeds of lovingkindness are replaced by peace. That this conclusion balances no. 2, and not the saying in no. 1, strongly suggests that no. 2 was originally the first saying in the list, and that the saying in no. 1 is a later addition, putting at the head of the whole list the fundamental principles of the rabbinic academy as a social form. But the fact that no. 18 was added to balance no. 2 raises the problem about no. 2 itself: Was it an integral part of the ("original") list? We saw that the fixed form characteristic of the list ("A + B received from them; A said [three sayings]; B said [three sayings]") begins only with no. 4. Thus on formal grounds there are strong reasons for thinking that nos. 2 and 3 were secondary accretions, and since the rabbinic traditions had no substantial legal materials from Simeon the Just and Antigonus – indeed, ignored Antigonus and treated Simeon primarily through legends – the case is clear. The original list began just as the rabbinic legal tradition began: with the two Yosé's. The appeal to Simeon the Just, perhaps known from Ben Sira, was motivated by the desire to attach this legal tradition to the last great member of the legitimate Jerusalem priesthood before its fall. Simeon's function is therefore the same as that of Moses etc., – he is part of the biblical (and Ben Sira) stemma of the tradition of the law. Antigonus as put in to bridge the temporal gap between Simeon and the Yosé's – a whole century! Whence did they get him? We have no idea.

Another mystery is the beginning of no. 4: the two Yosé's received from them, when the solitary Antigonus has preceded them. This probably is confirmation of our conjecture that Simeon and Antigonus have been added. The original referent of them will have been "the men of the great synagogue" – a single mythologumenon which bridged the gap from the prophets to the Pharisees. The original list was thus 1A, 4, 5A, 6, 7, 8, 9, 10, 11, 12, and 15. This elegant structure was broken to insert Simeon and thus claim connection with the last of the legitimate priesthood, and also to make the representation that the priesthood put the law ahead of the Temple service. After no. 18, M. Avot 2 begins with the yet later additions from the patriarch's circle, Rabbi, and Rabban Gamaliel III (M. Avot 2:1, 2:2ff), and then a collection of sayings of Hillel, purported ancestor of the patriarchal house, and then in Avot 2:8 comes an earlier addition to the list: Rabban Yohanan b. Zakkai received [the Torah] from Hillel and Shammai. This, which does have the form of the earlier entries, clearly is what has been displaced by the intervening (inserted) patriarchal material. The pre-70 list was therefore expanded by his pupils before it was taken over by the patriarchate. From the material following M. Avot. 2:8 (Yohanan's pupils and their sayings) we can see how it was developed in his school, by contrast to the patriarchal development. The Mishnah combines the two traditions. The names on the lists compare as follows:

M.Hag. 2:2	B. Shab. 14b = Y. Shab. 1:4	M. Avot 1:1
		Moses
		Joshua
		Elders
		Prophets
		Men of the Great Synagogue
		Simeon the Just
		Antigonus of Sokho
Yosé b. Yoezer	Yosé b. Yoezer	Yosé b. Yoezer
Yosé b. Yohanan	Yosé b. Yohanan	Yosé b. Yohanan
Joshua b. Perahiah		Joshua b. Perahiah
Nittai the Arbelite		Nittai the Arbelite
Judah b. Tabbai	Judah b. Tabbai	Judah b. Tabbai
Simeon b. Shetah	Simeon b. Shetah	Simeon b. Shetah
	Shemaiah	Shemaiah
	Abtalyon	Abtalyon
Hillel-Menahem	Shammai	Hillel
Shammai-Hillel	Hillel	Shammai
		Gamaliel
		Simeon b. Gamaliel

The second names in the first two pairs, Yosé b. Yohanan and Nittai the Arbelite, elsewhere are given no independent sayings whatever. They occur only in the context of the first-mentioned names, Yosé b. Yoezer and Joshua b. Perahiah. Further, Shemaiah and Abtalyon are rarely separated at all, but, except in Avot, normally appear as a pair, with remarkably few independent lemmas attributed to either the one or the other. They are given common ancestry. The first two Yosé's are not supplied with places of origin in M. Hag.

M. Avot corresponds to M. Hag. where the two coincide, except in the additions of the places of origin of Yosé's, and in the reversal of the order to Hillel-Shammai, making Hillel *nasi;* the subscription of M. Hag. serves the same purpose. The Babylonian version of the cleanness-decree lists does not conform. The names tacked on to the Avot-list obviously serve to complete the story back to Moses, on the one side, and to A.D. 170, on the other. Gamaliel is made the heir of Hillel's Torah.

Since no extant materials have either Simeon b. Gamaliel or Gamaliel I referring to Hillel, we may suppose that the claim of Hillel as an ancestor by the patriarchate came some time after the destruction of the Temple. My guess is that it was first alleged quite a long time later, since it first surfaces only in sayings attributed to, or attested by, figures in the time of Judah the Patriarch. Judah the Patriarch's circle probably is responsible for the additions of Gamaliel and Simeon b. Gamaliel to the Avot list. Since that same circle also produced the genealogy linking Hillel to David – presumably because the Babylonian exilarch did the same – the link between Gamaliel I and Hillel may have come some time before Judah the Patriarch, who is the first patriarch to refer to Hillel as his ancestor. The link is to be traced to the point at which the patriarchate made peace with the growing predominance of the Hillelite House, some time soon after the destruction of the Temple. Before then the Shammaites apparently predominated within Pharisaism, and Simeon b. Gamaliel probably was one of them, which accounts for the suppression of virtually all of his legal traditions. The first point at which Hillelite claim would have served the patriarchate therefore was the time of Gamaliel II. But, since Gamaliel II is represented as following Shammaite law (e.g. b. Yev. 15b), makes no reference to Hillel, plays no role in the Hillel-pericopae or in Hillel's House's materials, as I said, and tells how his father Simeon followed Shammaite rules, the Hillelite ancestry for the patriarchate founded by Gamaliel II may not have been established until ca. 150, by which time it seems to be settled. That is the point at which Meir had to revise the form of the earlier list to make Hillel *nasi.*

Yosé b. Halafta, Meir's contemporary, knew nothing about b. Shab. 14b, and said the decree about the uncleanness of glassware and the land of the people in fact was in force (with no authority given) eighty years before the destruction of the Temple. The masters certainly recognized that the two Yosé's long antedated Hillel and Shammai. Therefore Yosé

b. Halafta's tradition was separate from, and contradicted, that of b. Shab. He presumably knew no other. It therefore may be that that beraita comes well after ca. 150, as the names of Palestinian Talmud's authorities suggest. This brings us back to our starting point, the conception of an original tradition and how it tells us what really was thought, said, or done, to begin with. In line with our comparison of several versions of the chains of tradition and authority, we may reasonably maintain that the "original tradition" consisted of the following names:

1. Yosé b. Yoezer
   2. Yosé b. Yohanan
3. Joshua b. Perahiah
   4. Nittai the Arbelite
5. Judah b. Tabai
   6. Simeon b. Shetah
7. Shemaiah
   +
8. Abtalyon
9. Shammai
   10. Hillel
11. Yohanan b. Zakkai
12. Yohanan's disciples
    Replaced by
13. Gamaliel
14. Simeon b. Gamaliel

Of the foregoing, nos. 2 and 4 exist in the traditions only in association with nos. 1 and 3, nos. 7 and 8 are always connected. The relationships between nos. 5 and 6 are extremely complex, and it looks as if separate traditions of the two masters may have been put together for a post facto explanation of the union of two originally unrelated circles of disciples. To revert to the point at which we began, if we now have the "original" "tradition," it surely does not amount to much, just a list of names, on which people felt free to attach whatever they wanted: historical facts, legal rules, moral apophthegms. More important, the theory of the "original" "tradition" proves irrelevant to most of the data at hand. So if the theory is right, then, so what? And the answer is, so nothing.

II. Dating Stories through their Contents

A fixed trait of mind characteristic of the received, and uncritical, tradition in the use of talmudic tales for historical purposes instructs us to "date" stories by their contents. This works two ways, one positive, the other negative. If a story refers to the destruction of the temple, for example, then that story was made up after A.D. 70, a reasonable, if trivial, supposition. That positive evidence is uncommon and therefore solves few problems. The negative side tells us that if a story does not "know" about a certain important event or fact, then said story was made up, or reflects conditions, prior to that event. The possibility that the story teller may have chosen not to refer to that important event is not considered, and other explanations for the allegedly indicative negative trait of the story are not proposed.

Not only so, but in a given document, stories and sayings are treated as individual and autonomous units, without relationship to the larger document in which they are found. Consequently, if a given story or saying in a document omits reference to what is regarded as an emblematic event, then without any reference to the literary setting in which the saying occurs, that saying, raised up out of its context, is assigned to a provenience prior to the event at hand. In these two ways stories are not only dated through their silences, but they also are represented out of all relationship to the documents that now preserve said stories. There is yet a third trait of mind. If we have two or more versions of a given story, then both of them, of course, refer to things that really happened – but different events. Consequently, if a given story comes to us in diverse documents, and each document tells the tale in its own way, we may be asked to believe that each story describes its own event. These three principles of historical explanation derive from ancient times but go forward into the twenty-first century. And that is why it is important to review them, first, in their realization in the classical texts of Judaism. Only then shall we understand how, in the hands of contemporary, younger scholars, they live on.

Sages of ancient times recognized that sayings and stories appeared in diverse versions. They too proposed explanations of how a given saying or story could come down in more than a single statement. The principal approach to the question posited that each detail represented a different stage in the history of the story, or of the life of its hero in particular, with one version characteristic of one such stage, and another version attesting to a different, and later one. So the successive versions of a saying or story supply a kind of incremental history. How so? Each version tells something about concrete events and real lives (biographies) that earlier versions did not reveal. The classic Talmudic expression of the incremental theory takes up a passage of the Mishnah in which Rabban Yohanan ben Zakkai is called merely "Ben Zakkai:"

The precedent is as follows:

Ben Zakkai examined a witness as to the character of the stalks of figs [under which an incident now subject to court procedure was alleged to have taken place] [Mishnah Sanhedrin 5:2B].

As we shall now see, at paragraph N in the following talmudic analysis, exactly the same story is reported, on Tannaite authority. Now Rabban Yohanan ben Zakkai is alleged to have made exactly the same ruling, in exactly the same case. The item is worded in the same way except for the more fitting title. Then, at P-Q, the two versions are readily explained as facts of history. The one of Ben Zakkai was framed when he was a mere disciple. When, later on, he had become a recognized sage, the story was told to take account of that fact. So the theory I call "incremental history" is simple: each story related to, because it derives from, historical moments in a linear progression. The Talmudic passage, which appears at Babylonian Talmud Sanhedrin 41a-b, is as follows:

IX

- A. Who is this "Ben Zakkai"?
- B. If we should proposed that it is R. Yohanan ben Zakkai, did he ever sit in a sanhedrin [that tried a murder case]?
- C. And has it not been taught on Tannaite authority:
- D. The lifetime of R. Yohanan ben Zakkai was a hundred and twenty years. For forty years he engaged in trade, for forty years he studied [Torah], and for forty years he taught.
- E. And it has been taught on Tannaite authority: Forty years before the destruction of the Temple the sanhedrin went into exile and conducted its sessions in Hanut.
- F. And said R. Isaac bar Abodimi, "That is to say that the sanhedrin did not judge cases involving penalties."
- G. Do you think it was cases involving penalties? [Such cases were not limited to the sanhedrin but could be tried anywhere in the Land of Israel!]
- H. Rather, the sanhedrin did not try capital cases.
- I. And we have learned in the Mishnah:
- J. After the destruction of the house of the sanctuary, Rabban Yohanan b. Zakkai ordained ... [M. R.H. 4:1]. [So the final forty years encompassed the period after the destruction of the Temple, and Yohanan could not, therefore, have served on a sanhedrin that tried capital cases.]
- K. Accordingly, at hand is some other Ben Zakkai [than Yohanan b. Zakkai].
- L. That conclusion, moreover, is reasonable, for if you think that it is Rabban Yohanan ben Zakkai, would Rabbi [in the Mishnah-passage] have called him merely, "Ben Zakkai"? [Not very likely.]
- M. And lo, it has been taught on Tannaite authority:

N.   There is the precedent that Rabban Yohanan ben Zakkai conducted an interrogation about the stalks on the figs [so surely this is the same figure as at M. 5:2B].

The key-language is as follows, given in italics:

O.   *But [at the time at which the incident took place, capital cases were tried by the sanhedrin and] he was a disciple in session before his master. He said something, and the others found his reasoning persuasive, [41B] so they adopted [the ruling] in his name.*

P.   *When he was studying Torah, therefore, he was called Ben Zakkai, as a disciple in session before his master, but when he [later on] taught, he was called Rabban Yohanan ben Zakkai.*

Q.   *When, therefore, he is referred to as Ben Zakkai, it is on account of his being a beginning [student] and when he is called Rabban Yohanan b. Zakkai, it is on account of his status later on.*

On the basis of this analysis, not a few scholars of the life of Yohanan ben Zakkai present the two versions as formulations of his opinion at different stages in his career. The relevance of the Talmudic passage is simple, as I shall now explain. We have here the model, out of antiquity, for modes of thought characteristic of contemporary scholarship of an order I regard as primitive and uncritical.

Modern academic, not only ancient or yeshiva-based, scholars have claimed to explain diverse versions of a single saying or story by much the same thesis as we see before us. That is to say, they alleged that they know why a given detail is added here, dropped there, changed in the third place, built up and augmented in the fourth, and on and on. Accordingly, the modern, critical scholars accomplish a kind of incremental history. This is the history of what happened to account for changes in versions of a story, based on a theory of what might have impelled an author to add or revise a given detail. Indeed, practitioners of the incremental approach have not hesitated to declare that they know an entire history for which the text at hand supplies no evidence whatsoever. They then refer to this (entirely undocumented) history in order to explain shifts and changes in versions of a story. We shall now examine one among many instances of the mode of historical inquiry that yields sayings when Yohanan was young, sayings when he matured, based on different wordings of the same saying.

III. Making Up Traditions-History:
The Case of David J. Halperin

The single most current and choice example of the fantasy at hand is supplied by David J. Halperin, *The Merkabah in Rabbinic Literature* (New Haven: American Oriental Series 62, 1980). Halperin refers to the Merkavah-materials, with which we made our acquaintance, that expound

Ezekiel's vision of the Chariot.[1] What is important for our purpose is not his result but only his method. Halperin posits that, prior to the first written version there was an entire cycle of such stories ("presumably oral"!). True, we do not have any evidence whatever about this cycle. But not to worry: Halperin supplies evidence by making it up. For example Halperin tells us that one of these stories had a narrative framework, then lost a miraculous element, then got that miracle reinserted later on. This literary history, claiming to explain shifts and changes in the sequence of stories derives from not a shred of evidence of any kind. There is no version of these stories at all. The author just made it up and wrote it down, then the American Oriental Society printed it as "scholarship." True, as we shall note, Halperin introduces appropriate qualifications and caveats. But he pays little attention to them; they are mainly formalities. Here is how he states his conclusions (pp. 138-9):

> 1. I postulate the following development for the merkabah tradition involving R. Johanan b. Zakkai: (1) A cycle of merkabah stories, presumably oral, recounted the miracles that accompanied the expositions of one or another of R. Johanan's disciples; the stories of this cycle contained little beside the miracles. (This stage is purely hypothetical, and is not attested by any literary source.) (2) One of these stories, which involved R. Eleazar b. Arakh, was given a narrative framework, which suggested that R. Eleazar exemplified the "scholar" of M. Hag. 2:1 (Mek. Rashbi). (3) The miraculous element was "censored" from the story of R. Eleazar, possibly by the compiler of the mystical collection (Tosefta). (4) Miraculous details were reinserted, and stories of other disciples added, on the basis of the old merkabah stories (PT, BT)....
>
> 3. If my hypothesis is correct, the merkabah tradition is rooted in a cycle of miraculous legends. Some historical reality may hide behind these legends, but it is nearly inaccessible. Instead of trying to recover it, we should focus on what the legends can teach us about (maaseh) merkabah and the image of those reported to have been expert in it.

Halperin's exposition of his own theories omits all reference to how he conceives the character of the literature that contains these stories and its formation, if any. Yet even on the surface, it is clear, he proposes to make up explanations for diverse versions of the Merkavah-story. Each detail has its day. None is spared the ravages of Halperin's imaginative reconstruction of its individual life-history. Everything means something somewhere – and to Halperin it does not matter where. It follows that the theory of "incremental history," assigning a particular event or motive or other explanation for each change in a story as it moves from document

---

[1] I first presented the comparison of the various versions of these materials in my *Development of a Legend. Studies on the Traditions Concerning Yohanan ben Zakkai* (Leiden: E. J. Brill, 1971).

to document finds exemplification in Halperin's treatment of the Merkavah-story.

A systematic picture of what Halperin has done and why it is founded on false premises (or on no premises other than an undisciplined imagination) derives from William Scott Green's review of Halperin's book.

In his review (the *Second Century*, 1983, 3:113-115) Green observes:

> For reasons never specified, Halperin tends to construe each literary unit, each manuscript variant, and each textual version as a discrete historical moment. he then constructs his history by arranging these textual moments into chronological sequence.   By adopting this strategy, Halperin forces himself into the grueling exercise of determining the relative dates of decontextualized literary segments. Much is at stake in these demonstrations; the very possibility of Halperin's history depends on their rigor and cogency. Halperin uses a wide range of criteria to date his materials, and he sometimes deploys these inconsistently.

Green's critique moves beyond the matter of inconsistency. He presents considerable reason to maintain that Halperin is simply making things up as he goes along. He states:

> That is, he established his chronologies on the basis of the differences among versions of a passage. But the variables he deems decisive are not systematically applied. Rather, they seem to shift from case to case. This sort of unevenness undermines Halperin's demonstrations of chronology and makes at least some of them appear arbitrary.   The problems of particular chronologies aside, Halperin's method limits the kind of history of rabbinic, merkabah speculation he can write.   His catenae of textual events result in schematic accounts that flip and flop, sparse chronicles of unexpected reversals and inversions in which discrete passages undergo marked, sometimes radical shifts of meaning.

Finally, Green draws us back to the phenomenon of dating stories by their contents. But now that mode of thought takes on a new trait: we determine in advance three distinct meanings to a single phrase and impute dates to the usage of each meaning. Then we can posit that a story in which a given meaning occurs refer to or derives from a specified period. But all of this is simply invented for the occasion. So Green goes on:

> He argues, for instance, that the Mishnaic rule that the merkabah may not be expounded "by an individual [variant: to an individual], unless he is a scholar, understanding on his own" (M. Hagigah 2:1) had three distinct meanings before the time of Tosefta's redaction (ca. A.D.250). When the passage circulated independently, it allowed the sage, but not the disciple, "to undertake on his own an exegesis of Ezekiel's vision" (p. 35). When it was redacted into the Mishnah and incorporated into a list of other biblical passages whose exposition is restricted, "the effect was

to reverse the other biblical passages whose exposition is restricted, "the effect was to reverse the meaning of the merkabah ruling; solitary study of the merkabah was no longer the object of the restriction, but a concession granted to certain exceptional individuals" (p. 36). Still later, the meaning of the rule was changed again to make it "refer to instruction" (p. 36), an alteration reflected in the variant reading. This final meaning is apparent in a story about Yohanan b. Zakkai and Eleazar b. Arakh at T. Hagigah 2:1, which, ironically, preserves the earliest version of the Mishnaic rule.

Green turns, at the end, to the more fundamental questions of not only evidence but also historical explanation. Untrained as a historian and essentially an autodidact, Halperin leaves open a wide variety of questions that will have attracted attention from a more critical intellect, so Green:

> This kind of lean and linear history disappoints because it does not account for the changes it describes. Even if Halperin's textual sequences are correct, they leave too much unexplained. For instance, to whom within rabbinism were these changes important? Did the different meanings supersede one another or exist simultaneously? Are these changes literary, or do they reflect deeper theological, religious, and social diversions within rabbinism? Are such changes, particularly the reversal of meaning, accidental or deliberate, the result of misunderstanding or of manipulation? Without some theory of rabbinic culture and society, of textual transmission and tradition, and of literary tendencies, Halperin's textual sequences lead nowhere. They are merely chronologies masquerading as history.

I should contend that Halperin simply replicates the "traditional" mode of thought that tells us how each version of a story or saying represents a different period or event. That is to say, he is just making it up as he goes along. No wonder that he also does not undertake any sort of analytical explanation, in context, of the things he has invented: the explanation is self-evident. And so it is.

In singling Halperin out for his exemplification of what are, in fact, commonplace methods among a wide variety of uncritical scholars in the study of ancient Judaism, my intent is only to show what people are doing now. I do not want anyone to suppose that I have taken a particularly weak example of an otherwise vital theory. On the contrary, Halperin presents us with as capable an exercise of the incremental-historical theory as is in print – alas. For it seems he is talking to himself, in the privacy of his study. He clearly is not engaging in reasoned arguments with the generality of interested participants in the inquiry. Only by that theory can I explain how anyone can make up a "cycle" of Merkavah-stories ("presumably oral"), tell us what was in them, then what was removed from them – and only then relate the whole to the actual sources at hand. The theory that details in successive versions of a saying or story bear historical meanings deserves better than it has gotten to date.

The approach that seeks to account for shifts and changes by reference to the interests of later authors, tradents, and redactors, remains entirely open. Indeed, in due course we may look forward to the rehabilitation of the theory at hand. My criticism, like Green's, is that, so far as Halperin exemplifies the theory, he provides yet another instance of the dreary approach of made-up explanations, never subjected to tests of falsification or validation. That approach, suitable for talmudic exegesis, does not serve for historical and literary work in our day. While both the theory that "he often used to say ..." and the claim that there is an "original" "tradition," promise little for the future, the one at hand awaits rigorous attention, because, as we note, it still rules in circles that regard themselves as contemporary and critical. In this regard, scholarship on the earliest history of Christianity, which has long since abandoned the Sermon on the Mount and the Sermon on the Plain, shows the way for Judaic learning.

Chapter Seven

Wrong Ways in Historical Study [3]: Confusing the History of Judaism with the History of the Jews: The Case of S. J. D. Cohen's *Judaism from the Maccabees to the Mishnah*

Shaye J. D. Cohen, professor of Jewish history at the Jewish Theological Seminary of America and author of a first-rate monograph on *Josephus in Galilee* (his other published book), presents in his *Judaism from the Maccabees to the Mishnah* what he conceives to be a textbook for college students on Judaism: "the goal of this book is to interpret ancient Judaism: to identify its major ideas, to describe its salient practices, to trace its unifying patterns, and to assess its relationship to Israelite religion and society."[1] The importance of this textbook in the context of wrong ways of the religious study of ancient Judaism is simple. Cohen is trained as a historian, not as a historian of religions, and, as we shall see, his textbook fails because he lacks the necessary intellectual tools to carry out the task he has accepted. The result of the insufficiency of his categories is confusion. At the same time, the principal error of all wrong ways, which is identifying all Judaisms with a single Judaism and all Jews' histories, wherever and whenever they lived, with a single, linear, harmonious, and unitary "Jewish history" finds striking exemplification in his book. That is why I think it pertinent to pay more attention to the work at hand than its standing, as a mere textbook, would ordinarily gain for itself.

The book is arranged thematically rather than chronologically...." The themes are laid out as follows. Cohen begins with a general chronology of the history of the Jews and aspects of Jews' culture, politics, and, by the way, religion, and offers definitions thereof. He proceeds to "Jews and Gentiles," covering political matters, gentile domination, in

---

[1] *From the Maccabees to the Mishnah*. By Shaye J. D. Cohen. *Library of Early Christianity*. Wayne A. Meeks, General Editor. Philadephia: Westminster Press, 1987.

that section: the Maccabean rebellion, the rebellion against the Romans, the wars of 115-117 and 132-135; cultural: Judaism and Hellenism, covering "Hellenism," "Hellenization, and "Hellenistic Judaism and the like; social: Jews and gentiles, anti-Judaism and "Anti-Semitism" and Philo-Judaism; then the Jewish "Religion" (his quotation marks), practices and beliefs, in which he defines "religion" (again, his quotation marks), practices, worship of God, ritual observances, ritual, ethics, and the yoke of the law, legalism, beliefs, kingship of God, reward and punishment, redemption. Then comes "the community and its institutions," dealing with the public institutions of the land of Israel, the Temple and sanhedrin, the public institutions of the diaspora, the synagogue, private organizations, sects, professional guilds, schools. Then he treats "sectarian and normative," with attention to "sect and heresy," focal points of Jewish sectarianism," "orthodox and "normative," proto-sectarianism in the Persian period, Ezra and Nehemiah, Isaiah 65, Pharisees, Sadducees, and Essenes; other sects and groups, touching "fourth philosophy," Christians, Samaritans, Therapeutae. This is followed by "canonization and its implications," with attention to the history of the biblical canon. At the end is "the emergence of rabbinic Judaism," with the main point "from second temple Judaism to rabbinic Judaism." All of these topics – and many more not catalogued – are covered in 230 pages, with a few pages of notes, and a few more for further reading. As is clear, therefore, Cohen follows an ample outline of topics and covers a wide range of subjects.

Part of a textbook series in the study of the history of religion in late antiquity, with focus on Christianity, this textbook (in the words of the editor, Wayne A. Meeks) brings together "the results of a wide range of scholarship of fields often separate." (That claim will surely surprise, among many, the authors of the new *Schuerer,* Geza Vermes and his colleagues, who rightly claim to have covered precisely the same range of scholarship.) The editor explains that the author avoids "the kind of argument and documentation that is necessary in the scholarly monographs in which work as new as this is ordinarily presented. Nevertheless, the expert as well as the novice will recognize both the erudition that lies behind this book and the freshness of its presentation." We shall return to the implications of that statement for the value of this book in the class room, to which it is addressed. No other volume in the series dismisses sources and scholarship as Meeks claims is all right when we study "Judaism." That hardly bespeaks respect for Judaism as an academic problem.

Cohen for his part says the same: "In order to make this book accessible to students and other nonspecialists, I have kept the bibliographical annotation to a minimum." Since this book clearly intends to serve as a textbook, it should be evaluated as such, since – in their own words – neither the editor nor the author claims to make a contribution to scholarship. Still, on the plus side the book does cover a vast range of topics, and it does so concisely. The discussion moves swiftly and smoothly, though the array of dates and facts in the opening discussion may pose problems for students. Cohen has read very broadly in scholarly literature and his book has the merit of reporting the state of knowledge (as he views it to be sure) in a variety of areas. The book exhibits a number of substantial flaws in presentation, conception, and mode of argument. These are three, and each one is so fundamental as to turn the book into a good bit less than meets the eye.

First, Cohen's plan of organization yields pure chaos. The reason, in my view, is the inadequacy of his category-formation. Reading this book is like reading a sequence of encyclopaedia articles. That is why the first, and the principal minus is the mode of organization, which separates important components of the picture at any given moment. That is to say, in one chapter, Cohen treats "Jews and gentiles," in another, Jewish religion, yet in a quite separate chapter, "sectarianism," and so on. In that way we are denied a sense of the whole and complete picture, at any one time, of the religious world view and way of life of the Jews in the land of Israel.

Within the chapters, too, we find the same incapacity at forming a cogent and coherent statement of the whole. "Jews and gentiles" covers separate matters of political, cultural, and social policy, one by one. But these of course are not separate matters and never were. Within politics we move from Jeremiah to the Persians, the Maccabees, the Romans; then on the cultural agenda, we have Judaism and Hellenism, out of phase with the foregoing. And then we come to "social: Jews and gentiles," and yet a fresh set of issues. I find this rather confusing. The schematization has a certain logic to it, but the logic derives not from education – the lucid presentation of issues, sources, arguments – but from a program of a different sort altogether. In many ways – as I said – what we have is a sequence of encyclopaedia entries. I hasten to add that many of these entries are quite good and all of them are well-informed. No one can imagine Cohen has not done his homework. The incoherence of the book as a whole, however, does not really diminish the strength of the parts as summaries of knowledge of discrete topics.

What does make the book a failure lies elsewhere, in Cohen's disciplinary inadequacy. He is a historian, not a historian of religion, and he has not got the intellectual equipment to do the job he has undertaken, at Meeks's invitation, to accomplish. Why Meeks chose for Judaism a historian rather than a historian of religion I do not know, but it surely does not bespeak respect for Judaism as a religion. The second

principal failure of the book, therefore, derives from a simple
methodological incapacity. Cohen's knowledge of the study of religion is
remarkably shallow, with the result that he operates with crude and
unworkable definitions of principal categories and classifications.
Cohen's prior scholarship lies in history, not in religion. He simply has
not got the training in the field of the history of religion to develop an
interpretive framework adequate to his task. As a result he is left to try to
present cogently a vast array of diverse materials that are not cogent at all.
With this he simply cannot cope, and the result is a series of rather
unfortunate "definitions," which define nothing and lead nowhere. Let
me give two probative examples. In both of them he substitutes classical
philology for the history of religion. But, then, he was trained in ancient
history, including classical philology – and not in the field of religion at
all (which is why, I assume, he commonly places quotation marks around
the word religion, that is, "religion").

Cohen wishes to define religion. This he does by asking what the word
"religion" meant in antiquity. Using the words of Morton Smith, he says,
"If a contemplative person in antiquity sought systematic answers to
questions about the nature of the gods and their involvement in human
affairs, he would have studied philosophy, not 'religion.'" Placing
religion in quotation-marks does not solve any problems left unsolved by
this monumentally irrelevant definition. For when *we* study religion, it is
within the definition(s) of religion that we have formed and brought to
evidence we have identified as pertinent. That process is in part inductive
and in part deductive, but it is never defined wholly within the definitions
of another language and another age. There is a vast literature, from the
Enlightenment foward, on the definition of religion, a literature in
philosophy, history of religions, and a range of other fields. Cohen does
not seem to have followed the discussions on the nature and meaning of
religion that have illuminated studies in the nineteenth and twentieth
centuries, with the result that his discussion is monumentally ignorant.
The result is that he does not know how to deal with the data he is trying to
sift, organize, and present in a cogent way, and that accounts for the
book's wild incoherence.

As to "Judaism," the word occurs on every page and in nearly every
paragraph. It starts, "The goal of this book is to interpret ancient
Judaism." But I do not know what Cohen means by "Judaism." Only many
pages later does he tell us. Cohen recognizes, of course, that various
groups of Jews formulated matters, each in its own way, lived each in its
own pattern, defined each its own "Judaism." And yet from the opening
lines, "Judaism" is an "it," not a "they," and Cohen tells us "its major
ideas...its salient practices...its unifying patterns...its relationship to
Israelite religion" (which then is another, different "it"). But that is only

part of the story. Cohen recognizes that the data that fall into the category, "religion," hence "Judaism," are incoherent and diverse. He says so – but then he is stymied when he tries to justify treating many things as one thing. Cohen states, "Second temple Judaism was a complex phenomenon. Judaism changed dramatically during the Persian, Hellenistic, Maccabean, Roman, and rabbinic periods. Generalizations that may be true for one period may not be true for another. In addition, at any given moment, Jews practiced their religion in manifold different ways. The Jewish community of Egypt in the first century C.E. was far from uniform in practice and belief...." That then is the question.

How is it answered? "What links these diverse phenomena together and allows them all to be called *Judaism*? [Italics his.] The Jews saw (and see) themselves as the heirs and continuators of the people of pre-exilic Israel; the Jews also felt...an affinity for their fellow Jews throughout the world....This self-perception manifested itself especially in the relations of diaspora Jewry to the land of Israel and the temple....Thus, like the bumblebee which continues to fly, unaware that the laws of aerodynamics declare its flight to be impossible, the Jews of antiquity saw themselves as citizens of one nation and one religion, unaware of, or oblivious to, the fact that they were separated from each other by their diverse languages, practices, ideologies, and political loyalties. In this book I do not minimize the varieties of Jewish religious expression, but my goal is to see the unity within the diversity." That, sum and substance, is Cohen's solution.

As a matter of fact, it is wrong. There were groups of Jews who regarded themselves as the only Jews on earth; everyone else was not "Israel" at all. The Essenes of Qumran saw themselves in that way. But so too did the authorship of the Pentateuch, which treated as normative the experience of exile and return and excluded from the normative experience of their particular "Israel" the Samaritans, who had not gone into exile, and the Jews elsewhere, who never went back and who are totally ignored in the pentateuchal statement of 450 B.C. So the allegation that Cohen knows what all the Jews thought of themselves is called into question by his rather blithe failure to conduct a survey of opinion, to the degree that we know opinion at all. He seems to me to play somewhat fast and loose with facts – if there are any facts about affinities, public opinion, attitudes, and the like.

As a matter of definition, Cohen does not really answer the question of defining a single Judaism at all. Here again, the vacuity of his theoretical system – of which there is none – accounts for his failure. Historians do not ask the questions that historians of religion do. How people see themselves forms a fundamental fact for the description of their world-view – but not for the world they view. Cohen is correct to claim that the way in which a given group sees itself tells us something about their Judaism. But whether or not their views testify to other Judaisms he does not know. The reason is that he does not explain and unpack the theology within his allegations of a mutually supportive society throughout the world. Cohen claims that "this self-perception manifested itself especially in the relations of diaspora Jewry to the land of Israel and the temple." But diaspora Jews preserved a certain distance; they gave money to the temple, but when the Jews of the land of Israel went to war, diaspora Jews remained at peace, within the same empire – and vice versa. That hardly suggests that the perceived "affinity" made much difference in public policy. What we have is an excuse for not investigating the answers to a well-asked question – but not an answer to that question. Cohen does not have the equipment to answer the question, being a historian, not a historian of religion.

This matter of Cohen's limited knowledge of the study of religion lies at the heart of the book's failure. Lest Cohen's difficulty at conceptualization seems one episode in an otherwise well-crafted work, let me point to yet another example of how Cohen dismisses as trivial a central question of definition. Cohen has, of course, to address the issue of "sects," meaning (in my language) diverse Judaisms. He has to tell us the difference between the sectarian and the normative, and, to his credit, he devotes a whole chapter to the matter. Here too Cohen appeals to ancient usage in the solution of a problem of conceptualization – as though anybody any more is bound to word-usages of Greek or Latin. He contrasts the negative use of "sect" and "heresy," deriving from theology. "'Sects' and 'heresies' are religious groups and doctrines of which we disapprove." That is true, but only for the uninformed.

A vast literature on the definition of "sect" and "church" has been written. Cohen does not use it. Here is Cohen's definition: "A sect is a small, organized group that separates itself from a larger religious body and asserts that it alone embodies the ideals of the larger group because it alone understands God's will." A sect then seems to me in Cohen's mind to be no different from a religion, except that it is small ("small") and differs from a group that is larger ("a larger religious body"). How the sect relates to the "larger religious body" we do not know. If the "sect" dismisses the "larger group" because the sect claims alone to understand God's will, then why is the sect not a "religious body" on its own? It would seem to me to claim exactly that. Lest I appear to exaggerate the conceptual crudity at hand and to impute to Cohen opinions he does not hold, let me now cite Cohen's own words:

> A sect must be *small* enough to be a distinctive part of a *larger religious body*. If a sect grows to the extent that it is a large body in its own right, it is no longer a sect but a "religion" or a "church." The precise definition

of "large body" and "church" is debated by sociologists, but that question
need not be treated here.

The italics are all his. This, I submit, is pure gibberish. A small group is a
sect. A big one is a "religion" or a "church." That surely is a distinction
that yields only one difference – and the difference may not matter,
except where it matters (so to speak). What has led Cohen to this impasse
is simple. Since there is one "Judaism" we have to figure out some way to
deal with all the other Judaisms, and by calling them "little" we can find a
suitable pigeonhole for them; then we do not have to ask how "little" is
different from "big" except that it is little. So much for crude definitions
and unworkable classifications.

Third, the book is educationally not well-conceived and therefore not
very useful. The reason is that the students are not given the two things
that make a textbook a conversation – a dialogue between the learning
student and the problems that require mastery. The first thing a student
needs to know is, what is the problem? what is the evidence that requires
accurate description, analysis, and interpretation? and – above all –
*what do I know about solving problems when I have solved the
problem?* Cohen does not present sources in this book. He also does not
present scholarly arguments about sources, for example portraying the
reasoned approaches that one may take to the interpretation of a given
problem, as portrayed by pertinent sources. As a result, students who use
this book will never know, from the pages of this book, what the evidence
looks like for any given statement, how the evidence may be read one way
or another, why Cohen reads it in his way and not in some other. All of
these questions, critical to the educational process, find no answer in
Cohen's presentation. It is not clear to me that Cohen has thought
through the educational problem of presenting his subject, and the
disorganization of the whole, the inadequacy of definition of the parts,
the decision to present no sources at all – these traits of the book suggest to
me that he has no clear educational program at all. So Cohen's dual task –
to present a religion, and to present it to students – has not been carried
out. Not a historian of religion, he has not framed categories that serve
for presenting a religion. And not a college teacher, he has not got the
experience to present a religion to a college course in religion. (Alan
Segal, both a historian of religion and a college teacher, has done just that
in his far superior textbook, as I shall point out at the end.)

Still, it is not wholly Cohen's fault. The editor is partly at fault, for
asking Cohen, a historian who teaches in a rabbinical school, to do the
work of a historian of religion for the academic class room. Meeks further
bears responsibility – as he himself admits – for freeing Cohen from the
responsibility for reasoned argument in dialogue with learning, as he says
in the preface cited above. In doing so, Meeks has treated Judaism with

utter contempt. He has also dismissed a vast range of scholarship on Judaism as thought it did not exist. The depth of Meeks's contempt for the subject at hand is underlined by the way in which other authors in this same series have defined their work and carried out – with enormous respect for their subjects. For other volumes in this same series have accomplished precisely the work of a first-rate textbook. I point, first to, Abraham J. Malherbe's *Moral Exhortation. A Greco-Roman Sourcebook*, which is the fourth volume in the Library of Early Christianity, and to Stanley K. Stowers, *Letter Writing in Greco-Roman Antiquity*, which is the fifth. Malherbe presents a rich anthology of relevant writings, which he introduces carefully and thoughtfully, and through which he leads the reader with great care and sharp perception. Cohen just does not do this. Stowers' *Letter Writing* presents an original and stunning interpretation of classic Christian writings, particularly Paul's, as these should be read within the literary conventions of the time. Letters are letters and to be read as letters – and Stowers shows precisely what this means, by leading the student through letters and their conventions and then applying what is learned to the reading of Paul's letters.

Now Stowers chose the occasion to write a major and original work of scholarship, which Cohen could not have asked himself to do on the vast program he has selected. And Malherbe, the master-teacher, chose the occasion carefully and thoughtfully to lead students through a critical issue. That is why Cohen seems to me not to have asked himself what people are going to learn from his book, beyond the statement of his views of matters (with most of which, as a matter of fact, most scholars will concur, since they are commonplaces as they should be).

Once more we turn to Meeks for an explanation of this travesty. In Cohen's defense, I have to say that, while Christianity gets six and a half volumes, Judaism gets one volume and a half (the other half being Kugel's dreadful section of *Early Biblical Interpretation* by James O. Kugel and Rowan A. Greer, but that is another matter). Cohen had to cover in a few pages subjects for which Malherbe and Stowers were given whole books – and then some. Cohen, unlike Stowers, could not have given us original scholarship had he had any to give. But, forced to pick and choose, in my view he made the wrong choice. He passes his opinion, but he does not set forth his arguments, he makes a great many allegations, but he provides remarkably thin analysis of sources of a representative character. He thus made precisely those choices experienced teachers ordinarily do not make.

Yet a textbook does convey a message and a purpose, and this one surely does. What does Cohen give us in place of sources and the analysis of sources, argumentation and reasoned disposition of counterargument?

He gives us Cohen. Let me explain. Cohen's own opinions, on the one side, and Cohen's judgment of the state of "scholarly opinion," on the other, take the place of sources, analysis of sources, reasoned argument about sources, fair presentation of diverse possibilities implicit in sources. What a student learns, as a matter of method, from this book is that scholarship consists of learned gossip: what this one thinks about that one, what "scholarly opinion" has decided. Cohen places himself in front of his subject and so obscures the subject. Let me give a concrete example of the way in which Cohen, assuming a position of superiority over all other scholars, passes his opinion in place of presenting his proposition and argumentation.

Let me give a single example of how Cohen expresses his high opinion of his own opinion. He treats the subject of God-fearers. These were – it has commonly been alleged – gentiles who observed some Jewish practices, attended synagogue, and the like. In a major article, A. Thomas Kraabel has argued that there was no such group. How does Cohen confront this position? Here are his exact words, whole and complete: "A. Thomas Kraabel argues that the 'God-fearers' never existed, but this position is untenable; see his 'The Disappearance of the "God-Fearers,"' Numen, 28, 1981, 113-126." That, sum and substance, dismisses poor Professor Kraabel. Why untenable? Cohen does not tell us. Nor does he tell us why in his bibliography he cites the items he cites and ignores – through a familiar process of Todschweigen, or murder by silence – the items he ignores.

But there is a stunning problem, best left for the end. The text of his book covers a vast array of subjects investigated by other scholars, whose work Cohen uses. But Cohen never tells us, in footnotes, whom he cites and why. The utter absence of footnotes denies us knowledge of what Cohen has taken from others and what Cohen has made up on his own. Under other circumstances Cohen might find himself accused of plagiarism and charlatanism (charges levelled, for example, by James Kugel against Robert Alter in *Journal of Religion*, January, 1987). But once more, at fault is the editor, not the author. Meeks excuses this omission of the normal and expected apparatus of learning, as I said earlier: "he has avoided the kind of argument and documentation that is necessary in the scholarly monographs in which work as new as this is ordinarily presented." Meeks alleges that this is a new work. But this is not really new work. It is a survey of other peoples' work, not of Cohen's own ideas (except in a few places). And most of the work in this book is familiar to scholars throughout the world. Why not give people credit for their ideas where and as they are used? I do not know, and that explains why I think the editor and author have treated with utter contempt the entire scholarly literature of which the author has made ample use. What lesson this mode of scholarship teaches I would not wish to spell out.

Still, there are legitimate differences of opinion, just as there are horse races and elections. So let us hear from the other side. The blurbs on the cover salute Cohen's book as "the best brief account" (Morton Smith), "Fresh and distinctive" (John J. Collins), "masterful survey...to be counted among the very best single-volume introductions..." (David Levenson), "comprehensive and concise...an excellent one volume introduction to Judaism for courses in Christian origins" (Martha Himmelfarb), "useful to students in colleges and seminaries and to the general reader" (Jon Levenson), for educational purposes. For the three reasons I have spelled out with some care, I am inclined to differ. It is not masterful, not original, and not coherent. Quite to the contrary, the book is merely brief but not coherent; it is fresh only in its ample attention to the author's own opinions. That does not mark a useful textbook. And, as is clear, it is not a contribution to scholarship and is not meant to be (though, as I said, Stowers and Malherbe accomplished precisely that within the framework of the same series).

For my part, for an introduction for a course in Judaism in the period covered by this book, I much prefer Alan Segal's *The Children of Rebecca. Judaism and Christianity in the Roman World* (Harvard). Segal is a historian of religion, specializing in Judaism, who teaches in a college class room, and he has handled the problem of a textbook with sophistication both in conception and in presentation. The reason is in three parts. First, Segal's presentation is conceptually sophisticated, for it is based on a sure grasp of the theoretical literature of the history of religion and therefore addresses the sources with greater conceptual clarity and without the obfuscation that mars Cohen's book. But Segal is in the field of religion, not history, which is Cohen's discipline. Second, it is cogent and coherent, not a mishmash of subjects thrown hither and yon. Segal therefore exhibits the marks of a superior education. Third, Segal treats scholarship in a scholarly way and does not impose his own opinion in place of sources and argumentation, the considered and reasoned description, analysis, and interpretation that, properly construed, constitute the wherewithal of intellectual exercise. So much for wrong ways of studying Judaism. Now let me offer two examples of what I present as right ways of doing things.

Chapter Eight

Right Ways in Historical Study [1]:
Do Religions Ever Have Histories?
System or Tradition in the Case
of Formative Judaism

A systematic, and by nature, philosophical, religious statement or document presents its ideas as though they began with its author or authorship, rather than claiming to start "way way back," as a tradition, or even alluding to, let alone citing in a persistent way, a prior writing, e.g., Scripture. The form of a systematic statement ordinarily will be autonomous. The order of discourse will begin from first principles and build upon them. The presentation of a system may, to be sure, absorb within itself a given document, citing its materials here and there. But – and this forms the indicator as to conception, not form alone – the authorship in such a case imposes its program and its problem upon received materials, without the pretense that the program and order of those inherited ("traditional" "authoritative" "scriptures") has made any impact whatsoever upon its presentation. An instance of a systematic statement's use of received materials is Matthew chapter two, which wishes to make the point that the events in the early years of Jesus's life fulfilled the promises of prophecy. That point requires the authorship to cite various verses; these are, of course, chosen for the occasion, and there is no pretense at a reading of whole passages in their "own" terms and in accord with their "own" momentum of meaning. The Matthean authorship, rather, makes its point, which is part of its larger program and polemic, through an incidental, if important, allusion to prophecy.

The basic criterion of the systematic character of a document or statement, however, derives from a quite distinct trait. It is the authorship's purpose and whether, and how, a statement serves that purpose. How do we know that a statement, a sizable composition for instance, is meant to be systematic? In a well-composed system, every detail will bear the burden of the message of the system as a whole. Each component will make, in its terms, the statement that the system as a whole is intended to deliver. In order to understand that fact, we have to appreciate an important distinction in the analysis of systems. It is between a fact that is systemically vital, and one that is inert.

For the study of economics, this point has been made by Joseph A. Schumpeter as follows: "In economics as elsewhere, most statements of fundamental facts acquire importance only by the superstructures they are made to bear and are commonplace in the absence of such superstructures."[1] That is to say, a system of religious thought, comprising a world view, a way of life, and a definition of the social entity meant to adopt the one and embody the other, makes ample use of available facts. In order to make their statement, the authors of the documents of such a system speak in a language common to their age. Some of these facts form part of the background of discourse, like the laws of gravity. They are, if important, inert, because they bear no portion of the burden of the systemic message. I call such facts inert. Other of these facts form centerpieces of the system; they may or may not derive from the common background. Their importance to the system forms part of the statement and testimony of that system.

Now in a well-composed religious or philosophical system, every systemically generative fact will bear in its detail the message of the system as a whole, and, of course, inert facts will not. What I mean is simply illustrated. It is clear to any reader of Plato's *Republic,* Aristotle's *Politics* (and related corpus, to be sure), the Mishnah, or Matthew's *Gospel,* that these writers propose to set forth a complete account of the principle or basic truth concerning their subject, beginning, middle, and end. Accordingly, they so frame the details that the main point is repeated throughout. At each point in the composition, the message as a whole, in general terms, will be framed in all due particularity. The choices of topics will be dictated by the requirements of that prevailing systemic attitude and statement. We can even account, ideally, for the topical components of the program, explaining (in theory at least) why one topic is included and another not. A topic will find its place in the system because only through what is said about that *particular* topic the system can make the statement it wishes to make.[2] Silence on a topic requires

---

[1] Joseph A. Schumpeter, *History of Economic Analysis,* p. 54.
[2] That is the point of my *Economics of Judaism* (in press). Paul V. Flesher, *Oxen, Women, or Citizens? Slaves in the System of the Mishnah* (Atlanta: Scholars Press for Brown Judaic Studies, 1988) is able to demonstrate the same for the inclusion of slavery within the Mishnah's system. Flesher is able to point to a counterpart study by G. Vlastos, "Slavery in Plato's Republic," *Slavery in Classical Antiquity: Views and Controversies,* ed. M. I. Finley (Cambridge: Heffer, 1960), pp. 133-148, who shows how, in the system of Plato's *Republic,* slavery bears a systemic role and task. I should further point to Simon Schama's *Embarassment of Riches* (New York: Knopf, 1987) as an example of a systemic reading of detail. Schama's

explanation, as much as we must supply a systemic motive or reason for the selection of, and substantial disquisition on, some other topic.

The criterion for whether a document and the religion it represents is traditional or systematic, therefore systemic viewed as a construction, therefore allows us to test our judgment by appeal to facts of verification or falsification.   For the importance of recognizing the systemically generative facts is simple. When we can account for both inclusion and exclusion, we know not merely the topical program of the system but its fundamental intent and method, and we may assess the system-builders' success in realizing their program. A well-composed system will allow us to explain what is present and also what is absent. Consequently, we may come to a reasonable estimation of the system's coverage, its realization of its program and full, exhaustive, presentation of its encompassing statement. Not only so, but a well-crafted systemic statement will by definition form a closed system, and the criterion of whether or not a statement stands on its own or depends upon other sources, e.g., information not contained within its encompassing statement but only alluded to by that statement, serves a a second major indicator for taxonomic purposes. Let me spell this out.

Some systems say precisely what they want on exactly those topics that make it possible to make its full statement. These are what we may call "closed systems," in that the authors tell us – by definition – everything that they want us to know, and – again, by definition – nothing that they do not think we need to know. They furthermore do not as a matter of systemic exposition have to refer us to any other writing for a further explication of their meaning (even though for reasons of argument or apologetic, they may do so). When an authorship sets forth a topic and completely and exhaustively expounds that topic, it has given us a systematic statement. The authorship has laid out its program, described the structure of its thought, given us what we need to know to grasp the composition and proportion of the whole, and, of course, supplied the information that, in detail, conveys to us the statement in complete and exhaustive form, thus, a closed system. It has done more than simply add a detail to available information. Quite to the contrary, the authorship of a statement of a closed system will frame its statement in the supposition that that authorship will tell us not only what we need to know, but everything we need to know, about a given topic. And that is a solid indicator of a systematic statement. An open system, by contrast, requires the recipient of a statement to refer not only to what an authorship tells us, but also to what an authorship invokes. The program is partial, the

---

eye for the evocative visual symbol has given him the power to produce a masterpiece of cultural description, analysis, and interpretation.

statement truncated, the system incomplete and not in correct composition and proportion, if, indeed, there is a system at all. That will then mark a traditional, not a systemic, statement. A piece of writing that depends upon other writings, and that is not occasioned by subjective judgment of the reader but by objective, if implicit, direction of the author, then forms part of an open system, or is not a systematic statement at all, but a fragment of thought.

I. Explaining a Religion: System against History

Now in all that I have said, I have treated as an axiom the formal and putative autonomy of systemic thought, which is so represented as if it begins *de novo* every morning, in the mind, imagination, and also conscience, of the system-builders. But what of what has gone before: other systems and their literary, as well as their social, detritus? Let us turn to the relationships to prior writings exhibited by systematic and traditional authorships, respectively. How do we know the difference between a system and a tradition in respect to the reception of received systems and their writings? The critera of difference are characterized very simply. A systematic authorship will establish connections to received writings, always preserving its own autonomy of perspective. A traditional authorship will stand in a relationship of continuity, commonly formal, but always substantive and subordinate, with prior writings. The authorship of a document that stands in a relationship of connection to prior writings will make use of their materials essentially in its own way. The authorship of a document that works in essential continuity with prior writings will cite and quote and refine those received writings but will ordinarily not undertake a fundamentally original statement of its own framed in terms of its own and on a set of issues defined separately from the received writings or formulations. The appeal of a systematic authorship is to the ineluctable verity of well-applied logic, practical reason tested and retested against the facts, whether deriving from prior authorities, or emerging from examples and decisions of leading contemporary authorities.

A traditional authorship accordingly will propose to obliterate lines between one document and another. A systematic authorship in the form of its writing ordinarily will not merge with prior documents. It *cites* the received writing as a distinct statement – a document "out there" – and does not merely allude to it as part of an internally cogent statement – a formulation of matters "in here." The systematic authorship begins by stating its interpretation of a received writing in words made up essentially independent of that writing, for example, different in language, formulation, syntax, and substance alike. The marks of independent, post facto, autonomous interpretation are always vividly imprinted upon the systematic authorship's encounter with an inherited document. Such a writing never appears to be represented by internal evidence as the extension of the text, in formal terms the uncovering of the connective network of relations, as literature a part of the continuous revelation of the text itself, in its material condition as we know it "at bottom, another aspect of the text." Not only so, but a systematic statement will not undertake the sustained imitation of prior texts by earlier ones. And even when, in our coming survey, we find evidence that, superficially, points toward a traditional relationship between and among certain texts that present us with closed systems and completed, systematic statements, we should, indeed, be struck by the independence of mind and the originality of authorships that pretend to receive and transmit, but in fact imagine and invent.

A traditional document (therefore the mind and the religious system that it represents) recapitulates the inherited texts; that defines the traditionality of such a writing. A systematic writing may allude to, or draw upon, received texts, but does not recapitulate them, except for its own purposes and within its idiom of thought. Traits of order, cogency, and unity derive from modes of thought and cannot be imposed upon an intellect that is, intrinsically, subordinated to received truth. A traditional writing refers back to, goes over the given. The system for its part not only does not recapitulate its texts, it selects and orders them, imputes to them as a whole cogency that their original authorships have not expressed in and through the parts, expresses through them its deepest logic. The system – the final and complete statement – does not recapitulate the extant texts. The antecedent texts – when used at all – are so read as to recapitulate the system. The system comes before the texts and so in due course defines the canon. But in introducing the notion of canon, I have moved far beyond my story. At this point it suffices to claim that the thought processes of tradition and those of system building scarcely cohere. Where applied reason prevails, the one – tradition – feeds the other – the system – materials for sustained reconstruction.

The statement of a system is worked out according to the choices dictated by that authorship's sense of order and proportion, priority and importance, and it is generated by the problematic found by that authorship to be acute and urgent and compelling. When confronting the task of exegesis of a received writing, the authorship of a systematic statement does not continue and complete the work of antecedent writings within a single line of continuity ("tradition"). Quite to the contrary, that authorship makes its statement essentially independent of its counterpart and earlier document. In a systematic writing, therefore, the system comes first. The logic and principles of orderly inquiry take precedence over the preservation and repetition of received materials, however holy.

The mode of thought defined, the work of applied reason and practical rationality may get underway.

First in place is the system that the authorship through its considered, proportioned statement as a whole expresses and serves in stupefying detail to define. Only then comes that selection, out of the received materials of the past, of topics and even concrete judgments, facts that serve the system's authorship in the articulation of its system. Nothing out of the past can be shown to have dictated the systematic program, which is essentially the work of its authorship. The tradition is ongoing, and that by definition. Then, also by definition, the system begins exactly where and when it ends. Where reason reigns, its inexorable logic and order, proportion, and syllogistic reasoning govern supreme and alone, revising the received materials and restating into a compelling statement, in reason's own encompassing, powerful, and rigorous logic, the entirety of the prior heritage of information and thought. From the Pentateuch to the Bavli, Judaic authorships presented not stages or chapters in an unfolding tradition but closed systems, each one of them constituting a statement at the end of a sustained process of rigorous thought and logical inquiry, applied logic and practical reason. The only way to read a reasoned and systematic statement of a system is defined by the rules of general intelligibility, the laws of reasoned and syllogistic discourse about rules and principles.

And the correct logic for a systematic statement is philosophical and propositional, whether syllogistic or teleological. The way to read a traditional and sedimentary document by contrast lies through the *ad hoc* and episodic display of instances and examples, layers of meaning and eccentricities of confluence, intersection, and congruence. But I maintain that tradition and system cannot share a single throne, and a crown cannot set on two heads. Diverse statements of Judaisms upon examination will be seen to constitute not traditional but systemic religious documents, with a particular hermeneutics of order, proportion, above all, reasoned context, to tell us how to read each document. We cannot read these writings in accord with two incompatible hermeneutical programs, and, for reasons amply stated, I argue in favor of the philosophical and systemic, rather than the agglutinative and traditional, hermeneutics.

Whatever happens to thought, in the mind of the thinker ideas come to birth cogent, whole, complete – and on their own. Extrinsic considerations of context and circumstance play their role, but logic, cogent discourse, rhetoric – these enjoy an existence, an integrity too. If sentences bear meaning on their own, then to insist that sentences bear meaning only in line with their associates, their friends, companions, partners in meaning, contradicts the inner logic of syntax that, on its own, imparts sense to sentences. These are the choices: everything imputed, as against an inner integrity of logic and the syntax of syllogistic thought.[3] But there is no compromise. As between the philosophical heritage of Athens and the hermeneutics of the Judaic tradition known from classical times forward, I maintain that one document of the Jewish intellect after another in classical times demonstrates the power of the philosophical reading of mind. In the end, the Jewish intellect in its classic age appealed to the self-evidence of truth compelled by of the well-framed argument, the well-crafted sentence of thought, the orderly cadence of correct, shared, and public logic – that and not the (mere) authority of tradition.

II. When Religious Systems Begin, Why They Flourish

Systems begin in the social entity, whether one or two persons or two hundred or ten thousand – there and not in their canonical writings, which come only afterward, or even in their politics. The social group, however formed, frames the system, the system then defines its canon within, and addresses the larger setting, the *polis* without. We describe systems from their end products, the writings. But we have then to work our way back from canon to system, not to imagine either that the canon is the system, or that the canon creates the system. The canonical writings speak, in particular, to those who can hear, that is, to the members of the community, who, on account of that perspicacity of hearing, constitute the social entity or systemic community. The community then comprises that social group the system of which is recapitulated by the selected canon. The group's exegesis of the canon in terms of the everyday imparts to the system the power to sustain the community in a reciprocal and self-nourishing process. The community through its exegesis then imposes continuity and unity on whatever is in its canon.

While, therefore, we cannot account for the origin of a successful religious-social system, we can explain its power to persist. It is a symbolic transaction, as I said just now, in which social change comes to expression in symbol-change. That symbolic transaction, specifically, takes place in its exegesis of the systemic canon, which, in literary terms, constitutes the social entity's statement of itself. So, once more, the texts recapitulate the system. The system does not recapitulate the texts. The system comes before the texts and defines the canon. The exegesis of the canon then forms that ongoing social action that sustains the whole. A

---

[3]No one can maintain that the meanings of words and phrases, the uses of syntax, bear meanings wholly integral to discrete occasions. Syntax works because it joins mind to mind, and no one mind invents language, only gibberish. But that begs the question and may be dismissed as impertinent, since the contrary view claims far more than the social foundation of the language.

system does not recapitulate its texts, it selects and orders them. A religious system imputes to them as a whole cogency, one to the next, that their original authorships have not expressed in and through the parts, and through them a religious system expresses its deepest logic, *and it also frames that just fit that joins system to circumstance.*

The whole works its way out through exegesis, and the history of any religious system – that is to say, the history of religion writ small – is the exegesis of its exegesis. And the first rule of the exegesis of systems is the simplest, and the one with which I conclude: *the system does not recapitulate the canon. The canon recapitulates the system.* The system forms a statement of a social entity, specifying its world view and way of life in such a way that, to the participants in the system, the whole makes sound sense, beyond argument. So in the beginning are not words of inner and intrinsic affinity, but (as Philo would want us to say) the Word: the transitive logic, the system, all together, all at once, complete, whole, finished – the word awaiting only that labor of exposition and articulation that the faithful, for centuries to come, will lavish at the altar of the faith. A religious system therefore presents a fact not of history but of immediacy, of the social present.

The issue of why a system originates and survives, if it does, or fails, if it does, by itself proves impertinent to the analysis of a system but of course is necessary to our interpretation of it. A system on its own is like a language. A language forms an example of language if it produces communication through rules of syntax and verbal arrangement. That paradigm serves full well however many people speak the language, or however long the language serves. Two people who understand each other form a language community, even, or especially, if no one understands them. So too by definition religions address the living, constitute societies, frame and compose cultures. For however long, at whatever moment in historic time, a religious system always grows up in the perpetual present, an artifact of its day, whether today or a long-ago time. The only appropriate tense for a religious system is the present. A religious system always *is*, whatever it was, whatever it will be. Why so? Because its traits address a condition of humanity in society, a circumstance of an hour – however brief or protracted the hour and the circumstance.

When we ask that a religious composition speak to a society with a message of the *is* and the *ought* and with a meaning for the everyday, we focus on the power of that system to hold the whole together: the society the system addresses, the individuals who compose the society, the ordinary lives they lead, in ascending order of consequence. And that system then forms a whole and well composed structure. Yes, the structure stands somewhere, and, yes, the place where it stands will secure for the system either an extended or an ephemeral span of life. But the system, for however long it lasts, serves. And that focus on the eternal present justifies my interest in analyzing why a system works (the urgent agenda of issues it successfully solves for those for whom it solves those problems) when it does, and why it ceases to work (loses self-evidence, is bereft of its "Israel," for example) when it no longer works. The phrase, the *history* of a *system*, presents us with an oxymoron. Systems endure – and their classic texts with them – in that eternal present that they create. They evoke precedent, they do not have a history. A system relates to context, but, as I have stressed, exists in an enduring moment (which, to be sure, changes all the time). We capture the system in a moment, the worm consumes it an hour later. That is the way of mortality, whether for us one by one, in all mortality, or for the works of humanity in society. But systemic analysis and interpretation requires us to ask questions of history and comparison, not merely description of structure and cogency. So in this approach to the study of a religion – any religion – we have to undertake first description, that is, the text, then analysis, that is, the context, and finally, interpretation, that is, the matrix, in which a system has its being.

Chapter Nine

Right Ways in Historical Study [2]: Seeing Religions as Social Systems in the Instance of Formative Judaism

Religion is more than a system or belief. It is more, also, than a way of life. It combines these two – world view, way of life – by forming of them a social entity.[1] When we understand that religion does its work – all its work, everything that matters about it – in the social world, then we can begin to grasp why religion is the single most powerful social force in the life and politics of the world today, as in nearly the whole of recorded history.

Religions form social worlds and do so through the power of their rational thought, that is, their capacity coherently to explain data in a (to an authorship) self–evidently valid way. The framers of religious documents answer urgent questions, framed in society and politics to be sure, in a manner deemed self–evidently valid by those addressed by the authorships at hand. To study any vital religion is to address – as a matter of hypothesis – a striking example of how people explain to themselves who they are as a social entity. Religion as a powerful force in human society and culture is realized in society, not only or mainly in theology; religion works through the social entity that embodies that religion. Religions form social entities – "churches" or "peoples" or "holy nations" or monasteries or communities – that, in the concrete, constitute the "us," as against "the nations" or merely "them." And religions carefully explain, in deeds and in words, who that "us" is – and they do it every day. To see religion in this way is to take religion seriously as a way of realizing, in classic documents, a large conception of the world.

But how do we describe, analyze and interpret a religion, and how do we relate the contents of a religion to its context? These issues of method are worked out through the reading of texts, and, I underline, through

---

[1]This essay at a few points goes over issues treated in the preceding one, though the context is fresh. I beg the reader's indulgence on that account.

taking seriously and in their own terms the particularity and specificity of texts.

I. Are Religions Traditions or Systems?

Religion may represent itself as a tradition, meaning, the increment of the ages. Or it may come forth as a cogent statement, a well–crafted set of compelling answers to urgent questions. A religious tradition covers whatever the received sedimentary process has handed on. A religious system addresses in an orderly way a world view, a way of life, and a defined social entity. And both processes of thought, the traditional or the systematic, obey, each its own rules. The life of intellect may commence morning by morning. Or it may flow from an ongoing process of thought, in which one day begins where yesterday left off, and one generation takes up the task left to it by its predecessors.

A system of thought by definition starts fresh, defines first principles, augments and elaborates them in balance, proportion, above all, logical order. In a traditional process, by contrast, we never start fresh but only add, to an ongoing increment of knowledge, doctrine, and mode of making judgment, our own deposit as well. And, in the nature of such an ongoing process, we never start fresh, but always pick and choose, in a received program, the spot we choose to augment. The former process, the systematic one, begins from the beginning and works in an orderly, measured and proportioned way to produce a cogent, and neatly composed statement, a philosophy for instance. Tradition by its nature is supposed to describe not a system, whole and complete, but a process of elaboration of a given, received truth: exegesis, not fresh composition. And, in the nature of thought, what begins in the middle is unlikely to yield order and system and structure laid forth *ab initio*. In general terms, systematic thought is philosophical in its mode of analysis and explanation, and traditional thought is historical in its manner of drawing conclusions and providing explanations.

System and tradition as modalities of religious world–construction not only describe incompatible modes of thought but also generate results that cannot be made to cohere, in the aggregate, with one another. For the conflict between tradition and system requires us to choose one mode of thought about one set of issues and to reject the other mode of thought and also the things about which thought concerns itself. And that choice bears profound consequences for the shape of mind.

So far as "tradition" refers to the matter of process, it invokes, specifically, an incremental and linear process that step by step transmits out of the past statements and wordings that bear authority and are subject to study, refinement, preservation, and transmission. In such a traditional process, by definition, no one starts afresh to think things through. Each participant in the social life of intellect makes an episodic and ad hoc contribution to an agglutinative process, yielding, over time, (to continue the geological metaphor) a sedimentary deposit. The opposite process we may call systematic, in that, starting as if from the very beginning and working out the fundamental principles of things, the intellect, unbound by received perspectives and propositions, constructs a free–standing and well–proportioned system. In terms of architect the difference is between a city that just grows and one that is planned; a scrapbook and a fresh composition; a composite commentary and a work of philosophical exposition.

II. Religions as Systems, Not (Mere) Traditions

What sort of indicator tells us that we have a system, not a tradition? A systematic, and by nature, philosophical, statement or document, by contrast, presents its ideas as though they began with its author or authorship, rather than alluding to, let alone citing in a persistent way, a prior writing, e.g., Scripture. The form of a systematic statement ordinarily will be autonomous. The order of discourse will begin from first principles and build upon them. The presentation of a system may, to be sure, absorb within itself a given document, citing its materials here and there. But the authorship in such a case imposes its program and its problem upon received materials, without the pretense that the program and order of those inherited ("traditional" "authoritative" "scriptures") has made any impact whatsoever upon its presentation. An instance of a systematic statement's use of received materials is Matthew chapter two, which wishes to make the point that the events in the early years of Jesus's life fulfilled the promises of prophecy. That point requires the authorship to cite various verses; these are, of course, chosen for the occasion, and there is no pretense at a reading of whole passages in their "own" terms[2] and in accord with their "own" momentum of meaning. The Matthean authorship, rather, makes its point, which is part of its larger program and polemic, through an incidental, if important, allusion to prophecy.

The basic criterion of the systematic character of a document or statement, however, derives from a quite distinct trait. It is the authorship's purpose and whether, and how, a statement serves that purpose. How do we know that a statement, a sizable composition for instance, is meant to be systematic? In a well–composed system, every detail will bear the burden of the message of the system as a whole. Each component will make, in its terms, the statement that the system as a whole is intended to deliver. In order to understand that fact, we have to

---

[2]Whatever that can have meant in context!

appreciate an important distinction in the analysis of systems. It is between a fact that is systemically vital, and one that is inert.

Now in a well–composed system, every systemically generative fact will bear in its detail the message of the system as a whole, and, of course, inert facts will not. What I mean is simply illustrated. It is clear to any reader of Plato's *Republic,* Aristotle's *Politics* (and related corpus, to be sure), the Mishnah, or Matthew's *Gospel,* that these writers propose to set forth a complete account of the principle or basic truth concerning their subject, beginning, middle, and end. Accordingly, they so frame the details that the main point is repeated throughout. At each point in the composition, the message as a whole, in general terms, will be framed in all due particularity. The choices of topics will be dictated by the requirements of that prevailing systemic attitude and statement. We can even account, ideally, for the topical components of the program, explaining (in theory at least) why one topic is included and another not. A topic will find its place in the system because only through what is said about that *particular* topic the system can make the statement it wishes to make.[3] Silence on a topic requires explanation, as much as we must supply a systemic motive or reason for the selection of, and substantial disquisition on, some other topic.

The criterion for whether a document and the religion it represents is traditional or systematic, therefore systemic viewed as a construction, therefore allows us to test our judgment by appeal to facts of verification or falsification.[4] For the importance of recognizing the systemically generative facts is simple. When we can account for both inclusion and exclusion, we know not merely the topical program of the system but its

---

[3]That is the point of my *Economics of Judaism* (in press). Paul V. Flesher, *Oxen, Women, or Citizens? Slaves in the System of the Mishnah* (Atlanta: Scholars Press for Brown Judaic Studies, 1988) is able to demonstrate the same for the inclusion of slavery within the Mishnah's system. Flesher is able to point to a counterpart study by G. Vlastos, "Slavery in Plato's Republic," *Slavery in Classical Antiquity: Views and Controversies,* ed. M. I. Finley (Cambridge: Heffer, 1960), pp. 133-148, who shows how, in the system of Plato's *Republic,* slavery bears a systemic role and task. I should further point to Simon Schama's *Embarassment of Riches* (New York: Knopf, 1987) as an example of a systemic reading of detail. Schama's eye for the evocative visual symbol has given him the power to produce a masterpiece of cultural description, analysis, and interpretation.

[4]One example is the difficulty we face in classifying the writings of the Essene library of Qumran as a system at all. By contrast, we have no difficulty in representing the Mishnah as a systemic statement. I do not wish to enter into counterpart classification of Christian writings, e.g., Irenaeus, Origen, and Augustine, as to their traditional or systemic identification. I do maintain, that the Bible (Old and New Testaments together) forms a system and was meant to make a systemic statement, and that position rests on the function and purpose of the Bible as described in scholarship on the canon.

fundamental intent and method, and we may assess the system–builders' success in realizing their program. A well–composed system will allow us to explain what is present and what is absent, as I said. Consequently, we may come to a reasonable estimation of the system's coverage, its realization of its program and full, exhaustive, presentation of its encompassing statement. Not only so, but a well–crafted systemic statement will by definition form a closed system, and the criterion of whether or not a statement stands on its own or depends upon other sources, e.g., information not contained within its encompassing statement but only alluded to by that statement, serves as a second major indicator for taxonomic purposes. Let me spell this out.

Some systems say precisely what they want on exactly those topics that make it possible to make its full statement. These are what we may call "closed systems,"[5] in that the authors tell us – by definition – everything that they want us to know, and – again, by definition – nothing that they do not think we need to know. They furthermore do not as a matter of systemic exposition have to refer us to any other writing for a further explication of their meaning (even though for reasons of argument or apologetic, they may do so). When an authorship sets forth a topic and completely and exhaustively expounds that topic, it has given us a systematic statement. The authorship has laid out its program, described the structure of its thought, given us what we need to know to grasp the composition and proportion of the whole, and, of course, supplied the information that, in detail, conveys to us the statement in complete and exhaustive form, thus, a closed system. It has done more than simply add a detail to available information. Quite to the contrary, the authorship of a statement of a closed system will frame its statement in the supposition that that authorship will tell us not only what we need to know, but everything we need to know, about a given topic. And that is a solid indicator of a systemic statement. An open system, by contrast, requires the recipient of a statement to refer not only to what an authorship tells us, but also to what an authorship invokes. The program is partial, the statement truncated, the system incomplete and not in correct composition and proportion, if, indeed, there is a system at all. That will then mark a traditional, not a systemic, statement. A piece of writing that depends upon other writings, and that is not occasioned by subjective judgment of the reader but by objective, if implicit, direction of the

---

[5]On the Mishnah as a closed system, see my *Judaism: The Evidence of the Mishnah* (Second edition, augmented: Atlanta: Scholars Press for Brown Judaic Studies, 1988).

author, then forms part of an open system, or is not a systematic statement at all, but a fragment of thought.[6]

III. Systemic versus Traditional "Holy Scriptures"

A traditional authorship accordingly will propose to obliterate lines between one document and another. A systematic authorship in the form of its writing ordinarily will not merge with prior documents. It *cites* the received writing as a distinct statement – a document "out there" – and does not merely allude to it as part of an internally cogent statement – a formulation of matters "in here." The systematic authorship begins by stating its interpretation of a received writing in words made up essentially independent of that writing, for example, different in language, formulation, syntax, and substance alike. The marks of independent, post facto, autonomous interpretation are always vividly imprinted upon the systematic authorship's encounter with an inherited document. Such a writing never appears to be represented by internal evidence as the extension of the text, in formal terms the uncovering of the connective network of relations, as literature a part of the continuous revelation of the text itself, in its material condition as we know it "at bottom, another aspect of the text." Not only so, but a systematic statement will not undertake the sustained imitation of prior texts by earlier ones. And even when, in our coming survey, we find evidence that, superficially, points toward a traditional relationship between and among certain texts that present us with closed systems and completed, systematic statements, we should, indeed, be struck by the independence of mind and the originality of authorships that pretend to receive and transmit, but in fact imagine and invent.

A traditional document (therefore the mind and the religious system that it represents) recapitulates the inherited texts; that defines the traditionality of such a writing. A systematic writing may allude to, or draw upon, received texts, but does not recapitulate them, except for its own purposes and within its idiom of thought. Traits of order, cogency, and unity derive from modes of thought and cannot be imposed upon an intellect that is, intrinsically, subordinated to received truth. A traditional writing refers back to, goes over the given. The system for its part not only does not recapitulate its texts, it selects and orders them, imputes to them as a whole cogency that their original authorships have not expressed in and through the parts, expresses through them its deepest logic. The system – the final and complete statement – does not recapitulate the extant texts. The antecedent texts – when used at all – are

---

[6]True, such an open system may turn out to form part of a collage, but that is a different question.

so read as to recapitulate the system. The system comes before the texts and so in due course defines the canon. But in introducing the notion of canon, I have moved far beyond my story. At this point it suffices to claim that the thought processes of tradition and those of system building scarcely cohere. Where applied reason prevails, the one – tradition – feeds the other – the system – materials for sustained reconstruction.

The statement of a system is worked out according to the choices dictated by that authorship's sense of order and proportion, priority and importance, and it is generated by the problematic found by that authorship to be acute and urgent and compelling. When confronting the task of exegesis of a received writing, the authorship of a systematic statement does not continue and complete the work of antecedent writings within a single line of continuity ("tradition"). Quite to the contrary, that authorship makes its statement essentially independent of its counterpart and earlier document. In a systematic writing, therefore, the system comes first. The logic and principles of orderly inquiry take precedence over the preservation and repetition of received materials, however holy. The mode of thought defined, the work of applied reason and practical rationality may get underway.

First in place is the system that the authorship through its considered, proportioned statement as a whole expresses and serves in stupefying detail to define. Only then comes that selection, out of the received materials of the past, of topics and even concrete judgments, facts that serve the system's authorship in the articulation of its system. Nothing out of the past can be shown to have dictated the systematic program, which is essentially the work of its authorship. The tradition is ongoing, and that by definition. Then, also by definition, the system begins exactly where and when it ends. Where reason reigns, its inexorable logic and order, proportion, and syllogistic reasoning govern supreme and alone, revising the received materials and restating into a compelling statement, in reason's own encompassing, powerful, and rigorous logic, the entirety of the prior heritage of information and thought. From the Pentateuch to the Bavli, Judaic authorships presented not stages or chapters in an unfolding tradition but closed systems, each one of them constituting a statement at the end of a sustained process of rigorous thought and logical inquiry, applied logic and practical reason. The only way to read a reasoned and systematic statement of a system is defined by the rules of general intelligibility, the laws of reasoned and syllogistic discourse about rules and principles.

And the correct logic for a systematic statement is philosophical and propositional, whether syllogistic or teleological. The way to read a traditional and sedimentary document by contrast lies through the *ad hoc* and episodic display of instances and examples, layers of meaning and eccentricities of confluence, intersection, and congruence. But I maintain that tradition and system cannot share a single throne, and a crown cannot set on two heads. Diverse statements of Judaisms upon examination will be seen to constitute not traditional but systemic religious documents, with a particular hermeneutics of order, proportion, above all, reasoned context, to tell us how to read each document. We cannot read these writings in accord with two incompatible hermeneutical programs, and, for reasons amply stated, I argue in favor of the philosophical and systemic, rather than the agglutinative and traditional, hermeneutics.

The whole then works its way out through exegesis, and the history of any religious system – that is to say, the history of religion writ small – is the exegesis of its exegesis. And the first rule of the exegesis of systems is the simplest: *the system does not recapitulate the canon. The canon recapitulates the system.* The system forms a statement of a social entity, specifying its world view and way of life in such a way that, to the participants in the system, the whole makes sound sense, beyond argument. So in the beginning are not words of inner and intrinsic affinity, but (as Philo would want us to say) the Word: the transitive logic, the system, all together, all at once, complete, whole, finished – the word awaiting only that labor of exposition and articulation that the faithful, for centuries to come, will lavish at the altar of the faith. A religious system therefore presents a fact not of history but of immediacy, of the social present.

IV. Religion and the Fabric of Society

When we ask that a religious composition speak to a society with a message of the *is* and the *ought* and with a meaning for the everyday, we focus on the power of that system to hold the whole together: the society the system addresses, the individuals who compose the society, the ordinary lives they lead, in ascending order of consequence. And that system then forms a whole and well composed structure. Yes, the structure stands somewhere, and, yes, the place where it stands will secure for the system either an extended or an ephemeral span of life. But the system, for however long it lasts, serves. And that focus on the eternal present justifies my interest in analyzing why a system works (the urgent agenda of issues it successfully solves for those for whom it solves those problems) when it does, and why it ceases to work (loses self–evidence, is bereft of its "Israel," for example) when it no longer works. The phrase, the *history* of a *system*, presents us with an oxymoron. Systems endure – and their classic texts with them – in that eternal present that they create. They evoke precedent, they do not have a history. A system relates to context, but, as I have stressed, exists in an enduring moment (which, to be sure, changes all the time). We capture the system in a moment, the worm consumes it an hour later. That is the way of mortality, whether for us one by one, in all mortality, or for the works of humanity in society.

Part Four

HISTORY OF RELIGION:
SOME INITIAL RESULTS IN THE DESCRIPTION
OF THE JUDAISM OF THE DUAL TORAH
IN ITS FORMATIVE AGE

Chapter Ten

Judaism in the First Century

I. The Limits of Our Knowledge

When we invoke the word "Judaism" in the study of the religion of first century Jews in the Land of Israel, we introduce a category that no one at that time would have grasped. The "-ism" of Judaism defines this category. Through this classification we seek to describe that order, system, and encompassing doctrine which, all together, characterized Israel's common faith and holy way of life in the land of Israel. But the evidence that would make possible such a description of a common world view and way of life characteristic of the people, Israel, in its land, does not come to hand.

To list the range of our ignorance: we do not know what the people as a whole thought, or how they felt, or what they did, because of faith in God and in the Torah. On the basis of contemporary evidence we cannot describe, from beginning to end, the course of a single individual's life. We do not have access either to the shared convictions of the people as a whole or to the singular manner in which an individual mediated, into a private mode of living, the people's religion and culture. We lack descriptions by external observers in communication with, and subject to the correction of, insiders. We have no records, letters, diaries, and the like, of participants in the religious culture. By contrast from the second century onward, we can take up the life and thought of important figures of Christianity. In sheer volume we have more knowledge of Augustine, for example, than we do of all individual Jews of the Land of Israel in the first century. Later on, moreover, for the mode of Judaism that became dominant, the way of life and world view laid forth by the sages ("rabbis") of the Mishnah and its successor-documents down to the Talmud of Babylonia, (ca. A.D. 200-600), we do have an official record for guidance. Through these documents we can know how an important group of people saw things and how they instructed the people to live. Even though we know little about what people actually did, the literary record, augmented by the archeological testimonies, permits description of a world through the artifacts of people whose views we claim to portray. For first century Israel, by contrast, none of this is possible, since there is

scarcely an individual portrayed through his or her own documents, and
little evidence deriving from representative authors of the time and place.
It follows that we cannot describe either the common theology or the
shared piety, of the Jewish population of the country as a whole. There are
no direct sources for this.

II. The Nature of the Sources

What, then, is the kind of evidence for the piety of Judaism that we do
have? It consists, on the one side, of writings emerging from small groups
("sects"), and, on the other, of parts of libraries preserved by groups that
later enjoyed a dominance they could not have at first imagined possible.
Into the former category fall those parts of the Gospels that not only refer
to, but derive from, the land of Israel and its Jews, as well as those
components of the Essene library at Qumran that were written down in the
first century. In the latter category we find the canon of Judaism from the
Mishnah through the Talmud of Babylonia, which presents convictions
about ideas held in the first century, or portrays events that then took
place. These, it is claimed, were handed on through time. But they were
given authoritative status in writing only much later, as in the Mishnah and
its associated documents. Out of the land of Israel in the first century, we
have only the pseudepigraphic writings that appeal to the authority of
earlier holy men, such as Ezra or Baruch, and the works of Josephus.
There is practically nothing else deriving from the Land of Israel in the
first century.

What "Judaism" did or did not teach must, in the end, therefore be
garnered from evidence not for a single homogeneous and monolithic
"Judaism," as a national way of life and commonly-held world view.
Rather, we know about "Judaisms," ways of life and world views framed by
distinct and not necessarily representative groups. In no way did such
groups claim to speak about, or for, or even to, all Israel.

However, the absence of a recognized and well-documented
orthodoxy, such as did emerge in the Judaism defined by the later
authoritative canon of the ancient sages, that is, the orthodoxy system
summarized in the Talmud of Babylonia and associated writings, does not
present insuperable obstacles. Any sketch of the piety of the nation-
religion (to invoke the two appropriate, if anachronistic, categories), will
appeal to two distinct approaches to the available evidence.[1] First, we

---

[1]"Nation" is anachronistic for the period at hand, and "religion" also imposes a
distinction between secular and sacred that at this time few in Israel would have
grasped. Israel was a people of a shared Scripture and collective consciousness –
hence, we should invoke the term "nation." Israel assuredly framed its way of life
and world view in ways we should regard as religious, believing that God wanted

may ask about common denominators. Second, we may sort out the points of special emphasis, that is differences, characteristic of various groups ("sects"), whose writings we do have. In this way we may gain some perspective on the common denominators.

The principal common denominator must in social terms derive from the ordinary people called *am haares*.[2] The piety of Judaism comes to expression – speaking descriptively – when we know, or can credibly surmise, what the ordinary folk had in mind. Access to their wit and imagination, to the givens of their everyday lives as individuals and as a large and, in important aspects, homogeneous group, will permit us entry into the piety of Judaism. How so? As we stated, comparison between the generality of the people, on the one side, and the points of emphasis of particular groups, on the other, allows us to sort out differences and gain perspective on the totality. If we could have a grasp of the points of special interest of such groups, we might then hope to know what Israelites generally understood to be, and practiced as, the way of life of Judaism. Alongside, what people commonly perceived that way of life to have meant, the ethos of the religion, the people as a whole, will emerge.

III. From the Particular to the General

Where are we to begin? In seeking definitions, we do best to start with the negative. The piety of Judaism is not a "philosophy" nor the outcome of a philosophy. We must be guided by the excellent observations of Morton Smith, who states:

> It must be remembered that Judaism to the ancient world was a philosophy. That world had no general term for religion. It could speak of a particular system of rites or a particular set of beliefs or a legal code or a body of national customs or traditions; but for the peculiar synthesis of all these which we call a "religion," the one Hellenistic word which came closest was "philosophy."[3]

What we want to know, however, is not the "philosophy" of Judaism in the Graeco-Roman sense. Ours is a different question. We ask about the religious experience in the formation of culture, in the bonding of society, and in the conduct of everyday life, which was afforded by that

---

things as they were. But, as is clear, we have to take note of the imposition, by us, of a category at that time not available.

[2]The *am haares* – people of the land – would correspond in general to the Roman *paganus*. In the rabbinic writings they defined the category of "outsider," as distinct from the insider, who engaged in certain approved practices. Later on the term acquired the still more negative sense of "total ignoramus," ordinarily applied to anyone with whom a learned man does not agree.

[3]"Palestinian Judaism in the First Century," in M. Davis, ed. *Israel: Its Role in Civilization* (New York: Harper, 1956), p. 79.

cogent system, way of life, and world view, addressed to that single social group, Israel, we today evoke when we use the word "Judaism." For this quest the data of the Graeco-Roman philosophical vocabulary prove irrelevant. We may simply assume that, in the land of Israel in the first century, C.E. as through much of human history, nearly everywhere, such a religious system, such an "-ism," bearing doctrines about the supernatural, did serve to define culture, frame society, and impart order and meaning to the personal and common life.

Our second negative, yielding a more concrete and positive approach to piety, brings us to those distinctive points of emphasis that separated each group from others. We know not about the people at large but only about sects. I refer to the distinctive groups, separate from the commonality of Israel, about which we do have information. For if we do not know what the people as a whole believed, we have ample access to small groups, e.g., records deriving from the Essenes and Pharisees, and disciples of Jesus, contemporary stories concerning the activities of coherent political and social groups, and other data about distinctive and hardly representative elements of the nation as a whole. Our task in utilizing the data concerning, and even coming from, such special groups is simple. First, we must describe the emphases of small components of the larger social construct. Second, we have to ask how what we know about the particular groups may inform us about what was held in common.

Since we are seeking to describe and interpret modes of piety within the Israel of late antiquity, we seek to imagine from what people said and did, how things appeared to groups of people whom we now know only at a considerable distance. In doing this we have to treat the mixed as pure. To begin with, we have to sort out the different strands of these groups' faith and to characterize each one. The principal strands that are discernible emerge in the distinct types of holy men we know as priests, scribes, and messiahs, and in the definitive activities of cult, school and government offices, and (ordinarily) the battlefield. Ancient Israel's heritage yielded the cult with its priests, the Torah with its scribes and teachers, and the prophetic and apocalyptic hope for meaning in history and an eschaton mediated by messiahs and generals. From these derive the three elements indicated: Temple, school, and (in the apocalyptic expectation) battlefield on earth and in heaven.

IV. Three Ideal-Types of Israelite Piety

In positing these three ideal types of Israelite piety – the priestly, the scribal, the Messianic – we must suspend for the moment our disbelief that things can have ever been so simple. Indeed, we recognize the contrary, their complexity. Let me give one obvious example of the complexity involved in positing ideal types. The troops of a messianic army also observed Scripture's sacred calendar. Their goal was not only to enthrone the King-Messiah, their general, but also to rebuild the Temple, reestablish the priesthood, and restore the sacrificial cult. Moreover that the Messiah's army valued the scribal heritage, is readily apparent in the writings which Bar Kokhba's troops preserved.[4] These include women's carefully wrapped up documents covering divorces and marriage settlements, land titles, and other scribal deeds. The Essene community at Qumran also united the themes we treat as separate: priesthood, Messiah, Torah study. Among the earliest writers in Jewish Christianity, Jesus finds ample representation not only as King-Messiah, but as prophet, perfect priest, and sacrificial victim, and always as sage or rabbi (which is why most of the sublime ethical sayings ascribed to him in fact are commonplaces in other version of Judaism). Accordingly, none of the symbolic systems at hand, with their associated modes of piety, faith, and religious imagination, ever existed pure and unalloyed, ideal types awaiting singular description and interpretation as we treat them here.

As implied above, to seek a typology of the modes of Israelite piety, we must look for the generative symbol of each mode: an altar for the priestly ideal, a scroll of Scripture for the scribal ideal of wisdom, a coin marked "Israel's freedom: year one" for the messianic modality. In each of these visual symbols we perceive things we cannot touch, hearts and minds we can only hope to evoke. We seek to enter into people's imagination, long ago and far away. Our effort is to understand the way in which they framed the world, and encapsulated everything in some one thing: the sheep for the sacrifice, the memorized aphorism for the disciple, the stout heart for the soldier of light. Priest, sage, soldier – each figure stands for the whole of Israel. When all would meld into one, there would emerge a fresh and unprecedented Judaism, whether among the heirs of Scribes and Pharisees or among the disciples of Christ.

The issues of the symbols under discussion – Temple-altar, sacred scroll, victory wreath for the head of the King-Messiah – largely covered Jewish society. We need not reduce them to their merely social dimensions to recognize that in them we deal with the foundations of the organization of Israelite society and its interpretation of its history. Let us rapidly review the social groups envisaged and addressed by the framers of these symbols.

---

[4]See Yigael Yadin, *Bar Kokhba* (New York: Random House, 1971), and Peter Schaefer, "The Causes of the Bar Kokhba Revolt," in *Studies in Aggadah, Targum, and Jewish Liturgy in Memory of Joseph Heinemann* (Jerusalem: 1981), pp. 74-94. Schaefer provides an up-to-date bibliography on the topic, though he makes no original contribution to scholarship, other than through his collection of what various persons have said.

First, the priest viewed society as organized along lines of structure emanating from the Temple. His caste stood at the top of a social scale in which all things were properly organized, each with its correct name and proper place. The inherent sanctity of the people of Israel, through the priest's genealogy, came to its richest embodiment in the high priest. Food set aside for the priests' rations, at God's command, possessed that same sanctity; so, too, did the table at which priests ate their rations. To the priest, for the sacred society of Israel, history was an account of what happened in, and (alas) on occasion to, the Temple.[5]

Secondly, to the sage, the life of society demanded wise regulation. Relationships among people required guidance by the laws enshrined in the Torah and best interpreted by Scribes. The task of Israel was to construct a way of life in accordance with the revealed rules of the Torah. The sage, master of the rules, stood at the head.

Thirdly, as for prophecy's insistence that the fate of the nation depended upon the faith and moral condition of society, history testified both to events outside its borders and to the inner condition of Israel, viewed as a whole. While both sage and priest saw Israel from the aspect of eternity, the nation had to live out its life in this world, among other peoples coveting the very same land, and within the context of Roman imperial policies and politics. The messiah's kingship would resolve the issue of Israel's subordinate relationship to other nations and empires, establishing once and for all the desirable, correct context for priest and sage alike.

Implicit, therefore, in the messianic framework was a perspective on the world beyond Israel for which priest and sage cared not at all. The priest perceived the receding distances of the world beyond the Temple, as at, first, less holy, then, unholy, then, unclean, as at M. Kelim 1:6-9. All lands outside the Land of Israel were unclean with corpse uncleanness; all other peoples were unclean just as corpses were unclean. Accordingly, life abided within Israel, and, in Israel, within the Temple. Outside, in the far distance, were vacant lands and dead peoples, comprising an undifferentiated wilderness of death – a world of uncleanness. From such a perspective on the world, no doctrine about Israel among the nations, no interest in the history of Israel and its meaning, was apt to emerge.

The sagacity of the sage, in general, pertained to the streets, marketplaces, and domestic establishments (the household units) of Israel. What the sage said was wisdom, indeed, as much for gentiles as for Israel. This universal wisdom in the nature of things proved international, moving easily across the boundaries of culture and language, from eastern

---

[5]This viewpoint finds expression in the priestly narratives, e.g., in Leviticus and Chronicles.

to southern to western Asia. It focused, by definition, upon human experience common to all and undifferentiated by nation, essentially unaffected by the large movements of history. Wisdom spoke about fathers and sons, masters and disciples, families and villages, not about nations, armies, and destiny.

Because of their very diversity these three principal modes of Israelite existence might readily cohere. Each focused on a particular aspect of the national life, and none essentially contradicted any other. One could worship at the Temple, study the Torah, and fight in the army of the Messiah – and some did all three. Yet we must see these modes of being, and their consequent forms of piety, as separate, each with its own potentiality of full realization without reference to the others.

The three modes of human existence expressed in the symbolic systems of cult, Torah, and messiah demanded choices. If one thing was more important, then the others must have been less important. Either history matters, or it happens, without significance, "out there." The proper conduct of the cult determines the course of the seasons and the prosperity of the Land, or it is merely ritual. The messiah will save Israel, or he will ruin everything. Accordingly, while we take for granted that people could have lived within the multiple visions of priest, sage, and messiah, we also recognize such a life was vertiginous, inducing a blurred perception. Narratives of the war of 66-73 emphasize that priests warned messianists not to endanger their Temple. Later sages – talmudic rabbis – paid slight regard to the messianic struggle led by Bar Kokhba, and after 70 claimed the right to tell priests what to do.[6]

It must follow that the way in which symbols were arranged and rearranged was crucial. Symbol change is social change. A mere amalgam of all three symbols by itself hardly serves as a mirror for the mind of Israel. The particular way the three were bonded in a given system reflects an underlying human and social reality. That is how it should be, since, as we saw, the three symbols with their associated myths, the world views they projected, and the ways of life they defined, stood for different views of what really matters. In investigating the existential foundations of the several symbolic systems available to Jews in antiquity, we penetrate to the bedrock of Israel's reality, to the basis of the life of the nation and of each Israelite, to the ground of being – even to the existential core that we the living share with them.

---

[6]On the later rabbis' views of Bar Kokhba, note Y. Ta. 4:5 as a representative case. Bar Kokhba was held to have sinned through his arrogance, and, by the way, also to have mistreated and murdered sages. On rabbis' telling priests what to do, see J. Neusner, *Life of Yohanan ben Zakkai* (Leiden: 1970), pp. 196-227.

V. Responses to Time and Eternity

Let us unpack the two foci of existence, public history and private establishment of home and hearth. We may call the first focus "time." Its interest is in events that happen day by day in the here and now of continuing history. The other focus we may call "eternity." Its interest is in the recurrent patterns of life, birth and death, planting and harvest, the regular movement of the sun, moon, stars in heaven, night and day, Sabbaths, festivals and regular seasons on earth. The shared existential issue is this: How do we we respond to the ups and downs of life? Every group that survives experiences the noteworthy events we call "history." The events of the individual life – birth, maturing, marriage, death – do not make history, except for individuals. But the events of group life, the formation of groups, the development of social norms and patterns, depression and prosperity, war and peace – these do make history. When a small people coalesces and begins its course though history in the face of adversity, two things can happen. Either the group may disintegrate in the face of disaster and lose its hold on its individual members, or the group may fuse, being strengthened by trial, and so turn adversity into renewal.

The modes around which human and national existence were interpreted – those of priests, sages, and messianists (including prophets and apocalyptists) – emerge, we must remember, from the national and social consciousness of ancient Israel. The heritage of the written Torah (Tanakh, the Hebrew Scriptures or "Old Testament") was carried forward in all three approaches to Judaism. The Jewish people knew the mystery of how to endure through history. In ancient Israel adversity elicited self-conscious response. Things did not merely happen to Israelites. They shaped, reformulated, and interpreted them, and so treated events as raw material for renewing the life of the group. Israelites regarded their history as important, teaching significant lessons. History was not merely "one damn thing after another." It had a purpose and was moving somewhere. The writers of Leviticus and Deuteronomy, of the historical books from Joshua through Kings, and of the prophetic literature, agreed that, when Israel did God's will, it enjoyed times of peace, security, and prosperity; when it did not, it was punished at the hands of mighty kingdoms raised up as instruments of God's wrath. This conception of the meaning of Israel's life produced another question: How long? When would the great events of time come to their climax and conclusion? And as one answer to that question, there arose the hope for the messiah, the anointed of God, who would redeem the people and set them on the right path forever, thus ending the vicissitudes of history.

Now when we reach the first century A.D., we come to a turning point in the messianic hope. No one who knows the Gospels will be surprised to learn of the intense, vivid, prevailing expectation among some groups that the Messiah was coming soon. And that anticipation is hardly astonishing. People who fix their attention on contemporary events of world-shaking dimensions naturally look to a better future. That represents one context for the messianic myth.

More surprising is the development among the people of Israel of a second, quite different response to history. It is the response of those prepared once and for all to transcend historical events and to take their leave of wars and rumors of wars, of politics and public life. These persons undertook to construct a new reality beyond history, one that focused on the meaning of humdrum everyday life. After 70 there was no mere craven or exhausted passivity in the face of world-shaking events. We witness in particular among the sages after 70 ultimately represented in the Mishnah, the beginnings of an active construction of a new mode of being. Their decision was to exercise freedom uncontrolled by history, to reconstruct the meaning and ultimate significance of events. That is to seek a world not outside this one formed by ordinary history, but a different and better world. This second approach was a quest for eternity in the here and now, an effort to form a society capable of abiding amid change and stress. Indeed, it was a fresh reading of the meaning of history. The nations of the world suppose that they make "history" and think that their actions matter. But these sages in Israel knew that it is God who makes history, and that it is the reality formed in response to God's will that counts as history: God is the King of kings.

This conception of time and change, in fact, formed the focus of the earlier priestly tradition, which was continued later in the Judaism called rabbinic or talmudic. This sort of Judaism offered essentially a meta-historical approach to life. It lived above history and its problems. It expressed an intense inwardness. The Judaism attested in the rabbis' canon of writings emphasized the ultimate meaning contained within small and humble affairs. Rabbinic Judaism came in time to set itself up as the alternative to all forms of messianic Judaism – whether in the form of Christianity or militaristic zealotry and nationalism – which claimed to know the secret of history, the time of salvation and way to redemption. But paradoxically the canonical writings of rabbis also disclosed the answers to these questions. The messiah-myth was absorbed into the rabbis' system and made to strengthen it. The rabbinical canon defined in a new way the uses and purposes of all else that had gone before.[7]

---

[7]That is to say, the established categories, e.g., Torah, Messiah, priest, sacrifice, and the like, all were taken over by the rabbis of the two Talmuds and given new meaning. The study of Torah, for one instance, was held to be equivalent to making a Temple sacrifice; the Messiah was represented as a learned rabbi; the Torah was no longer a single, written Scripture but encompassed all of the

This approach to the life of Israel, stressing continuity and pattern and promising change only at the very end, when all would be in order at the last, represents the union of two trends. The one was symbolized by the altar, the other by the Torah scroll, the priest and the sage. In actual fact, the union was effected by a special kind of priest manqué, and a special kind of sage. The former was the Pharisee, the latter the scribe.

Let me give a clear and simple definition of Pharisaism. The Pharisees were a particular sect of people who pretended, in their homes, that they were priests in the Temple. The scribes, on the other hand, were members not of a sect but of a profession. The scribes knew and taught Torah. They took their interpretation of Torah very seriously, and the act of study for them had special importance. The Pharisees had developed, for their part, a peculiar perception of how to live and interpret life. We may call this an "as if" perception. In very specific ways the Pharisees claimed to live "as if" they were priests, "as if" they had to obey at home the laws that applied to the Temple. When the Temple was destroyed in 70, the Pharisees were prepared for that tremendous event. They continued to live "as if" the Temple stood, and "as if" there were a new Temple composed of the Jewish people. They united hearth with mode of looking at life the substance of the scribal ideal, the stress on learning Torah and carrying out its teachings.

These, then, represent the different ways in which great events were experienced and understood by special groups. One was the historical-messianic way, stressing the intrinsic importance of events and concentrating upon their weight and meaning. The other was the meta-historical, scribal-priestly-rabbinic way, which emphasized Israel's power of transcendence and the construction of an eternal, changeless mode of being in this world, capable of riding out the waves of history.

Once we have identified the principal strands of Judaic consciousness, we must deal with this pressing question. What made one particular focus – the priestly and the sagacious, or the messianic, trend – appear more compelling than the other? The answer becomes obvious when we realize that each kind of piety addressed its distinctive concern, speaking about different things to different people. We may sort out the types of piety from one another if we return to our earlier observations. Priests and sages turned inward, toward the concrete everyday life of the community. They addressed the sanctification of Israel. Messianists and their prophetic and apocalyptic teachers turned outward, toward the

---

writings of sages themselves, beginning with the Mishnah. So while the categories remained fixed, the meaning imputed to them vastly changed. As is clear, the Christians did the same thing, e.g., in Hebrews with the priest, sacrifice, and Temple.

affairs of states and nations. They spoke of the salvation of Israel. Priests saw the world of life in Israel, and death beyond. They knew what happened to Israel without concerning themselves with a theory about the place of Israel among the nations. For priests, the nations formed an undifferentiated realm of death. Sages, all the more, spoke of home and hearth, fathers and sons, husbands and wives, the village and enduring patterns of life. What place was there in this domestic scheme for the realities of history – wars and threats of war, the rise and fall of empires? It rather expressed the consciousness of a singular society amidst other societies. At issue for the priest was "being," for the prophet and Messiah, "becoming."

In the light of these distinctive and partial formulations of a world view and way of life, how shall we gain access to a general picture of the whole? For, as we have emphasized, we realize that what we know comes to us from distinct and special groups, each with its own emphasis, whether embodied in the messiah or the scribe or the priest – or in of them all together. Let me state with appropriate emphasis: To learn about Judaism, in particular the inner piety in the first century Jews, we have to place in perspective what we know, which concerns the special, and then proceed to extrapolate from the known to the unknown, which involves the general.

Specifically, let us ask how what is uncommon and sectarian testifies to what was shared, the common piety of the people in its land. Once more, for a definitive summary of what is known about first-century Judaism on the basis of the distinctive and special evidence in hand, we turn to Morton Smith, who states:

> In sum, then, the discoveries and research of the past twenty-five years have left us with a picture of Palestinian Judaism in the first century far different from that conceived by earlier students of the period. We now see a Judaism which had behind it a long period of thoroughgoing Hellenization – Hellenization modified, but not thrown off, by the revival of nationalism and nationalistic and antiquarian interest in native tradition and classic language (an interest itself typically Hellenistic). As the Greek language had permeated the whole country, so Greek thought, in one way or another, had affected the court and the commons, the Temple and the tavern, the school and the synagogue. If there was any such thing, then, as an "orthodox Judaism," it must have been that which is now almost unknown to us, the religion of the average "people of the land." But the different parts of the country were so different, such gulfs of feeling and practice separated Idumea, Judea, Caesarea, and Galilee, that even on this level there was probably no more agreement between them than between any one of them and a similar area in the Diaspora. And in addition to the local differences, the country swarmed with special sects, each devoted to its own tradition. Some of these, the followings of particular prophets, may have been spontaneous revivals of Israelite religion as simple as anything in Judges. But even what little

we know of these prophets suggests that some of them, at least, taught a complex theology. As for the major philosophic sects – the Pharisees, Sadducees, and Essenes – the largest and ultimately the most influential of them, the Pharisees, numbered only about 6000, had no real hold either on the government or on the masses of the people, and was, as were the others, profoundly Hellenized.

This period of Palestinian Jewish history, then, is the successor to one marked by great receptivity to outside influences. It is itself characterized by original developments of those influences. These developments, by their variety, vigor, and eventual significance, made this small country during this brief period the seedbed of the subsequent religious history of the Western world.

Smith's definitive picture leads us to the critical question. As stated, we must move from the particular to the general, from the evidence cherished by small groups to the larger totality taken for granted in that evidence but not attested in a particular by any of it. In the light of Smith's correct stress on the disagreements and differences characteristic of the country, its sects, and divided people, we have now to address the points they shared in common, we seek the bridges across diverse experiences and practices that characterized distinct regions, social groups, and layers and levels of society, however differentiated, and characterized by special traditions.

VI. "Orthodox" Judaism

Using the word in the loosest sense, we ask, therefore, how we may describe "orthodox" "Judaism." The use of "Judaism" has already been explained. What of "orthodox"? By "orthodox" we here understand simply the commonly practiced way of life, the generally-shared world view, characteristic – as a matter of fact – of the Jewish population in the Land of Israel. If we wish to choose the three critical elements in the common piety of a "religion-people", they should surely include mode of address to God, hence, prayer; mode of revelation from God, hence, the encounter with revelation; and mode of work-a-day expression of what is revealed, hence, those aspects of everyday life that imparted meaning to the whole. In the case of Israel in its land, we wish to know:

1. the prayers people generally said;

2. the revelation they commonly recognized and how they made it their own;

3. the cycle of the natural year and of history and how, at specified points, its turnings uniformly turned people to the divine.

In these three aspects, we gain some access to definitive traits of the world view and way of life and piety of the social group at hand. But how, in the light of what we know about special and particular groups and their Judaisms, do we justify the selection of the specified categories as the valid ones for the description of that piety? If we revert to the three foci of piety designated as distinctive or particular to special groups, represented by priest, sage, and messiah, we may see in the categories at hand a statement in general terms of the emphasis of a singular ideal-type. How so?

1. The address to God in prayer for the generality of Israel corresponds to the special case of the priests' service in the cult.

2. The inquiry into revelation and the hearing of God's message form the counterpart to the scribes' distinctive focus on learning.

3. The quest, in everyday life, for what imparted meaning to history brought Israelites to the Messiah-aspect. For the messiah-theme was one mode by which small groups of people imparted meaning to the historical life of the nation as a whole. So here, in each case, we find the bridge from the particular to the general.

VII. The Definitive Role of Scripture: The Tanakh and the Definition of the Common Faith of Judaism

Clearly, Scripture – Tanakh or the written Torah in Judaism, the Old Testament in Christianity – formed the principal source of information on what can have been held in common among all Israel in its land. Scripture, of course, provided not only what united, but also what divided, the community. Meanings imputed to verses served as indicators of what was defined as special to a group that was otherwise quite undifferentiated within the people as a whole. Each special group read the Scriptures in its own way. So too, the Temple and its cult, the focus of national institutions and politics, united most Israelites into a single community. At the same time, the group's definition of its relationship to the Temple indicated what was special about that small group. For example, imitating the Temple cult, by eating ordinary meals, in accord with the levitical regulations that dictated conduct of priests at the altar and in the holy place, in part defined what was particular about Pharisees and Essenes. Widely held convictions about the character of the people as especially loved by God found general acceptance in a shared view of the sanctified character of the people and the land, as well as of the heightened meaning of what happened to the one and in the other.

So when distinct groups took up positions of their own on questions of history and salvation, on procedures of the cult and sanctification, they stood on a single continuum. They adopted singular and special positions within categories characteristic of the people and shared by them as a whole. In turning to the general categories at hand – prayer, the encounter with revelation, the common way of life followed throughout the year – what do we find as a bridge from sect to nation-religion? We take up precisely those divisions in the classification of the world view and way of life of the nation-religion that differentiated and characterized distinct groups ("sects") about which we indeed are well-informed. That is how we work backward from the known, the special, to the besought, the general. We find that, in the distinctive, in fact we deal with extreme and special statements of what was shared and commonplace. These commonalities then defined the foci of special concern to distinct groups. So we turn to the components of the common piety of first-century Judaism.

VIII. Prayer

The worship of God encompassed sacrifice in the Temple and prayer outside. The Priestly code, Leviticus 1-15, lays out the requirements of the former, as these were defined by the time of Ezra and Nehemiah. The substance of the prayers outside the Temple presents a puzzle, because we do not have direct evidence of how people ordinarily prayed beyond the walls of the holy place. On the basis of the statement, "Simeon Happaqoli arranged the Eighteen Benedictions in their proper order under the authority of Rabban Gamaliel in Jamnia" (Bavli Berakot 28b), the acknowledged expert on the subject, Joseph Heinemann, states:

> We may safely conclude ... that the evolution of the fixed prayers began hundreds of years before the destruction of the Second Temple and reached the period of consolidation and editing ... in the generation following the destruction of the Temple. At that time the details of the principal obligatory prayers and the laws which govern them were fixed.... The basic structures and content of the prayers determined at that time have never since been altered, and to this very day constitute the essential components of the Jewish liturgy.[8]

Sayings attributed to authorities after 70 deal with the formalization of details of practices assumed, to be familiar and defined by that time. The authenticity of these attributions to authorities between 70 and 130 cannot be proved. But secondary opinions on the same matters make their appearance in the names of authorities a generation later, after 135. It

---

[8]Joseph Heinemann, *Prayer in the Period of the Tannaim and the Amoraim* (Jerusalem: 1976), p. 13.

therefore does not appear unreasonable to assume that the first two generations of authorities after 70, and assuredly the latter of the two, did legislate concerning the regularization of well-established practices. The intent of the legislation proves clearer than the final date of its literary formulation. That intent was to establish some sort of common order and practice from among diverse traditions.

If we turn to the particular prayers which people generally used, our evidence derives from the Mishnah, which attained closure only about a century and a quarter after the destruction. Recognizing the uncertainty involved, we note the prayers that the framers of the Mishnah, in the name of earlier authorities, catalogued. In its account of the Temple rites, the authorship of Mishnah-tractate Tamid provides the following:

A.   The superintendent said to them, "Say one blessing."
B.   They [the priests] said a blessing, pronounced the Ten Commandments, the Shema [Hear O Israel (Deut. 6:4-9)], And it shall come to pass if you shall hearken[Deut. 11:13-21], and And the Lord spoke to Moses [Num. 15:37-41].
C.   They said three blessings over the people: "True and sure," "Abodah," and the blessing of priests ["May the Lord bless you and keep you"].

M. Tamid 5:1A-C

There is no reason to doubt the existence of a formal liturgy in the Temple. Quite discrete discourse on the disposition of Temple rites after the destruction in 70, moreover, underlines the probability that prior to 70, a formal liturgy, though in diverse forms, did govern synagogue prayer.

Form-analysis makes possible the identification, within the Mishnah, of a handbook on prayer, handed on probably in written form and deriving from the period before 70. If we turn to the opening statements of a number of paragraphs in Mishnah-tractate Berakhot, we find a set of formalized rules governing the recitation of prayers required, in the Mishnah's authors' conception, of all Israelites, and not only of priests or of those sages who formulated the law. The tractate opens with the following:

A.   From what time do they read (qorin) the Shema in the evening? From the time that the priests go in to eat their Heave-offering.

M. Ber. 1:1A

Then follows the time at which one no longer may read the Shema:

B.   "Until the end of the first watch" – the word of R. Eliezer.
C.   Sages say, "Until midnight."
D.   Rabban Gamaliel says, "Until the morning star rises."

M. Ber. 1:1B-D

The three sayings in M. Ber 1:1.B-D have been formulated in the same way, *ad* (until) plus the specified time. They take for granted that the time from which the Shema may be recited requires no comment. That language is singularly inappropriate to ordinary folk. How so? Not everyone was a priest waiting the permissible time for eating Heave-offering. Most were not. The language of the opening clause is important, because it establishes as a pattern the use of the present participle in the plural: qorin in M. Ber 1:1A. This usage provides a key to how later passages continue the opening one, as we shall now see.

M. Berakhot 1:2 proceeds in the same formula, "From what time do they read the Shema in the morning?" Eliezer provides an answer different from that given anonymously. Then follows, "And he completes it before sunrise." Joshua gives a different opinion, which is glossed. M. Berakhot 1:3 now introduces a completed Houses-pericope, and M. Berakhot 1:4 tells us about the blessings said before and after reciting the Shema, with allusions to various customs.

The present participle in the plural next occurs in M. Berakhot 1:5, "They make mention of the going forth from Egypt at night." This then is glossed by a saying of Eleazar b. Azariah. So the whole of M. Berakhot Chapter One, when attributed at all, is assigned to early figures, just beyond A.D. 70, and the attested passages all use the same verbal construction.

The next available passage following the earlier participial construction, tells us that women, slaves, and children are free of the obligation of saying the Shema and putting on phylacteries (Tefillin), but they are liable to say The Prayer. That is to say, they are required to recite the Eighteen Benedictions of The Prayer, just now reviewed by us, but they are not required to put on phylacteries and to recite the Shema. This is unattested. (M. Ber. 3:4, 5, and 6 deal with unclean people in connection with the Shema. Chapter Four does not contain the important participial construction.) This brings us to M. Ber. 5:1, "They do not stand to say The Prayer (the Eighteen Benedictions) except reverentially ... They make mention of the Power of Rains in the [prayer for] the resurrection of the dead and ask for rains in the blessing of the years [this is the ninth benediction] and Havdalah [at the end of the Sabbath, marking the division of holy and ordinary time] in 'Who graciously grants knowledge.'" This is attested by Aqiba and Eliezer, who hold different opinions. M. Ber. 5:3-5 deal with other matters and do not use the present participle in the plural, which next occurs in M. Ber. 6:1: "How do they bless fruit?" This is answered with 'omer, "one blesses," and is attested by Judah b. Ilai. M. Ber. 7:2 has, "Women, slaves and children are not invited to participate in the Blessing of food after meals." Then M. Ber. 7:3, "How do they invite to participate in the blessing of food after meals?" This is answered, at some length, by Aqiba, Ishmael, and Yosé the Galilean. Chapter Eight deals with the purity rules of the Houses of Hillel and Shammai and how they affect meals. Only one is relevant to a catalogue of participial constructions. M. Ber. 8:6 reads, "They do not bless the light, spices of gentiles, nor the light or spices prepared for the dead." Chapter Nine is not relevant, for it does not exhibit the specified response verbal construction.

What is the upshot? Placed side by side, the passages which use the present participle in the plural, produce the following little enchiridion:

I. *The Shema*

1. Reciting the Shema, evening and morning.

2. Referring to the Exodus in the evening Shema.

3. Women, slaves, and children are not obligated to recite the Shema (etc.).

II. *The Prayer*

4. When they say the Prayer, they must do so with reverence.

5. They include Powers of Rain in the paragraph of the Prayer dealing with Resurrection, rains in the Blessing of the Years, and Habdalah in "Who graciously favors man with knowledge."

III. *Saying Blessings*

6. How do they say a blessing over fruit? [This shifts to "he says" [singular participle] and is attested only by Judah b. Ilai. The rest of the chapter ignores the present plural participle form, even where it might be used, e.g., 6:6.]

7. How do they invite [people] to say the Blessing of Food?

8. They bless the light and spices not of gentiles or of the dead etc. [in connection with Habdalah].

The foundations of tractate Berakhot as suggested by the specified verbal form, that is, the present participle in the plural, deals with the most fundamental matters of prayer: (1) the Shema, (2) The Prayer, (3) saying blessings over food and other substances of enjoyment and particularly the Grace after meals.

We cannot now know what other items were included in the list. But that we have, in the passages indicated, an enchiridion for the liturgical life seems likely. We deal with the three things people evidently were expected to know: Shema, The Prayer, and Grace after Meals. We have already observed that the more important items in the handbook, when attested at all, are attested by the earliest strata of authorities after A.D. 70. It would carry us too far afield to show how this list has been broken up and augmented, glossed, filled with interpolations, and otherwise expanded by later generations, beginning with the authorities who in the first place witness to its original elements. But that the Mishnah-tractate Berakhot starts here seems beyond serious question. The substance as well as the form of the later strata build upon foundational items that we have isolated. We do not know, was responsible for the original handbook (if that is what it was), why it was formulated in so consistent a way as seems (if our hypothesis is sound) to have been the case, or when it was originally composed. But it is very likely that it was composed before A.D. 70-80, that is, the time of Eliezer and Gamaliel, and this leads us to a period before A.D. 70, as Heinemann has persuasively maintained.

What of the the piety expressed generated in and by the recitation of the prayers at hand? We turn again to Heinemann:

> If each individual is required to pray daily at fixed times and in a set fashion, his prayer must in time become more than a mere device for giving expression to personal emotions and thoughts. It becomes, over and above this, a means for actually stimulating and arousing such emotions and thoughts. It is doubtful whether the average man, absorbed as he is in the monotonous routine of daily life, would ever turn his thoughts spontaneously to God, except perhaps in times of extreme joy or distress. It is, then, the aim of fixed prayer to provide man with a stimulus to turn his thoughts to God; to remove the individual from the realm of the mundane and the routine, and to elevate his thoughts and feelings to the level of the Divine and the Absolute. This objective of self-education is manifest not only in the obligation to say the Eighteen Benedictions three times daily, but even more explicitly in the manifold benedictions which the Sages instituted for the individual to recite during the performance of his everyday functions, and which permeate his daily routine. A man is obliged to recite a benediction upon beholding any overwhelming or fearsome aspect of nature; before and after enjoying food or drink; on particularly joyous occasions. The benediction which is to be recited before eating, for example, is certainly intended to lift that mundane daily activity from its biological level of significance, and to transform it into an act of divine worship. The benediction to be recited upon performing a ritual commandment is likewise geared to deepen the devotion and concentration of the individual, and to prevent him from performing the commandment mechanically. If the Sages saw fit to multiply the number of benedictions to the point where they said: "A man is obliged to recite one hundred benedictions each day" (B. Menahot 43b), their pedagogical intent would seem to be obvious: the benediction aims to sanctify man's daily activities by constantly infusing their performance with a sense of holiness and with the consciousness of the Divine Presence.[9]

---

[9]Heinemann, op. cit., pp. 17-18.

Heinemann is fully justified in turning to the act and substance of the liturgy in the description of the religious life of Judaism in the period at hand.

We come to the description of the other two foci of piety. The second focus is the study of the Torah which, in general, reached the people at large and, in particular, formed the point of scribal emphasis. The third focus of piety, the Temple and concerned services the meaning of the life of the people as a whole, in natural and historical terms. The quest in the Temple for the significance of the collective life of Israel constituted a common concern. This also found particular expression in the messianic movements of the day. These two matters require less detailed exposition than did the liturgical life.

IX. The Reading of the Scriptures

The piety of Israel in the Land of Israel encompassed not only prayer but the public recitation and exposition of the Scriptures. Scholars concur that, by the first century, people observed the rite of the reading of the Torah, that is the Pentateuch, as well as of prophetic lections in the synagogue. No one now can identify with certainty the lections in the prophets that accompanied various passages in the Pentateuch, nor do we know how long it took for the recitation of the whole Pentateuch, whether one year or three years. We do not know who took charge of the public reading of Scripture. Scribes, required in the preparation of governmental and other legal documents, and teachers of the law, cannot have found positions in every synagogue. We cannot know who would have taken their place and role in places where well-educated scribes did not exist.

On the work of the scribes in relationship to the life of the country we are better informed. On this matter, Schuerer-Vermes-Millar state (p. 330):

> In regard to the theoretical formation of the law itself, its basic principles were of course thought to be fixed, implicitly or explicitly, in the written Torah. But no legal code is so detailed that it requires no further interpretation. In any case, the directions provided by the law of Moses are in part very general. There was, therefore, wide scope for the work of the Torah scholars. They had to develop, with the help of careful casuistry, the general precepts given in the Torah in such a way as to guarantee that their bias was really understood in accordance with the precepts' full significance and extent. Where the written Torah advances no direct ruling, this had to be made good, either by determining the common law, or by reasoning from other legal regulations already valid. Owing to the assiduity with which this whole operation was carried on in the last centuries B.C., biblical law gradually became a complex and intricate branch of knowledge. And as this law was not fixed in writing but was mainly handed down by word of mouth, continuous study was

necessary even to become familiar with it. But knowledge of legal obligations was never more than the basis and prerequisite of the Torah scholar's professional activity. Their real business was to go on developing what was already lawful by continuous methodical work, in ever finer casuistical detail.

It is difficult to see how these special scribal interests bore much relationship to the general piety of the community. But the symbolism of the Torah, joined to the concrete lessons learned from it, assuredly did speak to everyone, not only specialists.

The interpretation of the contemporary meaning and requirements of the Torah and of the prophets not only occupies a principal place in accounts of such special groups as the disciples of Jesus and the Essenes. But it also formed the background of public life in a world that constantly and ubiquitously invoked the authority of the Torah as validation for the policies and practices of everyday life. The contribution of the Torah to the common piety derived, in the end, from the conviction that "God revealed Torah to Moses at Sinai" (M. Abot 1:1f). That meant that, when people acted rightly and in conformity to the Torah, they carried out the requirements of the covenant that Israel had made with God. Life under the Torah was a life of sanctification in the here and now and salvation in the age to come, because all life found meaning under the aspect of the covenant.

Clearly, the conception that the national life found definition in Scripture rests on the premise that education, formal and informal, constituted a broad opportunity for the population at large. Certainly people learned Scriptures, which formed the center of synagogue worship and defined the nation's sense of itself in the world. We have slight evidence deriving from the period under discussion on the basis of which to describe an institution so formal as a school-system. We cannot say what, beyond Scripture and aspects of piety such as formal prayer, people would have learned in such schools. The absence of concrete information on schooling, however, should not obscure the fact that the population at large, in every available account, is represented as informed about the Scripture and traditions of the nation. It must follow that these literary works found their way, through some institutional means, into the lives of the people. It is hardly far-fetched to call "a school-system" whatever media brought learning to the people at large. But beyond that simple surmise, nothing can presently be said.

Certainly one mode of popular education lay in the translation of Scripture into the vernacular, which was Aramaic in the countryside and Greek and Aramaic in the towns, such as Jerusalem. The Scriptures, read in Aramaic, gained access to the people that public recitation in a language no one spoke would have denied them. We do not now have the

Aramaic translations, or targumim, exactly as these would have been read in the synagogue in the first century. Nonetheless, successful, if limited, efforts at recovering the contents of such translations have produced solid results. Bruce Chilton's account of the version of Isaiah, in Aramaic, that underlies certain sayings ascribed to Jesus, for example, makes it clear that, with future progress, we may hope to gain a clearer picture than we now have of exactly how Scripture reached first-century Israelite synagogues.

To state matters simply, the life of Israel in its land in the first century found structure and meaning in the covenant between God and Israel as contained in the Torah revealed by God to Moses at Mount Sinai. The piety of Israel, defined by the Torah, in concrete ways served to carry out the requirements of the covenant. This holy life under the Torah has been properly called "covenantal nomism," a phrase introduced by E.P. Sanders to state in two words the complete and encompassing holy way of life and world view of Israel in its land in the first century.[10] Life under the Torah was so lived as to fulfill Israel's covenant with God, so one must state as the gist of Israel's piety in the first century (and not then alone).

X. The Temple and Pilgrimages

The third aspect of the piety of Israel in its Land entailed pilgrimages to the Temple on festivals in celebration of nature and in commemoration of historical events. Specifically, the encounter with God and the yearning for salvation at the end of time came to a climax in the coincidence of those turnings in the natural year, spring and fall, identified at the natural year's beginning and end, and explained in all forms of Judaism, as celebrations of great events in the life of historical Israel. At these intense moments of heightened reality during the natural year, Scripture required a pilgrimage to the Temple. Accordingly, in theory at least, "all Israel," or as many as could make it, assembled in the holy place, the Temple in Jerusalem. They then together celebrated the passage of the natural year, on the one hand, and the past and future of the people, on the other.

In the dimension of the future, of course, messianic hopes were associated with the pilgrim festivals, both Tabernacles and Passover, in particular. The pilgrim festivals, joined not only in sectarian doctrine to the moment at which the Messiah would come (as did Christ at Passover, and, as, in the sages' later writings, would the Messiah at Tabernacles), drew the nation to the Temple in Jerusalem. These festivals found their first definition in Scripture. Passover came in the spring. Tabernacles came in the fall. The festal season inaugurated at Passover, on the 15th of

---

[10]Cited in the next note.

Nisan (corresponding to April). That marks the first full moon after the vernal equinox. The festival continued through seven days, with a further festival coming fifty days after the beginning of the first on the 15th of Nisan. This second festival was Pentecost, in Hebrew, Shabuot.

The corresponding high point of the year in the autumn, Tabernacles, Sukkot, came to its climax on the first full moon after the autumnal equinox. It was on the 15th of Tishré, that is, the first full moon after September 21. However, the holy season began two weeks earlier, on the eve of the first of Tishré, and ended a week later, on the 21st of Tishré. The opening of the holy season of autumn, the 1st of Tishré, with the celebration of the New Year, then the Day of Atonement on the 10th of Tishré, marked (as is still the case) a penitential season of repentance, fasting, and charity.

Both pilgrim-festivals thus celebrated in particular the sun's movement around the earth relative to that of the moon (and so the seasons of the land). Especially important were dramatic shifts in the pattern of the rains in the Holy Land itself. The fall festival marked the beginning of the autumnal and winter rains, on which the life of the Land depended. The spring festival marked the end of the same rainy season. Scripture identified the Passover with the liberation of Israel from Egypt and the beginning of the life of the people. As indicated, the autumnal season focused upon the moral condition of individuals and of the people as a whole. In the pilgrim-festivals the affairs of the individual, the people, the natural and supernatural world, all reached a climax in a massive and impressive celebration in the cult.

The Temple, therefore, marked the point of the convergence of lines of historical, social, and political order and God as ruler on earth, corresponding to the rules of nature and of God as creator in heaven. Assembling within its walls, the priesthood, Levites, and Israelites, men, women, and children, as well as lower castes, embodied in one place and at one time the people as a whole. Symbolizing the social order, honoring the political structure, celebrating the regularity of nature, the people, corporate Israel drawn together as pilgrims, offered up to God what the Torah defined as appropriate service, in the smoke of burning meat and grain and the other offerings. Looking backward, the pilgrim-people, the assembly of Israel before God, celebrated its very formation in the exodus from Egypt. Looking forward, the nation prayed for the prosperity brought by rain in the autumnal season and for safe passage through the dry season to come. Clearly, in its pilgrim festivals, the people corporately brought to expression a piety encompassing all reality. In the pilgrim rites in the Temple, Israel corporately fulfilled what, as noted, Sanders properly calls "covenantal nomism."[11] But obedience to the covenant also expressed itself in fulfillment of the law, which promised sanctification in nature, salvation in history, and piety also reached expression in individual prayer and synagogue study of Torah.

XI. From Phenomenology to History of Judaism

Let me conclude this portrait of the beginning of Judaism by answering some narrowly historical questions. When, exactly, did the Judaism that became normative originate? What particular groups made their contribution to this Judaism? Above all, under what circumstances was the union of established elements in a striking new way accomplished? The Judaism under discussion, called "rabbinic" because of the title accorded to its principal hero, the rabbi or sage, is the creation of the meeting of Pharisee and scribe before the destruction of the Second Temple of Jerusalem in the year 70. It flows out of Pharisaism, a particular sect in the Judaism of ancient Palestine, as I shall explain. It is shaped by the convictions of the scribes, the professional class of teachers of Torah, petty officials and bureaucrats of that same period. The scribes knew and taught Torah. They took their interpretation of Torah very seriously, it goes without saying, and the act of study to them was of special importance.

The Pharisees had developed a peculiar perception of how to live and interpret life. The Pharisees claimed to live as if they were priests, as if they had to obey the laws that applied to the Temple. When the Temple itself was destroyed, it turned out that the Pharisees had prepared for that tremendous change in the sacred economy. Earlier, when the Temple stood, Pharisees had maintained that ordinary people, not priests, should eat everyday food, not shares of the Temple offerings, as if they were governed by the levitical rules applying to Temple priests eating holy things. So in Temple times the Pharisees were lay people pretending to be priests. Now they maintained that same pretense, only with much better reason. That is, they held that the holiness of the life of Israel, formerly centered on the Temple, endured and transcended the physical destruction of the building and the cessation of sacrifices. They therefore continued to live as if. They acted as if the Temple stood, as if there was a new Temple formed of the Jewish people. Joined to their mode of looking at life was the substance of the scribal ideal, the stress on learning of Torah and carrying out its teachings.

---

[11]E.P. Sanders, *Paul and Palestinian Judaism. A Comparison of Patterns of Religion* (Philadelphia: Fortress Press, 1977).

What brought the two components together – the one, the Pharisaic mode of experiencing everyday life; the other, the Scribal way of interpreting it through Tanakh? It was the impact of the destruction of the Temple itself.

In 66 A.D. a Jewish rebellion in the Land of Israel against Rome's rule of the country broke out in Jerusalem. Initially successful, the rebels in the end were pushed back into the holy city, which fell in August, 70. The Temple, destroyed in 586 B.C. and rebuilt three generations later, by the time of its second destruction had stood for five hundred years. In it the commandments of God to Moses concerning sacrifice reached fulfillment. With its destruction the foundations of Israel's national and social life in the Land of Israel were shaken. The Temple had constituted one of the primary, unifying elements in that common life. The structure not only of political life and of society, but also of the imaginative life of the country, depended upon the Temple and its worship and cult. It was there that people believed they served God. At the Temple the lines of structure – both cosmic and social – had converged. The Temple, moreover, had served as the basis for those many elements of autonomous self-government and political life left in the Jews' hands by the Romans. Consequently, the destruction of the Temple meant not merely a significant alteration in the cultic or ritual life of the Jewish people, but also a profound and far-reaching crisis in their inner and spiritual existence.

A viable cultural-religious existence was reconstructed during the next half-century. What exactly happened? Between ca. 70 and ca. 120 a number of elements of the religious-cultural structure of the period before 70 were put together into a new synthesis. This synthesis, ultimately joining scribal, priestly, and messianic points of emphasis, would come to expression in the writings of the rabbis of the first seven centuries A.D. We now know it as Judaism. We should call that synthesis by its own name, "the Torah." In more descriptive language, we may call it by the name of its ideal-type, the rabbi, hence Rabbinic Judaism.

In response to the disaster of the destruction Rabbinic Judaism took shape, and its success was in its capacity to claim things had not changed at all – hence the assertion that even at the start, Moses was "our rabbi." But the very destruction of the Temple itself served as the verification and vindication of the new structure. How so? Rabbinic Judaism claimed, like the scribes of old, that it was possible to serve God not only through sacrifice, but also through study of Torah. A priest is in charge of the life of the community, just as the priests had said. But now it was a new priest, the rabbi. The old sin-offerings still may be carried out. But today it would be the sacrifice of deeds of loving-kindness. In former times people revered the Temple. Now, if and when the whole Jewish people will fully carry out the teachings of the Torah, the Temple itself will be rebuilt. Like the prophets and historians in the time of the first destruction, in 586 B.C.E., the rabbis further claimed that it was because the people had sinned, had not kept the Torah, that the Temple had been destroyed. So the disaster itself was made to vindicate the rabbinic teaching and to verify its truth. When the people lived up to the teachings of the Torah as the rabbis expressed them, the Temple would be restored in response to the people's repentence and renewal.

Two primary components in the synthesis then are to be discerned: first, the emphases of Pharisaism, and second, the values of the scribal profession. How so? Pharisaism lay stress upon universal keeping of the law, obligating every Jew to do what only the elite – the priests – were normally expected to accomplish. The professional ideal of the scribes stressed the study of Torah and the centrality of the learned person in the religious system. The unpredictable, final element in the synthesis of Pharisaic stress on widespread law, including ritual-law, observance and scribal emphasis on learning, is what makes Rabbinic Judaism distinctive. That is the conviction that the community now stands in the place of the Temple. The ruins of the cult did not mark the end of the collective, holy life of Israel. What survived was the holy people. It was the genius of Rabbinic Judaism to recognize that the holy people might reconstitute the Temple in the sanctity of its own community life. Therefore the people had to be made holy, as the Temple had been holy. The people's social life had to be sanctified as the surrogate for what had been lost. That is why the rabbinic ideal further maintained that the rabbi served as the new priest, the study of Torah substituted for the Temple sacrifice, and deeds of loving-kindness were the social surrogate for the sin-offering – personal sacrifice instead of animal sacrifice. All things fit together to construct out of the old Judaisms the world view and way of life of the new and enduring Judaism of the Torah.

XII. Conclusion

All the radical claims of holiness-sects, such as Pharisees and Essenes, of professions such as the scribes, and of followers of messiahs, each in its particular manner, gave expression to an aspect or emphasis of the common piety of the nation. Priest, scribe, messiah – all stood upon the same continuum of faith and culture with the rest of Israel, the Jewish people. Each expressed in a particular and intense way a mode of piety all in common understood and shared. That is why we can move from the particular to the general in our description of the common faith of Israel in the first century in its land. That that common faith also distinguished Israel from all other peoples of the age, whatever the measure of "hellenization" of the country's life, hardly requires argument. There was no "common theology of the ancient Near East," so far as Israel was concerned, not then, not before, and not afterward.

No wonder then that the two new modes of the definition of Judaic piety to emerge from the period before 70 and to thrive long after that date, the Judaism framed by sages from before the first to the seventh century, and Christianity, both redefined the inherited categories while remaining true to emphases of these same categories. What happened was that the established classifications – priest, scribe, and messiah – were taken over and infused with new meaning, so that, while in categories nothing changed, in substance nothing remained what it had been. That is why both Christian and Judaic thinkers reread the received Scriptures – "the Old Testament" to the one, "the written Torah" to the other – and produced, respectively, "the New Testament" and "the Oral Torah." The common piety of the people Israel in its land defined the program of religious life for the Judaism and the Christianity to emerge beyond the caesura of the destruction of the Temple. The bridge to Sinai – worship, revelation, national and social eschatology – was open in both directions.

Thus Christ as perfect sacrifice, teacher, prophet, and King-Messiah, in the mind of the Church brought together but radically recast the three foci of what had been the common piety of Israel in Temple times. Still later on, the figure of the Talmudic sage would encompass but redefine all three categories as well. How so? After 70, study of Torah and obedience to it came to be a substitute, for the time being, for the Temple and its sacrifice. The government of the sages in accord with "the one whole Torah of Moses, our rabbi," revealed by God at Sinai, carried forward the scribes' conception of Israel's proper government. The Messiah would come when all Israel, through mastery of the Torah and obedience to it, had formed that holy community which, to begin with, the Torah prescribed in the model of Heaven revealed to Moses at Sinai. Jesus as perfect priest, rabbi, Messiah, was a protean figure. The talmudic rabbi as Torah incarnate, priest manqué, and, in the model of (Rabbi) David, progenitor and paradigm of the messiah, was also such. In both cases we find an unprecedented rereading of established symbols in new and striking ways.

The history of the piety of Judaism therefore is the story of successive rearrangements and revisioning of symbols. From ancient Israelite times onward, there would be no classification beyond the three established taxa. But no category in content would long be left intact. When Jesus asked people who they thought he was, the enigmatic answer proved less interesting than the question posed. For the task he set himself was to reframe everything people knew in the encounter with what they did not know: a taxonomic enterprise. When the rabbis of late antiquity rewrote in their own image and likeness the entire Scripture and history of Israel,

dropping whole eras as though they had never been, ignoring vast bodies
of old Jewish writing, inventing whole new books for the canon of Judaism,
they did the same thing. They reworked what they had received in light of
what they proposed to give. No mode of piety could be left untouched,
for all proved promising. But, in Judaism from the first century to the
seventh, every mode of piety would be refashioned in the light of the vast
public events represented by the religious revolutionaries at hand, rabbi-
clerk, rabbi-priest, rabbi-messiah. Accordingly, the piety of Israel in the
first century ultimately defined the structure of the two great religions of
Western civilization: Christianity, through its Messiah, for the gentile,
Judaism, through its definition in the two Torahs of Sinai and in its
embodiment in the figure of the sage, for Israel.

Chapter Eleven

The Second Century:
the Mishnaic Stage in the Formation of Judaism

I. "Jewish Law" or Laws of Jews?

Apart from the scriptural law codes, in antiquity no single system of law governed all Jews everywhere. So we cannot describe "Jewish law" as one encompassing system. The Scripture's several codes of course made their impact on the diverse systems of law that governed various groups of Jews, or Jewish communities in various places. But that impact never proved uniform. In consequence, in no way may we speak of "Jewish law," meaning a single legal code or even a common set of encompassing rules everywhere held authoritative by Jewry. The relationship between the legal system of one distinct group of Jews to that governing some other proves various.[1]

Certain practices to be sure characterized all. But these too do not validate the premise that such a thing as "Jewish law" operated, even in the points in common, pretty much everywhere. The fact that Jews ordinarily observed certain taboos, e.g., concerning the Sabbath day and forbidden foods, hardly changes the picture. On the basis of the prohibition of pork and the observance of a common calendar one can hardly describe a common law of Jewry, hence "Jewish law." Such evidence as we have of diverse Jews' laws points in the opposite direction. What these sets of laws shared in common in part derives from the Scripture all revered. What turns up in a number of contexts in further measure proves so general or so fragmentary as to yield no trace of a single, systematic, and comprehensive law common among Jews. An example of the latter – something too general to make much difference – is

---

[1]For the contrary view cf. Lawrence H. Schiffman, *Sectarian Law in the Dead Sea Scrolls. Courts, Testimony, and the Penal Code* (Chico: Scholars Press for Brown Judaic Studies, 1983), p. 3: "This system [referring to Judaism and its law] composed of interlocking and re-interlocking parts possessed of an organic connection one to another, is never really divisible." Schiffman does not demonstrate that claim.

the marriage-contract. It is a fact that marriage-contracts occur in the Jewish community records of Elephantine, in the fragments found from the time of Bar Kokhba, and in the setting of Mishnaic law. But in detail the contracts that have been found scarcely intersect.[2] The Mishnah's rules governing the scribal preparation of such contracts hardly dictated to the authorities of fifth century B.C. Elephantine[3] or second century C.E. Palestine how to do their work. So it is misleading to speak of "the halakhah," meaning a single system of law operative among all Jews.[4] It is still more confusing to treat as fragments of a single legal system all of the bits and pieces of information deriving from various and sundry communities, scattered throughout the territories of the Near and Middle East, and dated over a span of hundreds of years.

When, therefore, we wish to investigate the history of halakhah or Jewish law, in point of fact we must follow the course of distinct bodies of sources. Each of these several systems of law applying to diverse Jewish groups or communities emerges from its distinct historical setting, addresses its own social entity, and tells us, usually only in bits and pieces of detailed information, about itself alone. Whether whole or fragmentary, systems of Jewish law do not coalesce into one ideal system. That is why we may indeed propose to describe any of several legal systems governing one or more groups of Jews. It is possible to trace development of systems of halakhah characteristic of communities of Jews. To begin with, however, an account of the development of such systems will compare wholes, that is, one system to another system.

True, one might seek the lowest common denominator among all of the systems of law followed by Jewish groups. That then would be deemed "the halakhah," or "Jewish law." But details shared among a variety of Judaisms make sense only in their respective contexts. Each on its own matters in the system in which it makes its appearance and plays its role. So if we wish to consider the development of "the halakhah," we have first to decide whose halakhah, among a variety of candidates, we propose to describe and to analyze. Among a range of choices subject to documentation a choice is to be made. Systematic studies of the halakhah of the Jews in Alexandria,[5] the Jews in Elephantine, the Jews in the Essene

---

[2]Cf. R. Yaron, *The Law of the Aramaic Papyri.* Oxford: 961.

[3]In addition to Yaron, cf. B. Porten, *Archives from Elephantine. The Life of an Ancient Jewish Military Colony.* Berkeley and Los Angeles: Y. Muffs, 1968. *Studies in the Aramaic Legal Papyri from Elephantine.* Leiden, 1969.

[4]Compare the view of E.E. Urbach, *The Law. Its Sources and Development.* Jerusalem: 1984. (In Hebrew.)

[5]Erwin R. Goodenough, *The Jurisprudence of the Jewish Courts in Egypt. Legal Administration by the Jews under the Early Roman Empire as Described by Philo Judaeus.* New Haven: 1929.

community of Qumran,[6] and, of course, the Jews who stand behind the law now presented in the Mishnah and its successor documents,[7] all present appropriate foci of inquiry. Among these and other systems of law produced by Jews, the one of greatest importance is that first written down in the Mishnah, ca. 200 C.E.

II. The Mishnah's Halakhah and its Importance

The Mishnah is an encompassing law code brought to closure in ca. 200 C.E. under the sponsorship of Judah the Patriarch, ethnic ruler of the Jewish communities of the Land of Israel ("Palestine"). Laid forth in six divisions, the laws of the Mishnah take up the sanctity of the land and its use in accord with God's law ("Seeds" or agriculture), the differentiation and passage of sacred time and its impact upon the cult and the village ("Appointed Times"), the sacred aspects of the relationship between woman and man ("Women" or family law), civil law ("Damages"), the conduct of the cult in appropriate regularity and order ("Holy Things"), and the protection of food prepared under the rules of cultic taboos from contamination ("Purities"). The laws of the document throughout lay stress upon the sanctification of Israel's life in the natural world through conformity to the rules governing by the supernatural world. So the Mishnah's halakhah presents a very particular construction, one proposing to form Israel into a holy community in accord with God's holy law, revealed in the Torah given to Moses at Mount Sinai.

What makes the Mishnah important after its own time in the history of Judaism is a simple fact. The exegesis of the Mishnah became the center, after Scripture, of the articulation of Judaism in law and theology. In the next three hundred years, parts of its system, vastly articulated and reworked, would form the jurisprudential and theological foundations of the practical law, administration, world view, and way of life of Israel's inner affairs, both in the holy land and in the diaspora. Accordingly, the Mishnah contributed some of its tractates to what became the normative Jewish law and theology. That was in the very exact sense that nearly all Jews everywhere, for a long time, would live under a single law code and theological system.

Specifically, once the Mishnah had reached closure, four documents would take up the task of apologia and articulation. The first, tractate Abot, ca. 250, a generation or two beyond the Mishnah, explained the origin and authority of the Mishnah by attributing to its sages positions in the chain of tradition extending from Mount Sinai onward. When, as the

---

[6]Lawrence H. Schiffman, *The Halakhah at Qumran*. Leiden, 1975; idem., *Sectarian Law*. Joseph M. Baumgarten, *Studies in Qumran Law*. Leiden: 1977.

[7]J. Neusner, *Judaism: The Evidence of the Mishnah*. Chicago: 1981.

text states, "Moses received Torah at Sinai" (Abot 1:1), he thus stood at the head of a chain of sages, which ended among the just-deceased authorities of the Mishnah itself. So the new code, in its first and principal apologia, found its place in the setting of the revealed Torah of Moses. The second, third, and fourth dealt with the details of the concrete laws.

The second was the Tosefta, a composite of supplements to the Mishnah's rules, covering nearly the whole of the Mishnah's rules, item by item. That document is generally supposed to have reached closure in the later third or earlier fourth centuries, ca. 300-400.

The third, the Talmud of the Land of Israel, took up thirty-nine of the Mishnah's sixty-two tractates (omitting Abot from the count) and supplied them with paragraph-by-paragraph exegeses. The framers of these exegetical exercises contributed amplifications in one of three classifications. They, first, took up and explained phrases and sentences of the Mishnah-paragraph at hand. They, second, brought the Tosefta's supplementary formulations to bear and compared and contrasted them to those of the Mishnah. They, third, composed large-scale theoretical inquiries into the principles of the law, so joining one rule of the Mishnah to several others in a search for the deeper line of order and structure of the law as a whole.

The fourth of the four, the Talmud of Babylonia, ca. 600, contributed the same exegetical exercises to parts of the Mishnah, thirty-seven tractates in all (but not all of the same ones of interest to the compositors of the Talmud of the Land of Israel). While treating the fifth division, on Holy Things, the redactors extensively dealt with the three most practical parts of the Mishnah, the second, third, and fourth divisions, and so they created a complete and encompassing legal system, superimposed on the one of the Mishnah, dealing with everyday religious life, affairs of the individual and the family, and all aspects of civil law.

In one way the authors of the Talmud of Babylonia moved beyond the pattern established by those of the Talmud of the Land of Israel. For the purposes of large-scale organization of discourse, they made use not only of the Mishnah but also of Scripture. The authors of the Talmud of the Land of Israel had relied for order and sequence mainly upon the Mishnah's structure. Those of the other, later Talmud referred also to passages of Scripture. These they would subject to systematic exegesis along exactly those lines that guided their reading of the Mishnah. So the Talmud of Babylonia joined together extensive explanations of the Mishnah's paragraphs with sizable and quite orderly explanations of verses of Scripture. Since the sages by that time regarded the Mishnah as the Oral, or memorized, Torah, and Scripture as the Written Torah, we may define the intent of the framers of the Talmud of Babylonia. It was to join important components of the Torah that had come from Sinai in two media, writing and memorization. So the framers presented as one, whole and complete Torah this final and encompassing system of law and theology. The importance of the Mishnah in the history of Judaism derives from its position alongside Scripture as one of the two principal structures of organization and legal principles upon which the Talmud of Babylonia created its structure of Jewish law.

III. The Antiquity of the Mishnah's Halakhah

If we turn to the complementary question of why, looking backward from the Mishnah, the Mishnah constitutes the most important composition in Jewish law up to its own time, a simple answer suggests itself. The fact is that much of the law of the Mishnah derives from the age before its final closure. In the Mishnah we see how a group of jurisprudents drew together a rich heritage of legal and moral traditions and facts and made of them a single system. From Scripture onward, no other composition compares in size, comprehensive treatment of a vast variety of topics, balance, proportion, and cogency. Let us rapidly review the various types of evidence for the antiquity of numerous facts utilized by the Mishnah's framers in the construction of their system.

Some legal facts in the Mishnah, as in other law codes of its place and age, derive from remote antiquity. Categories of law and investment, for instance, prove continuous with Akkadian and even Sumerian ones. To cite a single instance, there are the sorts of investment classified as nikhse *melug* or *nikhse son barzel* (M. Yebamot 7:1-2), investments in which the investor shares in the loss or the profit, on the one side, or in which the investor is guaranteed the return of the capital without regard to the actual course of the investment-transaction, on the other. (The former would correspond to common stock, the latter to preferred or even to a government bond, a gilt, in British parlance.) It has been shown that the linguistic and legal datum of Mishnah's rules goes back to Assyrian law.[8] Other important continuities in the common law of the ancient Near East have emerged in a broad diversity of research, on Elephantine law for instance. The issue therefore cannot focus upon whether or not the Mishnah in diverse details draws upon established rules of jurisprudence. It assuredly does.

Yet another mode of demonstrating that facts in the Mishnah's system derive from a period substantially prior to that in which the Mishnah reached closure carries us to the data provided by documents redacted long before the Mishnah. For one example, details of rules in the law codes found in the library of the Essene community of Qumran intersect

---

[8]Baruch A. Levine, "Mulugu/Melug. The Origins of a Talmudic Legal Institution," *JAOS* 1968, 88:271-285.

with details of rules in the Mishnah. More interesting still, accounts of aspects of Israelite life take for granted that issues lively in the Mishnah came under debate long before the closure of the Mishnah. The Gospels' accounts of Jesus' encounter with the Pharisees, among others, encompass rules of law, or topics dealt with, important to the Mishnah.[9] It is, for instance, not merely the datum that a writ of divorce severs the tie between wife and husband. The matter of grounds for divorce proves important to sages whose names occur in the Mishnah, and one position of one of these sages turns out to accord with the position on the same matter imputed to Jesus.[10] It follows that not only isolated facts but critical matters of jurisprudential philosophy came to the surface long before the closure of the Mishnah.

That fact yields one incontrovertible result. The Mishnah's rules have to come into juxtaposition, wherever possible, with the rules that occur in prior law codes, whether Israelite or otherwise. That is the case, even though it presently appears that only a small proportion of all of the rules in the Mishnah fall within the frame of prior documents, remote or proximate. For every rule we can parallel in an earlier composition, the Mishnah gives us dozens of rules that in topic, logic, or even mere detail bear no comparison to anything now known in a prior composition, from Sumerian and Akkadian to Essene and Christian writers alike. (The sole exception, the Hebrew Scripture's law codes, comes under analysis in the next section.) Details of the law, wherever possible, still must stand in comparison with equivalent details in earlier documents, whether narrative or legislative. In that way we gain perspective on what, in the Mishnah, has come into the framers hands from an earlier period. At stake in such perspective is insight into the mind of the Mishnah's framers and the character of their system. We see what they have made out of available materials. What do we learn from the occurrence of facts by the time of the Mishnah more than two millenia old, or of issues important two centuries earlier? We review the resources selected by those who contributed to the traditions brought to closure in the Mishnah.

For the authors of the Mishnah in using available, sometimes very ancient, materials, reshaped whatever came into their hands. The document upon close reading proves systematic and orderly, purposive and well composed. It is no mere scrapbook of legal facts, arranged for purposes of reference. It is a document in which the critical problematic at the center always exercises influence over the peripheral facts, dictating how they are chosen, arranged, utilized. So even though some facts in the

---

[9]J. Neusner, "First Cleanse the Inside," *New Testament Studies*, 1976, 22:486-495, repr. in *Method and Meaning in Ancient Judaism. Third Series*. Chico: 1981.
[10]Cf. M. Git. 9:10 and Mt. 5:31-32, among numerous well-known points of intersection.

document prove very old indeed, on that basis we understand no more than we did before we knew that some facts come from ancient times. True halakhah as the Mishnah presents law derives from diverse sources, from remote antiquity onward. But the halakhah as it emerges whole and complete in the Mishnah, in particular, that is, the system, the structure, the proportions and composition, the topical program and the logical and syllogistic whole – these derive from the imagination and wit of the final two generations, in the second century C.E., of the authors of the Mishnah.

IV. The Originality of the Mishnah's Halakhah as a System

A simple exercise will show that, whatever the antiquity of rules viewed discretely, the meaning and proportionate importance of rules taken all together derive from the perspective and encompassing theory of the authors of the Mishnah themselves. That is what will show that the history of halakhah as the Mishnah presents the halakhah, can be traced, whole and cogent, only within the data of the Mishnah itself: systemically, not episodically. The desired exercise brings us to the relationship of the Mishnah to Scripture. For, as noted just now, that is the one substantial source to which the authors of the Mishnah did make reference. Accordingly, to demonstrate the antiquity of more than discrete and minor details of law of the Mishnah, we turn to Scripture. There, it is clear, we can find out whether the Mishnah constitutes merely a repository of ancient halakhah.

Indeed, proof that there was not merely law characteristic of a given group, but the halakhah, shared by all Israel, should derive solely from the Scripture common to all Israel everywhere. How so? The theory of a single, continuous halakhah rests upon the simple fact that all Israel by definition acknowledged the authority of Scripture, its law and theology. It must follow that, in diverse ways and within discrete exegetical processes, every group now known to us drew its basic legal propositions from Scripture and therefore contributes evidence on the unilinear formation of a single law, based upon a single source, common to all Israel, that is, the halakhah.

In examining the notion of the halakhah, as distinct from the theory, argued here, of diverse systems of halakhah, we turn to the critical issue. It concerns not whether a given rule derives from exegesis of Scripture. That issue, by itself, provides trivial and not probative insight. Rather we want to know how the several systems now known to us define their respective relationships to Scripture. That is to say, we ask about the nature of Scriptural authority, the use of Scripture's facts in a code, or system, of law. The answer to the question settles an important issue. If two (or more) systems of law governing groups of Israelites turn out to respond to, to draw upon, Scripture's rules in much the same way, then these discrete systems merge at their roots, in a generative and definitive aspect of their structure. In consequence, we may conclude the two (or more) systems do form part of a single common law, once more, the halakhah. But if two or more systems of law approach Scripture each in its own way and for its own purposes, then we have to analyze each system on its own terms and not as part of, and contributory to, the halakhah.

For the present purpose it will suffice to demonstrate one modest fact. The authors of the Mishnah read Scripture, as they read much else, in terms of the system and structure they proposed to construct. Their goals and conceptions told them what, in Scripture, they would borrow, what they would expand and articulate, what they would acknowledge but neglect and what they would simply ignore. That fact shows that law in the Mishnah, even though shared here and there with other codes, and even though intersecting with still other systems, constitutes a distinct and autonomous system of law, a halakhah on its own. So, to review, the Mishnah then does not absorb and merely portray in its own way established rules of law out of a single, continuous and cogent legal system, the halakhah. Why not? Because, as we shall now see, the Mishnah's authors turn out to have taken from Scripture what they chose in accord with the criterion of the one thing they wished to accomplish. This was the construction of their system of law with its distinctive traits of topical and logical composition: their halakhah, not the halakhah.

In order to show the preeminence, in the encounter with Scripture's laws, of the perspective and purpose of the authors of the Mishnah, we simply review the Mishnah's tractates and ask how, overall, we may characterize their relationships to Scripture. Were these wholly dependent, wholly autonomous, or somewhere in-between? That is, at the foundations in fact and generative problematic of a given tractate, we may discover nothing more than facts and interests of Scripture's law. The tractate's authors may articulate the data of Scripture. Or when we reach the bed rock of a tractate, the point at which the articulation of the structure of the tractate rests, we may find no point of contact with facts, let alone interests, of Scripture's laws. And, third, we may discover facts shared by Scripture but developed in ways distinctive to the purposes of the framers of the Mishnah-tractate at hand. These three relationships, in theory, encompass all possibilities. Let us turn to the facts.[11]

First, there are tractates which simply repeat in their own words precisely what Scripture has to say, and at best serve to amplify and complete the basic ideas of Scripture. For example, all of the cultic

---

[11]These are summarized in detail in my *Method and Meaning in Ancient Judaism. Second Series*. Chico: 1981, pp. 101-214.

tractates of the Second Division, the one on Appointed Times, which tell what one is supposed to do in the Temple on the various special days of the year, and the bulk of the cultic tractates of the Fifth Division, which deals with Holy Things, simply restate facts of Scripture.   For another example all of those tractates of the Sixth Division, on Purities, which specify sources of uncleanness, depend completely on information supplied by Scripture.   Every important statement in Niddah, on menstrual uncleanness, and the most fundamental notions of Zabim, on the uncleanness of the person with flux referred to in Lev. 15, as well as every detail in Negaim, on the uncleanness of the person or house suffering the uncleanness described at Lev. 13 and 14 – all of these tractates serve only to restate the basic facts of Scripture and to complement those facts with other important ones.

There are, second, tractates which take up facts of Scripture but work them out in a way in which those scriptural facts cannot have led us to predict.   A supposition concerning what is important about the facts, utterly remote from the supposition of Scripture, will explain why the Mishnah tractates under discussion say the original things they say in confronting those scripturally provided facts.   For one example, Scripture takes for granted that the red cow will be burned in a state of uncleanness, because it is burned outside the camp, meaning the Temple.   The priestly writers cannot have imagined that a state of cultic cleanness was to be attained outside of the cult.   The absolute datum of tractate Parah, by contrast, is that cultic cleanness not only can be attained outside of the "tent of meeting."   The red cow was to be burned in a state of cleanness exceeding even that cultic cleanness required in the Temple itself.   The problematic which generates the intellectual agendum of Parah, therefore, is how to work out the conduct of the rite of burning the cow in relationship to the Temple: Is it to be done in exactly the same way, or in exactly the opposite way?   This mode of contrastive and analogical thinking helps us to understand the generative problematic of such tractates as Erubin and Besah, to mention only two.

And third, there are, predictably, many tractates which either take up problems in no way suggested by Scripture, or begin from facts at best merely relevant to facts of Scripture.   In the former category are Tohorot, on the cleanness of foods, with its companion, Uqsin; Demai, on doubtfully tithed produce; Tamid, on the conduct of the daily whole offering; Baba Batra, on rules of real estate transactions and certain other commercial and property relationships, and so on.   In the latter category are Ohalot, which spins out its strange problems with the theory that a tent and a utensil are to be compared to one another (!); Kelim, on the susceptibility to uncleanness of various sorts of utensils; Miqvaot, on the sorts of water which effect purification from uncleanness, and many others. These tractates draw on facts of Scripture. But the problems confronted in these tractates in no way respond to problems important to Scripture. What we have here is a prior program of inquiry, which will make ample provision for facts of Scripture in an inquiry to begin with generated essentially outside of the framework of Scripture.

Some tractates merely repeat what we find in Scripture. Some are totally independent of Scripture. Some fall in between. Scripture confronts the framers of the Mishnah as revelation, not merely as a source of facts. But the framers of the Mishnah had their own world with which to deal. They made statements in the framework and fellowship of their own age and generation. They were bound, therefore, to come to Scripture with a set of questions generated elsewhere than in Scripture. They brought their own ideas about what was going to be important in Scripture. This is perfectly natural.

The philosophers of the Mishnah conceded to Scripture the highest authority. At the same time what they chose to hear, within the authoritative statements of Scripture, will in the end form a statement of its own. To state matters simply: all of Scripture is authoritative. But only some of Scripture is relevant. And what happened is that the framers and philosophers of the tradition of the Mishnah came to Scripture when they had reason to. That is to say, they brought to Scripture a program of questions and inquiries framed essentially among themselves. So they were highly selective. Their program itself constituted a statement upon the meaning of Scripture. They and their apologists of one sort hastened to add, their program consisted of a statement of and not only upon the meaning of Scripture.

The authority of Scripture therefore for the Mishnah is simply stated. Scripture provides indisputable facts. It is wholly authoritative – once we have made our choice of which part of Scripture we shall read. Scripture generated important and authoritative structures of the community, including disciplinary and doctrinal statements, decisions, and interpretations – once people had determined which part of Scripture to ask to provide those statements and decisions. Community structures envisaged by the Mishnah were wholly based on Scripture – when Scripture had anything to lay down. But Scripture is not wholly and exhaustively expressed in those structures which the Mishnah does borrow. Scripture has dictated the character of formative structures of the Mishnah. But the Mishnah's system is not the result of the dictation of close exegesis of Scripture, except after the fact.

V. History of the Mishnah's Halakhah: Methodological Program

The Mishnah's formulation derives from the work of redaction.[12] So we cannot show that sizable components of the Mishnah were written down, pretty much as we have them, long before the closure of the document as a whole. On formal and literary grounds, the opposite is the fact: most of the Mishnah conforms to a single program of formulation, and that set of rules on formulation derives from encompassing decisions concerning redaction. We can, however, demonstrate that legal issues or principles in the Mishnah, if not the original wording of those ideas, did derive from periods prior to the age of redaction and formulation.

That demonstration rests on two facts. The first is that numerous statements in the Mishnah bear attributions to particular sages, who lived – it is generally assumed – over the period of approximately two centuries prior to the closure of the document. Since we cannot show that the sages to whom sayings are attributed actually said what is assigned to them, on the surface we do not know the historical value of the attributions. But a second fact makes possible a test of falsification and verification. It is that groups of names appear always with one another and never with names found in other distinct groups. Sages A, B, C, D, commonly believed to have lived at one time, occur in dispute with one another. But rarely, if ever, does sage A, B, C, or D, appear with sages W, X, Y, and Z. Those latter sages likewise stay together and rarely intersect with other groups of names. That indicates a simple and obvious fact. The system of attributions works itself out by groups, or generations. To begin with we may collect sayings assigned to sages A, B, C, and D, and treat them as distinct from sayings assigned to W, X, Y, and Z. But what difference does that distinction make?

The answer rests upon the test of falsification or verification. How so? Two or more groups of sayings, each set drawn together on the basis of the appearance of groups of names may intersect in the treatment of a common theme or even problem. In the consideration of that problem we may readily isolate the stages in the argument, identify the components of a theme. We may further show, on grounds of logic, that a given element of a problem or component of a theme takes precedence over some other element or component. The matter is very simple. For example, if we do not know that a woman requires a writ of divorce, we shall not ask about how the writ is supposed to be written. Again, if we do not know that rules dictate the correct composition of the writ of divorce, we are not likely to ask about the consequences of a scribal error in the writing of the document. So we see three stages in the simple problem

---

[12]Cf. my *History of the Mishnaic Law of Purities*. Leiden: 1977. XXI. *The Redaction and Formulation of the Order of Purities in Mishnah and Tosefta.*

before us: (1) we must know that if a husband wishes to divorce a wife, he must supply her with written evidence that the marriage is severed, and then (2) we must know that such written evidence conforms to a given formula, before we may ask (3) whether, if the document does not conform, the woman is deemed properly divorced. Yet a further stage in the unfolding of the issue will bring us to the question of how (4) we dispose of the offspring of the woman who, on the basis of a divorce accomplished through an improper document, has remarried and become pregnant.

Now recognizing the obvious stages in the unfolding of an issue, we cannot conclude that these stages in logic correspond to sequences of temporal periods. Why not? Because no one would claim that the logical stages outlined just now mark off fifty-year periods in the history of the law. In a single morning, someone can have thought the whole thing through. But what shall we say if we observe a sequence of correspondences between the order in which groups of sages engage in a discussion of a problem and the logic by which the problem itself unfolds? For example, to revert to the case at hand, we may be able to show that sages A, B, C, and D appear in units of discourse, or pericopes, concerning stage (1) of the issue, sages G, H, I, and J participate in units of discourse on the matter of stage (2), M, N, O, and P at stage (3), and W, X, Y, and Z at stage (4). Then we may propose the thesis that the issue unfolded in the sequence of historical periods in which the groups of sages lived. Why so? Because the order of logical steps not only corresponds to, but also correlates with, the order of the groups of sages to whom pertinent sayings are attributed. Can that thesis undergo a test of falsification? Of course it can, because we may ask whether to a later group of sages, e.g., M, N, O, and P, are attributed sayings that concern an issue, principle, or premise already supposedly settled among an earlier group of sages, e.g., A, B, C, and D.

Admittedly, the facts at hand do not demand a historical explanation. One may account in other ways for the correlation of logical stages with sequences of groups, or generations, of sages. The method allows the proposed historical results – the picture of the history of the halakhah of the Mishnah's larger system – to undergo tests of falsification and verification. It does not rest on total credulousness in accepting as fact all attributions. But a more critical approach in time to come will improve upon the method outlined here.

I have applied this procedure in a study of the entire Mishnah, each tractate and every unit of discourse of each tractate. The results proved not entirely uniform for two reasons. The first and the more important, the character of the materials did not invariably permit the test of falsification at hand. Some issues arise for the first time in the names of the final group of authorities, the one that would correspond, in my example above, to W, X, Y, and Z. That meant I had no basis other than the attributions on which to assign to the period of those sages the rules attributed to them. But since the sages at hand flourished one generation prior to the closure of the Mishnah, it did not appear an act of mere credulity in assigning what was attributed to that last stage in the formation of the Mishnah's system of halakhah.

The second, the less important matter was that, on rare occasions, it did appear that what was assumed in discourse among an earlier group of sages, e.g., A, B, C, and D, in fact produced substantial dispute among a later group, e.g, W, X, Y, and Z. These few exceptions often centered on the figure of a critical figure in the attributions, namely, Aqiba, an early second century authority, who is believed to have flourished prior to the Bar Kokhba War and to have trained the principal authorities of the period after the War. In any event where the test of falsification or verification could be met, an item had to be set aside and not included in an account of the history of the law.

To state the upshot of the procedure, we may work out the history of the halakhah of the Mishnah through three principal periods: before 70, from 70 to 130, from 140 to 170, that is, before the first war with Rome, between the two wars, and after the Bar Kokhba War. Obviously, we want to know how far before 70 the Mishnah's laws extend their roots. If we rely on the attributions at hand and make use only of those units of discourse in which we can verify or falsify the attributions, the answer is simple. The earliest layers of the laws ultimately joined together in the system of the Mishnah rest upon foundations laid forth somewhat before or at the beginning of the Common Era. No unit of discourse in the entire Mishnah can be shown to contain ideas or facts originating in the Mishnah's system prior to the turn of the first century C.E. To be sure numerous facts and ideas extend back to Scripture; some go back to Sumerian or Akkadian times. But so far as facts or ideas serve a purpose distinctive to the Mishnah's system and so may be called systemic, not merely episodic and routine, all facts and ideas begin at the designated period. To state the matter simply: the system of the Mishnah's halakhah begins at the turn of the first century C.E., though details, commonly routine facts of a common law, may originate as much as two thousand years earlier than that.

VI. The Mishnah's Halakhah Before 70

The halakhah of the Mishnah takes shape in a twofold process. Once a theme is introduced early in the history of law, it will be taken up and refined later on. Also, in the second and third stages in the formation of the Mishnah, many new themes with their problems will emerge. These then are without precedent in the antecedent thematic heritage. The common foundations for the whole always are Scripture, of course, so that I may present a simple architectural simile. The halakhah of the Mishnah is like a completed construction of scaffolding. The foundation is a single plane, the Scriptures. The top platform also is a single plane, the Mishnah itself. But the infrastructure is differentiated. Underneath one part of the upper platform will be several lower platforms, so that the supporting poles and pillars reach down to intervening platforms; only the bottom platform rests upon pillars set in the foundation. Yet another part of the upper platform rests upon pillars and poles stretching straight down to the foundation, without intervening platforms at all. So viewed from above, the uppermost platform of the scaffolding forms a single, uniform, and even plane. That is the Mishnah as we have it, six Divisions, sixty-three tractates, five hundred thirty-one chapters. But viewed from the side, that is, from the perspective of analysis, there is much differentiation, so that, from one side, the upper platform rises from a second, intermediate one, and, in places, from even a third, lowest one. And yet some of the pillars reach directly down to the bedrock foundations.

To reveal the result at the outset: what is new in the period beyond the wars is that part of the ultimate plane – the Mishnah as a whole – which in fact rests upon the foundations not of antecedent thought but of Scripture alone. What is basic in the period before 70 C.E. is the formation of that part of the Mishnah which sustains yet a second and even a third layer of platform construction. What emerges between the two wars, of course, will both form a plane with what comes before, that platform at the second level, and yet will also lay foundations for a level above itself. But this intermediate platform also will come to an end, yielding that space filled only by the pillars stretching from Scripture on upward to the ultimate plane of the Mishnah's completed and whole system. So let me now describe what I believe to be the state of the law as a whole before 70.

The Mishnah as we know it originated in its Division of Purities. The striking fact is that the Sixth Division is the only one that yields a complete and whole statement of a topic dating from before the wars. Its principal parts are (1) what imparts uncleanness; (2) which kinds of objects and substances may be unclean; and (3) how these objects or substances may regain the status of cleanness. Joined to episodic rulings elsewhere, the principal parts of the Sixth Division speak, in particular, of cleanness of meals, food and drink, pots and pans. It then would appear that the ideas ultimately expressed in the Mishnah began among people who had a special interest in observing cultic cleanness, as dictated by the Priestly Code. There can be no doubt, moreover, that the context for such cleanness is the home, not solely the Temple, about which Leviticus speaks. The issues of the law leave no doubt on that score. Since priests ate heave-offering at home, and did so in a state of cultic cleanness, it was a small step to apply the same taboos to food which was not a consecrated gift to the priests.

What is said through the keeping of these laws is that the food eaten at home, not deriving from the altar and its provision for the priesthood of meat not burned up in the fire, was as holy as the meal offerings, meat offerings, and drink offerings, consecrated by being set aside for the altar and then, in due course, partly given to the priests and partly tossed on the altar and burned up. If food not consecrated for the altar, not protected in a state of cleanness (in the case of wheat), or carefully inspected for blemishes (in the case of beasts), and not eaten by priests in the Temple, was deemed subject to the same purity-restrictions as food consecrated for the altar, this carries implications about the character of that food, those who were to eat it, and the conditions in which it was grown and eaten. First, all food, not only that for the altar, was to be protected in a state of levitical cleanness, thus holiness, that is, separateness. Second, the place in the Land, in which the food was grown and kept was to be kept cultically clean, holy, just like the Temple. Third, the people, Israel, who were to eat that food were holy, just like the priesthood, in rank behind the Temple's chief caste. Fourth, the act of eating food anywhere in the Holy Land was analogous to the act of eating food in the Temple, by the altar.

All of these obvious inferences point to a profound conviction about the Land, people, produce, condition, and context of nourishment. The setting was holy. The actors were holy. And what, specifically, they did which had to be protected in holiness was eating. For when they ate their food at home, they ate it the way priests did in the Temple. And the way priests ate their food in the Temple, that is, the cultic rules and conditions observed in that setting, was like the way God ate his food in the Temple. That is to say, God's food and locus of nourishment were to be protected from the same sources of danger and contamination, preserved in the same exalted condition of sanctification. So by acting, that is, eating like God, Israel became like God: a pure and perfect incarnation, on earth in the Land which was holy, of the model of heaven. Eating food was the critical act and occasion, just as the priestly authors of Leviticus and Numbers had maintained when they made laws governing slaughtering beasts and burning up their flesh, baking pancakes and cookies with and without olive oil and burning them on the altar, pressing grapes and making wine and pouring it out onto the altar. The nourishment of the Land – meat, grain, oil, and wine – was set before God and burned ("offered up") in conditions of perfect cultic antisepsis.

In context this antisepsis provided protection against things deemed the opposite of nourishment, the quintessence of death: corpse matter, people who looked like corpses (Lev. 13), dead creeping things, blood when not flowing in the veins of the living, such as menstrual blood (Lev. 15), other sorts of flux (semen in men, nonmenstrual blood in women) which yield not life but then its opposite, so death. What these excrescences have in common, of course, is that they are ambivalent. Why? Because they may be one thing or the other. Blood in the living is the soul; blood not in the living is the soul of contamination. The corpse was once a living person, like God; the person with skin like a corpse's and who looks dead was once a person who looked alive; the flux of the zab (Lev. 15) comes from the flaccid penis which under the right circumstances, that is, properly erect, produces semen and makes life. What is at the margin between life and death and can go either way is what is the source of uncleanness. But that is insufficient. For the opposite, in the priestly code, of unclean is not only clean, but also holy. The antonym is not to be missed: death or life, unclean or holy.

So the cult is the point of struggle between the forces of life and nourishment and the forces of death and extinction: meat, grain, oil, and wine, against corpse matter, dead creeping things, blood in the wrong setting, semen in the wrong context, and the like. Then, on the occasions when meat was eaten, mainly, at the time of festivals or other moments at which sin offerings and peace offerings were made, people who wished to live ate their meat, and at all times ate the staples of wine, oil, and bread, in a state of life and so generated life. They kept their food and themselves away from the state of death as much as possible. And this heightened reality pertained at home, as much as in the Temple, where most rarely went on ordinary days. The Temple was the font of life, the bulwark against death.[13]

Once the meal became a focus of attention, the other two categories of the law which yield principles or laws deriving from the period before the wars present precisely the same sorts of rules. Laws on growing and preparing food will attract attention as soon as people wish to speak, to begin with, about how meals are to be eaten. That accounts for the obviously lively interest in the biblical taboos of agriculture.[14] Since, further, meals are acts of society, they call together a group. Outside of the family, the natural unit, such a group will be special and cultic. If a group is going to get together, it will be on a Sabbath or festival, not on a workday. So laws governing the making of meals on those appointed

---

[13]Cf. my *History of the Mishnaic Law of Purities*. Leiden: 1974-1977. I-XXII.
[14]Cf. Alan J. Avery-Peck, *History of the Mishnaic Law of Agriculture*. Chico: 1985.

times will inevitably receive attention.[15] Nor is it surprising that, in so far as there are any rules pertinent to the cult, they will involve those aspects of the cult which apply also outside of the cult, that is, how a beast is slaughtered, rules governing the disposition of animals of a special status (e.g., firstborn), and the like.[16]

That the rules for meals pertain not to isolated families but to a larger group is strongly suggested by the other area which evidently was subjected to sustained attention before the wars, laws governing who may marry whom. The context in which the sayings assigned to the authorities before the wars are shaped is the life of a small group of people, defining its life apart from the larger Israelite society while maintaining itself wholly within that society. Three points of ordinary life formed the focus for concrete, social differentiation: food, sex, and marriage. What people ate, how they conducted their sexual lives, and whom they married or to whom they gave their children in marriage would define the social parameters of their group. These facts indicate who was kept within the bounds, and who was excluded and systematically maintained at a distance. For these are the things – the only things – subject to the independent control of the small group. The people behind the laws, after all, could not tell other people than their associates what to eat or whom to marry. But they could make their own decisions on these important, but humble, matters. By making those decisions in one way and not in some other, they moreover could keep outsiders at a distance and those who to begin with adhered to the group within bounds. Without political control, they could not govern the transfer of property or other matters of public interest. But without political power, they could and did govern the transfer of their women. It was in that intimate aspect of life that they firmly established the outer boundary of their collective existence. The very existence of the group and the concrete expression of its life, therefore, comes under discussion in the transfer of women. It therefore seems no accident at all that those strata of Mishnaic law which appear to go back to the period before the wars, well before 70, deal specifically with the special laws of marriage (in Yebamot), distinctive rule on when sexual relations may and may not take place (in Niddah), and the laws covering the definition of sources of uncleanness and the attainment of cleanness, with specific reference to domestic meals (in certain parts of Ohalot, Zabim, Kelim, and Miqvaot). Nor is it surprising that for the conduct of the cult and the sacrificial system, about which the group may have had its own doctrines but over which it neither exercised

---

[15]Cf. my *History of the Mishnaic Law of Appointed Times*. Leiden: 1981-1983. I-V.
[16]Cf. my *History of the Mishnaic Law of Holy Things*. Leiden: 1979. I-VI.

control nor even aspired to, there appears to be no systemic content or development whatsoever.

Once the group take shape around some distinctive, public issue or doctrine, as in odd taboos about eating, it also must take up the modes of social differentiation which will ensure the group's continued existence. For the group, once it comes into being, has to aspire to define and shape the ordinary lives of its adherents and to form a community expressive of its larger world view. The foundations of an enduring community will then be laid down through rules governing what food may be eaten, under what circumstances, and with what sort of people; whom one may marry and what families may be joined in marriage; and how sexual relationships are timed. Indeed, to the measure that these rules not only differ from those observed by others but in some aspect or other render the people who keep them unacceptable to those who do not, as much as, to the sect, those who do not keep them are unacceptable to those who do, the lines of difference and distinctive structure will be all the more inviolable.

VII. The Mishnah's Halakhah between the Wars of 66-70 and 132-135

The period between the wars marks a transition in the unfolding of the Mishnaic law and system. The law moved out of its narrow, sectarian framework. But it did not yet attain the full definition, serviceable for the governance of a whole society and the formation of a government for the nation as a whole, which would be realized in the aftermath of the wars. The marks of the former state remained. But those of the later character of the Mishnaic system began to make their appearance. Still, the systemic fulfillment of the law would be some time in coming. For, as I shall point out in the next section, the system as a whole in its ultimate shape would totally reframe the inherited vision. In the end the Mishnah's final framers would accomplish what was not done before or between the wars: make provision for the ordinary condition of Israelite men and women, living everyday lives under their own government. The laws suitable for a sect would remain, to be joined by others which, in the aggregate, would wholly revise the character of the whole. The shift after the Bar Kokhba War would be from a perspective formed upon the Temple mount to a vision framed within the plane of Israel, from a cultic to a communal conception, and from a center at the locative pivot of the altar, to a system resting upon the utopian character of the nation as a whole.[17]

When we take up the changes in this transitional period, we notice, first of all, continuity with the immediate past. What was taking place after

---

[17]Cf. my *History of the Mishnaic Law of Women*. Leiden: 1979-1980. I-VI.

70 is encapsulated in the expansion, along predictable and familiar lines, of the laws of uncleanness, so to these we turn first.

If the destruction of Jerusalem and the Temple in 70 marks a watershed in the history of Judaism, the development of the system of uncleanness does not indicate it. The destruction of the Temple in no way interrupted the unfolding of those laws, consideration of which is well attested when the Temple was standing and the cult maintained. Development is continuous in a second aspect as well. We find that, in addition to carrying forward antecedent themes and supplying secondary and even tertiary conceptions, the authorities between the wars develop new areas and motifs of legislation. These turn out to be both wholly consonant with the familiar ones, and, while fresh, generated by logical tensions in what had gone before. If, therefore, the destruction of the Temple raised in some minds the question of whether the system of cleanness at home would collapse along with the cult, the rules and system before us in no way suggest so. To be sure, the destruction of the Temple does mark a new phase in the growth of the law. What now happens is an evidently rapid extension of the range of legislation, on the one side, and provision of specific and concrete rules for what matters of purity were apt to have been taken for granted but not given definition before 70, on the other. So the crisis of 70 in the system of uncleanness gives new impetus to movement along lines laid forth long before.

Let us first dwell upon the points of continuity, which are many and impressive. The development of the rules on the uncleanness of menstrual blood, the zab, and corpse uncleanness is wholly predictable on the basis of what has gone before. The principal conceptual traits carry forward established themes. For example, if we have in hand an interest in resolving matters of doubt, then, in the present age, further types of doubts will be investigated. Once we know that a valid birth is not accompanied by unclean blood, we ask about the definition of valid births. The present thought on the zab (Lev. 15) depends entirely on the materials assigned to the Houses, which, moreover, appear to be prior to, and independent of, what is attributed to the authorities after 70. The transfer of the zab's uncleanness through pressure, forming so large and important a part of the tractate of Zabim, begins not with a reference to the zab at all, but to the menstruating woman. The fresh point in this regard is to be seen as a step beyond Scripture's own rule, a shift based on analogical thinking. Rulings on corpse contamination dwell upon secondary and derivative issues. One new idea is the interest in projections from a house and how they too overshadow and so bring corpse uncleanness. It is from this point that an important development begins. Once we treat the tent as in some way functional, it is natural to focus upon the process or function of overshadowing in general. A major innovation in regard to transfer of the contamination of corpse matter through the tent is the notion that the tent takes an active role, combining the diverse bits and pieces and corpse uncleanness into a volume sufficient to impart corpse uncleanness. What is done is to treat the overshadowing as a function, rather than the tent as a thing. Here the mode of thought is both contrastive and analogical.

What is new now requires attention. The comparison of the table in the home to the cult in the Temple is an old theme in the Mishnaic system. What is done at just this time appears to have been the recognition of two complementary sequences, the removes of uncleanness, the degrees of holiness. The former involves several steps of contamination from the original source of uncleanness. The latter speaks of several degrees of sanctification, ordinary food, heave offering, food deriving from the altar (holy things), and things involved in the preparation of purification water. Each of the latter is subject to the effects of contamination produced by each of the former, in an ascending ladder of sensitivity to uncleanness.

An essentially new topic for intense analysis was Holy Things. At issue now is the formation, between the wars, of laws governing the cult. The principal statement of this new system is as follows: the Temple is holy. Its priests therefore are indispensable. But the governance of the Temple now is to be in accord with Torah, and it is the sage who knows Torah and therefore applies it. Since a literal reading of Scripture prevented anyone's maintaining that someone apart from the priest could be like a priest and do the things priests do, it was the next best thing to impose the pretense that priests must obey laymen in the conduct even of the priestly liturgies and services. This is a natural step in the development of the law. A second paramount trait of the version of the system between the wars is its rationalization of those uncontrolled powers inherent in the sacred cult as laid forth by Leviticus. The lessons of Nadab and Abihu and numerous other accounts of the cult's or altar's intrinsic mana (inclusive of the herem) are quietly set aside. The altar sanctifies only what is appropriate to it, not whatever comes into contact with its power. In that principle, the sacred is forced to conform to simple conceptions of logic and sense, its power uncontrollably to strike out dramatically reduced. This same rationality extends to the definition of the effective range of intention. If one intends to do improperly what is not in any event done at all, one's intention is null. Third, attention is paid to defining the sorts of offerings required in various situations of sin or guilt. Here too the message is not to be missed. Sin still is to be expiated, when circumstances permit, through the sacrificial system. Nothing has changed. There is no surrogate for sacrifice, an exceedingly important affirmation of the cult's continuing validity among people burdened with sin and aching for a mode of atonement. Finally, we observe that the established habit of thinking about gifts to be paid to the priest accounts for the choices of topics on fees paid to maintain the cult. All pertain to priestly gifts analogous to tithes and heave offerings. Tithe of cattle is an important subject, and the rules of firstlings and other gifts to the priests are subject to considerable development. The upshot is that the principal concerns of the Division of Holy Things are defined by the end of the age between the wars.[18]

Systematic work on the formation of a Division of Appointed Times did not get under way in the aftermath of the destruction of the Temple. The established interest in rules governing meals, however, was carried forward in laws reliably assigned to the time between the wars. There is some small tendency to develop laws pertinent to the observance of the Sabbath; a few of these laws were important and generated later developments. But the age between the wars may be characterized as a period between important developments. Work on legislation for meals on Sabbaths and festivals had begun earlier. The effort systematically and thoroughly to legislate for the generality of festivals, with special attention to conduct in the Temple cult, would begin later on. In the intervening generations only a little work was done, and this was episodic and random.

When fully worked out, the Mishnah's Division of Women would pay close attention to exchanges of property and documents attendant upon the transfer of a woman from her father's to her husband's house. Authorities between the wars provided only a little guidance for such matters. For a very long time before 70 the national, prevailing law must have defined and governed them. What is significant is that broader and nonsectarian matters, surely subject to a long history of accepted procedure, should have been raised at all. It means that, after the destruction, attention turned to matters which sectarians had not regarded as part of their realm of concern. This may have meant that others who had carried responsibility for the administration of public affairs, such as scribes, now made an appearance. And it also may have meant that the vision of the sectarians themselves had begun to broaden and to encompass the administration of the life of ordinary folk, not within the sect. Both meanings are to be imputed to the fact of interest in issues of public administration of property transfers along with the transfer of women to and from the father's home. Concern for definition of personal status devolves upon genealogical questions urgent to the priesthood, and, it follows, in the present stratum are contained matters of deep concern to yet a third constituency. But these matters of interest

---

[18]Cf. M. Tohorot 2:2-7, for instance.

to scribes and priests do not predominate. It is their appearance, rather than their complete expression and articulation, which is of special interest. Whoever before 70 had settled those disputes about real estate, working conditions, debts and loans, torts and damages, and other sorts of conflicts which naturally came up in a vital and stable society, the group represented in the Mishnah did not.[19] That is why the Division of Damages, dealing with civil law and government, contains virtually nothing assigned to authorities before the wars. Scribes in Temple times served as judges and courts within the Temple government, holding positions in such system of administration of the Israelite part of Palestine as the Romans left within Jewish control. The Division of Damages is remarkably reticent on what after the destruction they might have contributed out of the heritage of their earlier traditions and established practices. Materials of this period yield little evidence of access to any tradition prior to 70, except (predictably) for Scripture. When people at this time did take up topics relevant to the larger system of Damages, they directed their attention to the exegesis of Scriptures and produced results which clarify what Moses laid down, or which carry forward problems or topics suggested by the Torah. That is not evidence that thinkers of this period had access (or wished to gain access) to any source of information other than that one, long since available to the country as a whole, provided by Moses. It follows that, in so far as any materials at all relevant to the later Mishnaic system of Damages did come forth between the wars, the work appears to have begun from scratch. And not much work can have been done to begin with. There is no evidence of sustained and systematic thought about the topics assembled in the Division of Damages. We find some effort devoted to the exegesis of Scriptures relevant to the Division. But whether or not those particular passages were selected because of a large-scale inquiry into the requirements of civil law and government, or because of an overriding interest in a given set of Scriptures provoked by some other set of questions entirely, we cannot say.

The net result of the stage in the law's unfolding demarcated by the two wars is that history – the world-shattering events of the day – is kept at a distance from the center of life. The system of sustaining life shaped essentially within an ahistorical view of reality, goes forward in its own path, a way above history. Yet the facts of history are otherwise. The people as a whole can hardly be said to have accepted the ahistorical ontology framed by the sages and in part expressed by the systems of Purities, Agriculture, and Holy Things. The people followed the path of Bar Kokhba and took the road to war once more. When the three

---

[19]Cf. My *History of the Mishnaic Law of Damages*. Leiden: 1983-1985. I-V.

generations had passed after the destruction and the historical occasion for restoration through historical – political and military – action came to fulfillment, the great war of 132 to 135 broke forth. A view of being in which people were seen to be moving toward some point within time, the fulfillment and the end of history as it was known, clearly shaped the consciousness of Israel after 70 just as had been the case in the decades before 70. So if to the sages of our legal system, history and the end of history were essentially beside the point and pivot, the construction of a world of cyclical eternities being the purpose and center, and the conduct of humble things like eating and drinking the paramount and decisive focus of the sacred, others saw things differently. To those who hoped and therefore fought, Israel's life had other meanings entirely.

The Second War proved still more calamitous than the First. In 70 the Temple was lost, in 135, even access to the city. In 70 the people, though suffering grievous losses, endured more or less intact. In 135 the land of Judah – surely the holiest part of the holy Land – evidently lost the bulk of its Jewish population. Temple, Land, people – all were gone in the forms in which they had been known. In the generation following the calamity of Bar Kokhba, what would be the effect upon the formation of the system of halakhah of the Mishnah? It is to that question that we now turn.

VIII. The Mishnah's Halakhah after the Wars: The System as a Whole

The halakhah reached its full and complete statement, as the Mishnah would present it, after the Bar Kokhba War. Over the next sixty years, from ca. 140 to ca. 200, the system as a whole took shape. To describe the completed halakhah, we survey the six divisions and their tractates and the main points covered in each.

The Division of Agriculture treats two topics, first, producing crops in accord with the scriptural rules on the subject, second, paying the required offerings and tithes to the priests, Levites, and poor. The principal point of the Division is that the Land is holy, because God has a claim both on it and upon what it produces. God's claim must be honored by setting aside a portion of the produce for those for whom God has designated it. God's ownership must be acknowledged by observing the rules God has laid down for use of the Land. In sum, the Division is divided along these lines: (1) Rules for producing crops in a state of holiness – tractates Kilayim, Shebiit, Orlah; (2) Rules for disposing of crops in accord with the rules of holiness – tractates Peah, Demai, Terumot, Maaserot, Maaser Sheni, Hallah, Bikkurim, Berakhot.

The Mishnaic Division of Appointed Times forms a system in which the advent of a holy day, like the Sabbath of creation, sanctifies the life of the Israelite village through imposing on the village rules on the model of those of the Temple. The purpose of the system, therefore, is to bring into alignment the moment of sanctification of the village and the life of the home with the moment of sanctification of the Temple on those same occasions of appointed times. The underlying and generative theory of the system is that the village is the mirror image of the Temple. If things are done in one way in the Temple, they will be done in the opposite way in the village. Together the village and the Temple on the occasion of the holy day therefore form a single continuum, a completed creation, thus awaiting sanctification.

The village is made like the Temple in that on appointed times one may not freely cross the lines distinguishing the village from the rest of the world, just as one may not freely cross the lines distinguishing the Temple from the world. But the village is a mirror image of the Temple. The boundary lines prevent free entry into the Temple, so they restrict free egress from the village. On the holy day what one may do in the Temple is precisely what one may not do in the village. So the advent of the holy day affects the village by bringing it into sacred symmetry in such wise as to effect a system of opposites; each is holy, in a way precisely the opposite of the other. Because of the underlying conception of perfection attained through the union of opposites, the village is not represented as conforming to the model of the cult, but of constituting its antithesis.

The world thus regains perfection when on the holy day heaven and earth are united, the whole completed and done: the heaven, the earth, and all their hosts. This moment of perfection renders the events of ordinary time, of "history," essentially irrelevant. For what really matters in time is that moment in which sacred time intervenes and effects the perfection formed of the union of heaven and earth, of Temple, in the model of the former, and Israel, its complement. It is not a return to a perfect time but a recovery of perfect being, a fulfillment of creation, which explains the essentially ahistorical character of the Mishnah's Division on Appointed Times. Sanctification constitutes an ontological category and is effected by the creator.

This explains why the Division in its rich detail is composed of two quite distinct sets of materials. First, it addresses what one does in the sacred space of the Temple on the occasion of sacred time, as distinct from what one does in that same sacred space on ordinary, undifferentiated days, which is a subject worked out in Holy Things. Second, the Division defines how for the occasion of the holy day one creates a corresponding space in one's own circumstance, and what one does, within that space, during sacred time. The issue of the Temple and cult on the special occasion of festivals is treated in tractates Pesahim, Sheqalim, Yoma, Sukkah, and Hagigah. Three further tractates, Rosh

Hashshanah, Taanit, and Megillah, are necessary to complete the discussion. The matter of the rigid definition of the outlines in the village, of a sacred space, delineated by the limits within which one may move on the Sabbath and festival, and of the specification of those things which one may not do within that space in sacred time, is in Shabbat, Erubin, Besah, and Moed Qatan.

While the twelve tractates of the Division appear to fall into two distinct groups, joined merely by a common theme, in fact they relate through a shared, generative metaphor. It is, as I said, the comparison, in the context of sacred time, of the spatial life of the Temple to the spatial life of the village, with activities and restrictions to be specified for each, upon the common occasion of the Sabbath or festival. The Mishnah's purpose therefore is to correlate the sanctity of the Temple, as defined by the holy day, with the restrictions of space and of action which make the life of the village different and holy, as defined by the holy day.

The Mishnaic system of Women defines the position of women in the social economy of Israel's supernatural and natural reality. That position acquires definition wholly in relationship to men, who impart form to the Israelite social economy. It is effected through both supernatural and natural, this-worldly action. What man and woman do on earth provokes a response in heaven, and the correspondences are perfect. So the position of women is defined and secured both in heaven and here on earth, and that position is always and invariably relative to men.

The principal interest for the Mishnah is the point at which a woman becomes, and ceases to be, holy to a particular man, that is, enters and leaves the marital union. These transfers of women are the dangerous and disorderly points in the relationship of woman to man, therefore, as I said, to society as well. Five of the seven tractates of the Division of Women are devoted to the formation and dissolution of the marital bond. Of them, three treat what is done by man here on earth, that is, formation of a marital bond through betrothal and marriage contract and dissolution through divorce and its consequences: Qiddushin, Ketubot, and Gittin. One of them is devoted to what is done by woman here on earth: Sotah. And Yebamot, greatest of the seven in size and in formal and substantive brilliance, deals with the corresponding heavenly intervention into the formation and end of a marriage: the effect of death upon both forming the marital bond and dissolving it through death. The other two tractates, Nedarim and Nazir, draw into one the two realms of reality, heaven and earth, as they work out the effects of vows, perhaps because vows taken by women and subject to the confirmation or abrogation of the father or husband make a deep impact upon the marital life of the woman who has taken them. So, in sum, the Division and its system delineate the natural and supernatural character of the woman's role in the social economy framed by man: the beginning, end, and middle of the relationship.

The Mishnaic system of Women thus focuses upon the two crucial stages in the transfer of women and of property from one domain to another, the leaving of the father's house in the formation of a marriage, and the return to the father's house at its dissolution through divorce or the husband's death. There is yet a third point of interest, though, as is clear, it is much less important than these first two stages: the duration of the marriage. Finally, included within the Division and at a few points relevant to women in particular are rules of vows and of the special vow to be a Nazir. The former is included because, in the scriptural treatment of the theme, the rights of the father or husband to annul the vows of a daughter or wife form the central problematic. The latter is included for no very clear reason except that it is a species of which the vow is the genus.

There is in the Division of Women a clearly defined and neatly conceived system of laws, not about women in general, but concerning what is important about women to the framers of the Mishnah. This is the transfer of woman and property associated with that same transfer from one domain, the father's, to another, the husband's, and back. The whole constitutes a significant part of the Mishnah's encompassing system of sanctification, for the reason that heaven confirms what men do on earth. A correctly prepared writ of divorce on earth changes the status of the woman to whom it is given, so that in heaven she is available for sanctification to some other man, while, without that same writ, in heaven's view, should she go to some other man, she would be liable to be put to death. The earthly deed and the heavenly perspective correlate. That is indeed very much part of larger system, which says the same thing over and over again.

The formation of the marriage comes under discussion in Qiddushin and Ketubot, as well as in Yebamot. The rules for the duration of the marriage are scattered throughout, but derive especially from parts of Ketubot, Nedarim, and Nazir, on the one side, and the paramount unit of Sotah, on the other. The dissolution of the marriage is dealt with in Gittin, as well as in Yebamot. We see very clearly, therefore, that important overall are issues of the transfer of property, along with women, covered in Ketubot and to some measure in Qiddushin, and the proper documentation of the transfer of women and property, treated in Ketubot and Gittin. The critical issues therefore turn upon legal documents – writs of divorce, for example – and legal recognition of changes in the ownership of property, e.g., through the collection of the settlement of a marriage contract by a widow, through the provision of a dowry, or through the disposition of the property of a woman during the period in which she is married. Within this orderly world of documentary and procedural concerns a place is made for the disorderly conception of the marriage not formed by human volition but decreed in heaven, the levirate connection. Yebamot states that supernature sanctifies a woman to a man (under the conditions of the levirate connection). What it says by indirection is that man sanctifies too: man, like God, can sanctify that relationship between a man and a woman, and can also effect the cessation of the sanctity of that same relationship.

The Division of Damages comprises two subsystems, which fit together in a logical way. One part presents rules for the normal conduct of civil society. These cover commerce, trade, real estate, and other matters of everyday intercourse, as well as mishaps, such as damages by chattels and persons, fraud, overcharge, interest, and the like, in that same context of everyday social life. The other part describes the institutions governing the normal conduct of civil society, that is, courts of administration, and the penalties at the disposal of the government for the enforcement of the law. The two subjects form a single tight and systematic dissertation on the nature of Israelite society and its economic, social, and political relationships, as the Mishnah envisages them.

The main point of the first of the two parts of the Division is expressed in the sustained unfolding of the three Babas, Baba Qamma, Baba Mesia, and Baba Batra. It is that the task of society is to maintain perfect stasis, to preserve the prevailing situation, and to secure the stability of all relationships. To this end, in the interchanges of buying and selling, giving and taking, borrowing and lending, it is important that there be an essential equality of interchange. No party in the end should have more than what he had at the outset, and none should be the victim of a sizable shift in fortune and circumstance. All parties' rights to, and in, this stable and unchanging economy of society are to be preserved. When the condition of a person is violated, so far as possible the law will secure the restoration of the antecedent status.

An appropriate appendix to the Babas is at Abodah Zarah, which deals with the orderly governance of transactions and relationships between Israelite society and the outside world, the realm of idolatry, relationships which are subject to certain special considerations. These are generated by the fact that Israelites may not derive benefit (e.g., through commercial transactions) from anything which has served in the worship of an idol. Consequently, commercial transactions suffer limitations on account of extrinsic considerations of cultic taboos. While these cover both special occasions, e.g., fairs and festivals of idolatry, and general matters, that is, what Israelites may buy and sell, the main practical illustrations of the principles of the matter pertain to wine. The Mishnah supposes that gentiles routinely make use, for a libation, of a drop of any sort of wine to which they have access. It therefore is taken for granted that wine over which gentiles have had control is forbidden for Israelite use, and also that such wine is prohibited for Israelites to buy and sell. This other matter – ordinary everyday relationships with the gentile world, with special reference to trade and commerce – concludes what the Mishnah has to say about all those matters of civil and criminal law which together define everyday relationships within the Israelite nation and between that nation and all others in the world among whom, in Palestine as abroad, they lived side by side.

The other part of the Division describes the institutions of Israelite government and politics. This is in two main aspects, first, the description of the institutions and their jurisdiction, with reference to courts, conceived as both judicial and administrative agencies, and, second, the extensive discussion of criminal penalties. The penalties are three: death, banishment, and flogging. There are four ways by which a person convicted of a capital crime may be put to death. The Mishnah organizes a vast amount of information on what sorts of capital crimes are punishable by which of the four modes of execution. That information is alleged to derive from Scripture. But the facts are many, and the relevant verses few. What the Mishnah clearly contributes to this exercise is a first-rate piece of organization and elucidation of available facts. Where the facts come from we do not know. The Mishnah tractate Sanhedrin further describes the way in which trials are conducted in both monetary and capital cases and pays attention to the possibilities of perjury. The matter of banishment brings the Mishnah to a rather routine restatement by flogging and application of that mode of punishment conclude the discussion.

These matters, worked out at Sanhedrin-Makkot, are supplemented in two tractates, Shebuot and Horayot, both emerging from Scripture. Lev. 5 and 6 refer to various oaths which apply mainly, though not exclusively, in courts. Lev. 4 deals with errors of judgment inadvertently made and carried out by the high priest, the ruler, and the people; the Mishnah knows that these considerations apply to Israelite courts too. What for Leviticus draws the chapters together is their common interest in the guilt offering, which is owing for violation of the rather diverse matters under discussion. Now in tractates Shebuot and Horayot the materials of Lev. 5-6 and 4, respectively, are worked out. But here is it from the viewpoint of the oath or erroneous instruction, rather than the cultic penalty. In Shebuot the discussion is intellectually imaginative and thorough, in Horayot, routine. The relevance of both to the issues of Sanhedrin and Makkot is obvious. For the matter of oaths in the main enriches the discussion of the conduct of the courts. The possibility of error is principally in the courts and other political institutions. So the four tractates on institutions and their functioning form a remarkable unified and cogent set.

The goal of the system of civil law is the recovery of the prevailing order and balance, the preservation of the established wholeness of the social economy. This idea is powerfully expressed in the organization of the three Babas, which treat first abnormal and then normal transactions. The framers deal with damages done by chattels and by human beings, thefts and other sorts of malfeasance against the property of others. The Babas in both aspects pay closest attention to how the property and person of the injured party so far as possible are restored to their prior condition, that is, a state of normality. So attention to torts focuses upon penalties paid by the malefactor to the victim, rather than upon penalties inflicted by the court on the malefactor for what he has done. When speaking of damages, the Mishnah thus takes as its principal concern the restoration of the fortune of victims of assault or robbery. Then the framers take up the complementary and corresponding set of topics, the regulation of normal transactions. When we rapidly survey the kinds of transactions of special interest, we see from the topics selected for discussion what we have already uncovered in the deepest structure of organization and articulation of the basic theme.

The other half of this same unit of three tractates presents laws governing normal and routine transactions, many of them of the same sort as those dealt with in the first half. Bailments, for example, occur in both wings of the triple tractate, first, bailments subjected to misappropriation, or accusation thereof, by the bailiff, then, bailments transacted under normal circumstances. Under the rubric of routine transactions are those of workers and householders, that is, the purchase and sale of labor; rentals and bailments; real estate transactions; and inheritances and estates. Of the lot, the one involving real estate transactions is the most fully articulated and covers the widest range of problems and topics. The Babas all together thus provide a complete account of the orderly governance of balanced transactions and unchanging civil relationships within Israelite society under ordinary conditions.

The character and interests of the Division of Damages present probative evidence of the larger program of the philosophers of the Mishnah. Their intention is to create nothing less than a full-scale Israelite government, subject to the administration of sages. This government is fully supplied with a constitution and bylaws (Sanhedrin, Makkot). It makes provision for a court system and procedures (Shebuot, Sanhedrin, Makkot), as well as a full set of laws governing civil society (Baba Qamma, Baba Mesia, Baba Batra) and criminal justice (Sanhedrin, Makkot). This government, moreover, mediates between its own community and the outside ("pagan") world. Through its system of laws it expresses its judgment of the others and at the same time defines, protects, and defends its own society and social frontiers (Abodah Zarah). It even makes provision for procedures of remission, to expiate its own errors (Horayot).

The (then non-existent) Israelite government imagined by the second-century philosophers centers upon the (then non-existent) Temple, and the (then forbidden) city, Jerusalem. For the Temple is one principal focus. There the highest court is in session; there the high priest reigns. The penalties for law infringement are of three kinds, one of which involves sacrifice in the Temple. (The others are compensation, physical punishment, and death.) The basic conception of punishment, moreover, is that unintentional infringement of the rules of society, whether "religious" or otherwise, is not penalized but rather expiated through an offering in the Temple. If a member of the people of Israel intentionally infringes against the law, to be sure, that one must be removed from society and is put to death. And if there is a claim of one member of the people against another, that must be righted, so that the prior, prevailing status may be restored. So offerings in the Temple are given up to appease heaven and restore a whole bond between heaven and Israel, specifically on those occasions on which without malice or ill will an Israelite has disturbed the relationship. Israelite civil society without a Temple is not stable or normal, and not to be imagined. And the Mishnah is above all an act of imagination in defiance of reality.

The plan for the government involves a clear-cut philosophy of society, a philosophy which defines the purpose of the government and ensures that its task is not merely to perpetuate its own power. What the Israelite government, within the Mishnaic fantasy, is supposed to do is to preserve that state of perfection which, within the same fantasy, the society to begin with attains and expresses. This is in at least five aspects. First of all, one of the ongoing principles of the law, expressed in one tractate after another, is that people are to follow and maintain the prevailing practice of their locale. Second, the purpose of civil penalties, as we have noted, is to restore the injured party to his prior condition, so far as this is possible, rather than merely to penalize the aggressor. Third, there is the conception of true value, meaning that a given object has an intrinsic worth, which, in the course of a transaction, must be paid. In this way the seller does not leave the transaction any richer than when he entered it, or the buyer any poorer (parallel to penalties for damages). Fourth, there can be no usury, a biblical prohibition adopted and vastly enriched in the Mishnaic thought, for money ("coins") is what it is. Any pretense that it has become more than what it was violates, in its way, the conception of true value. Fifth, when real estate is divided, it must be done with full attention to the rights of all concerned, so that, once more, one party does not gain at the expense of the other. In these and many other aspects the law expresses its obsession with the perfect stasis of Israelite society. Its paramount purpose is in preserving and ensuring that that perfection of the division of this world is kept inviolate or restored to its true status when violated.

The Division of Holy Things presents a system of sacrifice and sanctuary: Matters concerning the praxis of the altar and maintenance of the sanctuary. The praxis of the altar, specifically, involves sacrifice and things set aside for sacrifice and so deemed consecrated. The topic covers these among the eleven tractates of the present Division: Zebahim and part of Hullin, Menahot, Temurah, Keritot, part of Meilah, Tamid, and Qinnim. The maintenance of the sanctuary (inclusive of the personnel) is dealt with in Bekhorot, Arakhin, part of Meilah, Middot, and part of Hullin.

Viewed from a distance, therefore, the Mishnah's tractates divide themselves up into the following groups (in parentheses are tractates containing relevant materials): (1) Rules for the altar and the praxis of the cult – Zebahim Menahot, Hullin, Keritot, Tamid, Qinnim (Bekhorot, Meilah); (2) Rules for the altar and the animals set aside for the cult – Arakhin, Temurah, Meilah (Bekhorot); and (3) Rules for the altar and support of the Temple staff and buildings – Bekhorot, Middot (Hullin, Arakhin, Meilah, Tamid). In a word, this Division speaks of the sacrificial cult and the sanctuary in which the cult is conducted. The law pays special attention to the matter of the status of the property of the altar and of the sanctuary, both materials to be utilized in the actual sacrificial rites, and property the value of which supports the cult and sanctuary in general. Both are deemed to be sanctified, that is: qodoshim, "holy things."

The system of Holy Things centers upon the everyday and rules always applicable to the cult: the daily whole offering, the sin offering and guilt offering which one may bring any time under ordinary circumstances; the right sequence of diverse offerings; the way in which the rites of the whole, sin, and guilt offerings are carried out; what sorts of animals are acceptable; the accompanying cereal offerings; the support and provision of animals for the cult and of meat for the priesthood; the support and material maintenance of the cult and its building. We have a system before us: the system of the cult of the Jerusalem Temple, seen as an ordinary and everyday affair, a continuing and routine operation. That is why special rules for the cult, both in respect to the altar and in regard to the maintenance of the buildings, personnel, and even the holy city, will be elsewhere – in Appointed Times and Agriculture. But from the perspective of Holy Things, those Divisions intersect by supplying special rules and raising extraordinary (Agriculture: land-bound;

Appointed Times: time-bound) considerations for that theme which
Holy Things claims to set forth in its most general and unexceptional way:
the cult as something permanent and everyday.

The order of Holy Things thus in a concrete way maps out the
cosmology of the sanctuary and its sacrificial system, that is, the world of
the Temple, which had been the cosmic center of Israelite life. A later
saying states matters as follows: "Just as the navel is found at the center of a
human being, so the land of Israel is found at the center of the world ...
and it is the foundation of the world. Jerusalem is at the center of the land
of Israel, the Temple is at the center of Jerusalem, the Holy of Holies is at
the center of the Temple, the Ark is at the center of the Holy of Holies,
and the Foundation Stone is in front of the Ark, which spot is the
foundation of the world." (Tanhuma Qedoshim 10).

The Division of Purities presents a very simple system of three
principal parts: sources of uncleanness, objects and substances
susceptible to uncleanness, and modes of purification from uncleanness.
So it tells the story of what makes a given sort of object unclean and what
makes it clean. The tractates on these several topics are as follows: (1)
sources of uncleanness – Ohalot, Negaim, Niddah, Makhshirin, Zabim,
Tebul Yom; (2) objects and substances susceptible to uncleanness –
Kelim, Tohorot, Uqsin; and (3) modes of purification – Parah, Miqvaot,
Yadayim.

Viewed as a whole, the Division of Purities treats the interplay of
persons, food, and liquids. Dry inanimate objects or food are not
susceptible to uncleanness. What is wet is susceptible. So liquids activate
the system. What is unclean, moreover, emerges from uncleanness
through the operation of liquids, specifically, through immersion in fit
water of requisite volume and in natural condition. Liquids thus
deactivate the system. Thus, water in its natural condition is what
concludes the process by removing uncleanness. Water in its unnatural
condition, that is, deliberately affected by human agency, is what imparts
susceptibility to uncleanness to begin with. The uncleanness of persons,
furthermore, is signified by body liquids or flux in the case of the
menstruating woman (Niddah) and the zab (Zabim). Corpse uncleanness
is conceived to be a kind of effluent, a viscous gas, which flows like liquid.
Utensils for their part receive uncleanness when they form receptacles
able to contain liquid. In sum, we have a system in which the invisible
flow of fluidlike substances or powers serve to put food, drink, and
receptacles into the status of uncleanness and to remove those things from
that status. Whether or not we call the system "metaphysical," it certainly
has no material base but is conditioned upon highly abstract notions.
Thus in material terms, the effect of liquid is upon food, drink, utensils,
and man. The consequence has to do with who may eat and drink what

food and liquid, and what food and drink may be consumed in which pots and pans. These loci are specified by tractates on utensils (Kelim) and on food and drink (Tohorot and Uqsin).

The human being is ambivalent. Persons fall in the middle, between sources and loci of uncleanness, because they are both. They serve as sources of uncleanness. They also become unclean. The zab, the menstruating woman, the woman after childbirth, the tebul yom, and the person afflicted with *nega* (Scripture: leprosy) – all are sources of uncleanness. But being unclean, they fall within the system's loci, its program of consequences. So they make other things unclean and are subject to penalties because they are unclean. Unambiguous sources of uncleanness never also constitute loci affected by uncleanness. They always are unclean and never can become clean: the corpse, the dead creeping thing, and things like them. Inanimate sources of uncleanness and inanimate objects are affected by uncleanness. Systemically unique, man and liquids have the capacity to inaugurate the processes of uncleanness (as sources) and also are subject to those same processes (as objects of uncleanness). The Division of Purities, which presents the basically simple system just now described, is not only the oldest in the Mishnah. It also is the largest and contains by far the most complex laws and ideas.

IX. The Outcome of the Development of the Halakhah Down to the Mishnah: Statement of the Whole

The critical issue in economic life, which means, in farming, is in two parts. First, Israel, as tenant on God's holy land, maintains the property in the ways God requires, keeping the rules which mark the Land and its crops as holy. Next, the hour at which the sanctification of the Land comes to form a critical mass, namely, in the ripened crops, is the moment ponderous with danger and heightened holiness. Israel's will so affects the crops as to mark a part of them as holy, the rest of them as available for common use. The human will is determinative in the process of sanctification. Second, what happens in the Land at certain times, at "appointed times," marks off spaces of the Land as holy in yet another way. The center of the Land and the focus of its sanctification is the Temple. There the produce of the Land is received and given back to God, the one who created and sanctified the land. At these unusual moments of sanctification, the inhabitants of the Land in their social being in villages enter a state of spatial sanctification. That is to say, the village boundaries mark off holy space. This is expressed in two ways. First, the Temple itself observes and expresses the special, recurring holy time. Second, the villages of the Land are brought into alignment with the Temple, forming a complement and completion to the Temple's sacred being. The advent of the appointed times precipitates a spatial reordering of the Land, so that the boundaries of the sacred are matched and mirrored in village and in Temple. At the heightened holiness marked by these moments of appointed times, therefore, the occasion for an effective sanctification is worked out. Like the harvest, the advent of an appointed time such as a pilgrim festival is also a sacred season and is made to express that regular, orderly, and predictable sort of sanctification for Israel which the system as a whole seeks.

The counterpart of the Divisions of Agriculture and Appointed Times are Holy Things and Purities, dealing with the everyday and the ordinary, as against the special moments of harvest, on the one side, and special time or season, on the other. The Temple, the locus of sanctification, is conducted in a wholly routine and trustworthy, punctilious manner (Holy Things). The one thing which may unsettle matters is the intention and will of the human actor. This is subjected to carefully prescribed limitations and remedies. The Division of Holy Things generates its companion, the one on cultic cleanness, Purities. A system of cleanness, taking into account what imparts uncleanness and how this is done, what is subject to uncleanness, and how that state is overcome – that system is fully expressed, once more, in response to the participation of the human will. Without the wish and act of a human being, the system does not function. It is inert. Sources of uncleanness, which come naturally and not by volition, and modes of purification, which work naturally and not by human intervention, remain inert until human will has imparted susceptibility to uncleanness, that is, introduced into the system food and drink, bed, pot, chair, and pan, which to begin with form the focus of the system. The movement from sanctification to uncleanness takes place when human will and work precipitate it.

The middle Divisions, the Third and Fourth, on Women and Damages, finally, take their place in the structure of the whole by showing the congruence, within the larger framework of regularity and order, of human concerns of family and farm, politics and workaday transactions among ordinary people. For without attending to these matters, the Mishnah's system does not encompass what, at its foundations, it is meant to comprehend and order. So what is at issue is fully cogent with the rest. In the case of Women, attention focuses upon the point of disorder marked by the transfer of that disordering anomaly, woman, from the regular status provided by one man, to the equally trustworthy status provided by another. That is the point at which the Mishnah's interests are aroused: once more, predictably, the moment of disorder. In the case of Damages, there are two important concerns. First, there is the paramount interest in preventing, so far as possible, the disorderly rise of one person and fall of another, and in sustaining the status quo of the economy of Israel, the holy society in stasis.   Second, there is the necessary concomitant in the provision of a system of political institutions to carry out the laws which preserve the balance and steady state of persons.

The halakhic system presented by the Mishnah consists of a coherent logic and topic, a cogent world view and comprehensive way of living.   It is a world view which speaks of transcendent things, a way of life in response to the supernatural meaning of what is done, a heightened and deepened perception of the sanctification of Israel in deed and in deliberation.   Sanctification means two things, first, distinguishing Israel in all its dimensions from the world in all its ways; second, establishing the stability, order, regularity, predictability, and reliability of Israel at moments and in contexts of danger.   Danger means instability, disorder, irregularity, uncertainty, and betrayal.   Each topic of the system as a whole takes up a critical and indispensable moment or context of social being.   Through what is said in regard to each of the Mishnah's principal topics, what the halakhic system as a whole wishes to declare is fully expressed.   Yet if the parts severally and jointly give the message of the whole, the whole cannot exist without all of the parts, so well joined and carefully crafted are they all.

Chapter Twelve

The Fourth Century: The Talmudic Stage in the Formation of Judaism

I. The Initial Statement of a Judaism Despite Christianity

Changes in hermeneutics, symbolic structure, and teleology, characteristic of the fourth- and early fifth-century components of the canon of Judaism, contrast strikingly with the stability in the doctrine of emotions and the symbolization of the outsider, characteristic of that same canon. A theory that explains why the one changed must account also for the constancy of the other. Early, middle, and late, a single doctrine and program dictated what sages represented in the canonical literature of formative Judaism had to say on how Israel should tame its heart. So far as the unfolding components of the canon of Judaism, from ca. A.D. 200, in the Mishnah, through ca. A.D. 600, in the Talmud of Babylonia, portray matters, emotions form part of an iron tradition. That is, a repertoire of rules and relationships handed on from the past, always intact and ever unimpaired, governed the issue. As successive documents came to closure, we see each one adding its improvements, leaving doctrine on religious affections basically the same.

By contrast, in the components of the same canon that reached closure in the late third and fourth centuries, we observe striking changes from how the Mishnah's authors two centuries earlier had formulated critical principles of Judaism. If we follow the same books in the same order and ask about the fundamental hermeneutical method of Judaism, the symbolic structure of the system, and the teleology assigned to the whole, we see striking changes. How so? The Mishnah and its successor documents represent matters in one way, the Talmud of the Land of Israel, coming 200 years later, redirects thought in different paths.

To take one important example, the teleology of the Mishnah does not invoke the eschatological issue. The coming of the Messiah does not serve as the goal and purpose of the holy way of life and world view defined by the Mishnah's sages' Judaism. The Yerushalmi and the writings that follow supply the same system with an eschatological teleology, symbolized by the person of the Messiah. To give a second example, the Mishnah and its successor documents know little, if anything about the doctrine associating the Mishnah with Scripture as a single Torah, that is, the myth of the dual Torah, one given in writing, the other formulated for memorization and transmitted orally. The Yerushalmi, by contrast, lays forth the main lines of that myth of the Torah. Until the age in which the Yerushalmi took shape, third, the hermeneutical system of the sages did not encompass the making of verse-by-verse exegetical compilations serving books of the Scripture in the way in which the sages worked out sentence-by-sentence exegesis of paragraphs of the Mishnah. In the same age as the formation of the Yerushalmi, in the end of the fourth century, the work of compiling such exegeses of Scripture, parallel to the work of organizing exegeses of Scripture, began within the circles of sages that stand behind the canon of Judaism.

So, as is clear, substantial shifts in the definition of the principles and methods of Judaism took place in the fourth century. What changed? Fundamentals of Judaism, the generative exegetical method, the critical symbol, the teleological doctrine. What remained the same? The program of emotions, the sages' statement of how people should feel and why they should take charge of their emotions. The same books, read in the same order, that reveal the one in flux portray the other in stasis. The unchanging repertoire of feelings strikingly contrasts with the shifts and turns of critical components of Judaism as these emerge in the same authoritative writings. Writings that reveal stunning shifts in doctrine, teleology, and hermeneutical method lay forth from beginning to end the one picture of the emotional life of the ideal Israelite.

II. The Impact of the Political Triumph of Christianity

In my view the reason that some things underwent radical revision while others did not derives from the particular character of change fundamental in the politics and social life of the Land of Israel, as of the rest of the Roman East, marked by the fourth century. When Rome became Christian, and when Christianity became first licit, then established, and finally triumphant, the condition of Israel changed in some ways but not in others. What remained the same? The politics and social context of a defeated nation. What changed? The circumstance and context of the religious system of Judaism. The situation of Israel did not change. The setting of Judaism did. How so? Israelites in the Land of Israel persisted as a subject-people. But Judaism now confronted a world in which its principal components – hermeneutics, teleology, symbol – confronted an effective challenge in the corresponding components of the now-triumphant faith in Christ.

Specifically, the Hebrew Scriptures, the written Torah, now demanded a reading as the Old Testament, predicting the New. Why? Because history now proved that Scripture's prophetic promises of a king-Messiah to begin with had pointed toward Jesus, now Christ enthroned. Concommitantly, the teleology of the Israelite system of old, focused as it was on the coming of the Messiah, now found confirmation and realization in the rule of Jesus, again, Christ enthroned. And the symbol of the whole – hermeneutics, teleology alike – rose in heaven's heights: the cross that had triumphed at the Milvian Bridge. No wonder, then, that the three critical components of the Mishnaic system of Judaism now came under sharp revision.

The written Torah found completion in the oral one. So Judaism's extra-scriptural traditions found legitimacy. The system as a whole pointed toward an eschatological teleology, to be realized in the coming of the Messiah when Israel's condition, defined by the one whole Torah of Sinai, itself warranted. And, it would necessarily follow, the symbol of the Torah would expand to encompass the teleology and hermeneutic at hand. Salvation comes from the Torah, not the cross. So point by point, the principles of the Judaism turn out, in the fresh reading of the Talmud of the Land of Israel, coming to closure at the end of the fourth century, to respond point by point to the particular challenge of the principal event of that century.

So the fourth century turns out to have marked the first century of Judaism as it would flourish in the West. It further indicated the first century of Christianity as Christianity enthroned would define and govern the civilization of the West. That thesis demands exposition and demonstration in its own terms. I here offer it in a preliminary way. My intent is merely to account for the points of change and stability revealed in the canonical history of ideas we have now surveyed. Christianity accounts for change in Judaism. Social and political stability explains the constancy of those symbols or modes of symbolic behavior that do not change in Israel.

Let us turn back and rapidly review just what mattered to Israel in the Land of Israel in the history of the fourth century, beginning with Constantine's conversion and ending with the ultimate dissolution of the institutions and social foundations of paganism. Since the several fundamental shifts in symbolic system appear at one point, namely, in the movement, from the Mishnah and its nearby exegetical and apologetic literature to the Talmuds, and in particular, to the Yerushalmi, as is clear we turn our gaze to the fourth century. We ask for details of what had happened so radically to redefine Israel's social and political circumstances. Obviously, the answer for the Land of Israel was the same in the fourth century as it was in the second. The change that marked the advent of the Mishnah, a revolution in its age, was the same as the one that had accompanied the appearance of the Yerushalmi (viewed as a process of approximately a century). It was a considerable political turning.

In both the second and the fourth centuries, the matter reached to full symbolic realization in the name by which the Land of Israel would be known. In the second century the Land of Israel became "Palestine." Israel was defeated, so Rome renamed the Land. In the fourth century the Land of Israel became, for Christian Rome that ruled, "the Holy Land." Israel was now vanquished in heaven as much as on earth, so triumphant Christianity would now rename the Land. (But for Israel, let me say, the Land for Israel would always be what it was for Israel from the beginning and what it is once more in our day, namely, the Land of Israel, now the State, if not the condition, of Israel.) That symbolic order, that rule for unknown ages ahead, stood for all else.

For nearly everyone in the Roman world the most important events of the fourth and fifth centuries, the period in which the Talmud of the Land of Israel and collections of exegeses such as Leviticus Rabbah were coming into being, were, first, the legalization of Christianity, followed very rapidly, second, by the adoption of Christianity as the state's most favored religion, and, third, by the delegitimization of paganism and systematic degradation of Judaism. The astonishing advent of legitimacy and even power provoked Christian intellectuals to rewrite Christian and world history, and work out theology as a reflection on this new polity and its meaning in the unfolding of human history. A new commonwealth was coming into being, taking over the old and reshaping it for the new age. In 312 Constantine achieved power in the West. In 323 he took the government of the entire Roman empire into his own hands. He promulgated the edict of Milan in 313, whereby Christianity attained the status of toleration. Christians and all others were given "the free power to follow the religion of their choice." In the next decade Christianity became the most favored religion. Converts from Judaism were protected and could not be punished by Jews. Christians were freed of the obligation to perform pagan sacrifices. Priests were exempted from certain taxes. Sunday became an obligatory day of rest. Celibacy was permitted. From 324 onward Constantine ceased to maintain a formal impartiality, now intervening in the affairs of the Church, settling quarrels among believers, and calling the Church Council at Nicaea (325) to settle issues of the faith. He was baptized only on the eve of his death in 337. Over the next century the pagan cults were destroyed, their priests deprived of support, their intellectuals bereft of standing.

So far as the Jews of the Land of Israel were concerned, not much changed at the Milvian Bridge in 312, when Constantine conquered in the sign of Christ. The sages' writings nowhere refer explicitly to that event.

They scarcely gave testimony to its consequences for the Jews, and continued to harp upon prohibited relationships with "pagans" in general, as though nothing had changed from the third century to the fourth and fifth. Legal changes affecting the Jews under Constantine's rule indeed were not substantial. Jews could not proselytize; they could not circumcise slaves when they bought them; Jews could not punish other Jews who became Christians. Jews, finally, were required to serve on municipal councils wherever they lived, an onerous task involving responsibility for collecting taxes. But those who served synagogues, patriarchs, and priests were still exempted from civil and personal obligations. In the reign of Constantius III (337-361), further laws aimed at separating Jews from Christians were enacted, in 339 in the Canons of Elvira. These forbade intermarriage between Jews and Christians, further protected converts, and forbade Jews to hold slaves of Christian or other gentile origin.

III. The Repression of Paganism, and, By the Way, Judaism

The reversion to paganism on the part of the emperor Julian, ca. 360, involved a measure of favor to Jews and Judaism. To embarrass Christianity, he permitted the rebuilding of the Temple at Jerusalem, but he died before much progress could be made. In the aftermath of the fiasco of Julian's reversion to paganism, the Christians, returning to power, determined to make certain such a calamity would never recur. Accordingly over the next century they undertook a sustained attack on institutions and personnel of paganism in all its expressions. The long-term and systematic effort in time overspread Judaism as well. From the accession of Theodosius II in 383 to the death of his son, Arcadius in 408, Judaism came under attack. In the earlier part of the fifth century, Jews' rights and the standing of their corporate communities were substantially affected. The patriarchate of the Jews of the Land of Israel, the ethnarch and his administration, was abolished. So from the turn of the fifth century, the government policy was meant to isolate Jews, lower their status, and suppress their agencies of self-rule.

Laws against intermarriage posed no problem to the Jews. The ones limiting proselytism and those protecting converts from Judaism, did not affect many people. But the edicts that reduced Jews to second-class citizenship did matter. They were not to hold public office, but still had to sit on city councils responsible for the payment of taxes. Later, they were removed from the councils, though still obligated, of course, for taxes. Between 404 and 438 Jews were forbidden to hold office in the civil service, represent cities, serve in the army or at the bar, and they ultimately were evicted from every public office. In all, the later fourth and fifth centuries for Israel in its land marked a time of significant change.   Once a mere competing faith, Christianity now became paramount.   The period from Julian's fall onward, moreover, presented to Israel problems of a profoundly religious character.   To these we now turn.

There were, then, five events of fundamental importance for the history of Judaism in the fourth and fifth centuries.   All of them except for the last were well known in their day.   These were as follows: (1) the conversion of Constantine; (2) the fiasco of Julian's plan to rebuild the Temple of Jerusalem; (3) the depaganization of the Roman empire, a program of attacks on pagan temples and, along the way, synagogues; (4) the Christianization of the majority of the population of Palestine; and (5) the creation of the Talmud of the Land of Israel and of the earlier compositions of scriptural exegeses, symbolized by Genesis Rabbah.   The Talmud and the exegetical compilations came into being in an age of crisis, high hope, and then disaster.   Vast numbers of Jews now found chimerical the messianic expectation, as they had framed it around Julian's plan to rebuild the Temple.   So it was a time of boundless expectations followed by bottomless despair.

Let us briefly review from the present perspective, that of Jews and Judaism, the four events that framed the setting for the fifth, starting with Constantine's conversion.   The first point is that we do not know how Jews responded to Constantine's establishment of Christianity as the most favored religion.   But in the Land of Israel itself, his works were well known, since he and his mother purchased many sites believed connected with Israel's sacred history and built churches and shrines at them.   They rewrote the map of the Land of Israel.   Every time they handled a coin, moreover, Jews had to recognize that something of fundamental importance had shifted, for the old pagan images were blotted out as Christian symbols took their place – public events indeed!

A move of the empire from reverence for Zeus to adoration of Mithra meant nothing; paganism was what it was, lacking all differentiation in the Jewish eye.   As I have stressed, Christianity was something else.   It was different.   Why?   Because it was like Judaism.   Christians read the Torah and claimed to declare its meaning.   Accordingly, the trend of sages' speculation cannot have avoided the issue of the place, within the Torah's messianic pattern, of the remarkable turn in world history represented by the triumph of Christianity.   Since the Christians vociferously celebrated confirmation of their faith in Christ's messiahship and, at the moment, Jews were hardly prepared to concur, it falls surely within known patterns for us to suppose that Constantine's conversion would have been identified with some dark moment to prefigure the dawning of the messianic age.

Second, if people were then looking for a brief dawn, the emperor Julian's plan to rebuild the ruined Temple in Jerusalem must have dazzled their eyes. For while Constantine surely raised the messianic question, for a brief hour Emperor Julian appeared decisively to answer it. In 361 the now-pagan Julian gave permission to rebuild the Temple. Work briefly got underway, but stopped because of an earthquake. The intention of Julian's plan was quite explicit. Julian had had in mind to falsify the prophecy of Jesus that "not one stone of the temple would be left upon another." We may take for granted that, since Christ's prophecy had not been proven false, many surely concluded that it indeed had now been shown true. We do not know that Jews in numbers then drew the conclusion that, after all, Jesus really was the Christ. Many Christians said so. But in the next half century, Palestine gained a Christian majority. Christians were not slow to claim their faith had been proved right. We need not speculate on the depth of disappointment felt by those Jews who had hoped that the project would come to fruition and herald, instead of the Christian one, the Messiah they awaited.

Third, the last pagan emperor's threat to Christianity made urgent the delegitimization of paganism. In the formation of a new and aggressive policy toward outsiders, Judaism, too, was caught in the net. To be sure, Jews were to be protected but degraded. But the sword unsheathed against the pagan cult-places, if sharp, was untutored. It was not capable of discriminating among non-Christian centers of divine service. Nor could those who wielded it, zealots of the faith in church and street, have been expected to. The now-Christian Roman government protected synagogues and punished those who damaged them. Its policy was to extirpate paganism but protect a degraded Judaism. But the faithful of the church had their own ideas. The assault against pagan temples spilled over into an ongoing program of attacking synagogue property.

Still worse from the Jews' viewpoint, a phenomenon lacking much precedent over the antecedent thousand years now came into view: random attacks on Jews by reason of their faith, as distinct from organized struggles among contending and equal forces, Jewish and other mobs. The long-established Roman tradition of toleration of Judaism and of Jews, extending back to the time of Julius Caesar and applying both in law and in custom, now drew to a close. A new fact, at this time lacking all basis in custom and in the policy of state and Church alike, faced Jews: physical insecurity in their own villages and towns. So Jews' synagogues and their homes housed the same thing, which was to be eradicated: Judaism. A mark of exceptional piety came to consist in violence against Jews' holy places, their property and persons. Coming in the aftermath of the triumph of Christianity on the one side, and the decisive disproof of the Jews' hope for the rebuilding of the Temple on the other, was the hitherto-unimagined war against the Jews. In the last third of the fourth century and the beginning of the fifth, this war raised once again those questions about the meaning and end of history that Constantine, at the beginning of the age at hand, had forced upon Israel's consciousness.

Fourth, at this time there seems to have been a sharp rise in the numbers of Christians in the Holy Land. Christian refugees from the West accounted for part of the growth. But we have some stories about how Jews converted as well. The number of Christian towns and villages dramatically increased. If Jews did convert in sizeable numbers, then we should have to point to the events of the preceding decades as ample validation in their eyes for the Christian interpretation of history. Jews had waited nearly three hundred years, from the destruction in 70 to the promise of Julian. Instead of being falsified, Jesus' prophecy had been validated. No stone had been left on stone in the Temple, not after 70, not after 361, just as Jesus had said. Instead of a rebuilt temple, the Jews looked out on a world in which now even their synagogues came under threat and, along with them, their own homes and persons. What could be more ample proof of the truth of the Christians' claim than the worldly triumph of their Church? Resisted for so long, that claim called into question, as in the time of Bar Kokhba, whether it was worth waiting any longer for a messiah that had not come when he was most needed. With followers proclaiming the messiah who had come now possessing the world, the question could hardly be avoided.

IV. The Issues of the Fourth Century, the Response of Talmudic Judaism

Now that we understand the context, we appreciate the issues at hand. What happened was a world-historical change, one that could not be absorbed into Israel's available system of theories on the Torah, on teleology, hermeneutics, and symbolism, in general, and the meaning of the history of the great empires, in particular. The Christian empire was fundamentally different from its predecessor in two ways. First, it shared with Israel reverence for exactly the same Holy Scriptures on which Jewry based its existence. So it was no longer a wholly other, entirely alien empire that ruled over the horizon. It was now a monotheist, formerly persecuted, biblical empire, not awfully different from Israel in its basic convictions about all important matters of time and eternity. And it was near at hand and interested. Second, established policies of more than a half a millenium, from the time of the Maccabees' alliance with Rome to the start of the fourth century, now gave way. Tolerance of Judaism and an accommodation with the Jews in their Land – disrupted only by the Jews' own violation of the terms of the agreement in 70 and 132 – now no longer governed. Instead, we find intolerance of Judaism and persecution of Jews through attacks on their persons and property.

Whatever the world may have said, Jews themselves surely had to wonder whether history was headed in the right direction, and whether indeed the Christians, emerging from within Israel itself, may not initially have been right. For the Empire now was Christian. Israel's most recent bout with the messianic fever had proved disastrous. Julian's Temple had not been built. If, as is surely likely, some Jews thought that the building of that Temple would mean the Messiah was near at hand – or in fact had come – then the failure to build the Temple meant the Messiah was not near, or never would come in the way Jews expected. The requirement to construct an apologetics therefore emerged from the condition of Israel, whether or not, in addition, Christian polemicists had a hearing among Jews.

If, now, we inquire into what in fact sages did at that time, the answer is clear. They composed the Talmud of the Land of Israel as we know it. They collected exegeses of Scripture and made them into systematic and sustained accounts of, initially, the meaning of the Pentateuch (assuming dates in these centuries, late third through early fifth, for Sifra, the two Sifres, Genesis Rabbah and Leviticus Rabbah).

When we recall what Christians had to say to Israel, we may find entirely reasonable the view that compiling scriptural exegeses constituted part of a Jewish apologetic response. For one Christian message had been that Israel "after the flesh" had distorted and continually misunderstood the meaning of what had been its own Scripture. Failing to read the Old Testament in the light of the New, the prophetic promises in the perspective of Christ's fulfillment of those promises, Israel "after the flesh" had lost access to God's revelation to Moses at Sinai. If we were to propose a suitably powerful, yet appropriately proud, response, it would have two qualities. First, it would supply a complete account of what Scripture had meant, and always must mean, as Israel read it. Second, it would do so in such a way as not to dignify the position of the other side with the grace of an explicit reply at all. The compilations of exegeses and the Yerushalmi accomplished at this time assuredly take up the challenge of restating the meaning of the Torah revealed by God to Moses at Mount Sinai. This the sages did in a systematic and thorough way.

At the same time, if the charges of the other side precipitated the work of compilation and composition, the consequent collections in no way suggest so. The issues of the documents are made always to emerge from the inner life not even of Israel in general, but of the sages' estate in particular. Scripture was thoroughly rabbinized, as earlier it had been Christianized. None of this suggests the other side had won a response for itself. Only the net effect – a complete picture of the whole, as Israel must perceive the whole of revelation – suggests the extraordinary utility for apologetics, outside as much as inside the faith, served by these same compilations.

It follows, I think, that the changes at the surface, in articulated doctrines of teleology, hermeneutics, and symbolism, respond to changes in the political condition of Israel as well as in the religious foundations of the politics of the day. Paganism had presented a different and simpler problem to sages. Christianity's explicit claims, validated in world-shaking events of the age, demanded a reply. The sages of the Talmud of the Land of Israel provided it. So it is at those very specific points at which the Christian challenge met head-on old Israel's world view that sages' doctrines change from what they had been. What did Israel have to present to the cross? The answer is in three aspects of the Torah: (1) the Torah, in the doctrine, first, of the status, as oral and memorized revelation, of the Mishnah, and, by implication, of other rabbinical writings; (2) the Torah, moreover, in the encompassing symbol of Israel's salvation; (3) the Torah, finally, in the person of the Messiah who, of course, would be a rabbi. The Torah in all three modes confronted the cross, with its doctrine of the triumphant Christ, Messiah and king, ruler now of earth as of heaven.

So what changed? Those components of sages' world view that now stood in direct confrontation with counterparts on the Christian side. What remained the same? Doctrines governing fundamental categories of Israel's social life to which the triumph of Christianity made no material difference. And with what outcome? A stunning success for that society for which, to begin with, sages, and, in sages' view, God, cared so deeply: eternal Israel after the flesh. For Israel did endure in the Christian West, enjoying the secure conviction of constituting that Israel after the flesh to which the Torah continued to speak. How do we know sages' Judaism won? Because when, in turn, Islam gained its victory, Christianity throughout the Middle East and North Africa gave way. But sages' Judaism in those same vast territories retained the loyalty and conviction of the people of the Torah. The cross would rule only where the crescent and its sword did not. But the Torah of Sinai everywhere and always sanctified Israel in time and promised secure salvation for eternity. So Israel believed and so does Israel, the Jewish people, believe today.

Index